BANKING AND BUSINESS IN THE ROMAN WORLD

In the first century BC lending and borrowing by senators – starting with Caesar and Crassus – was the talk of Rome and even provoked political crises. During this same period, the state tax-farmers, the famous *publicani*, were handling enormous sums and exploiting the provinces of the empire. Until now no book has presented a synthetic view of Roman banking and financial life as a whole, from the time of the appearance of the first bankers' shops in the Forum between 318 and 310 BC down to the end of the Principate in AD 284. Professor Andreau writes of the business deals of the elite and the professional bankers and also of the interventions of the state. To what extent did the spirit of profit and enterprise predominate over the traditional values of the city of Rome? And what economic role did these financiers play? How should we compare that role to that of their counterparts in the late Middle Ages and the early modern period?

JEAN ANDREAU is Directeur d'Etudes at the Ecole des Hautes Etudes en Sciences Sociales, Paris. He is the author of *Les Affaires de Monsieur Jucundus* (Rome 1974), *Vie financière dans le monde romain, les métiers de manieurs d'argent* (Rome 1987) and *Patrimoines, échanges et prêts d'argent: l'économie romaine* (Rome 1997).

KEY THEMES IN ANCIENT HISTORY

Edited by P. A. CARTLEDGE *Clare College, Cambridge* and
P. D. A. GARNSEY *Jesus College, Cambridge*

Key Themes in Ancient History aims to provide readable, informed and original studies of various basic topics, designed in the first instance for students and teachers of Classics and Ancient History, but also for those engaged in related disciplines. Each volume is devoted to a general theme in Greek, Roman, or where appropriate, Graeco-Roman history, or to some salient aspect or aspects of it. Besides indicating the state of current research in the relevant area, authors seek to show how the theme is significant for our own as well as ancient culture and society. By providing books for courses that are oriented around themes it is hoped to encourage and stimulate promising new developments in teaching and research in ancient history.

Other books in the series

Death-ritual and social structure in classical antiquity, by Ian Morris
0 521 37465 0 (hardback), 0 521 37611 4 (paperback)

Literacy and orality in ancient Greece, by Rosalind Thomas
0 521 37346 8 (hardback), 0 521 37742 0 (paperback)

Slavery and society at Rome, by Keith Bradley
0 521 37287 9 (hardback), 0 521 37887 7 (paperback)

Law, violence, and community in classical Athens, by David Cohen
0 521 38167 3 (hardback), 0 521 38837 6 (paperback)

Public order in ancient Rome, by Wilfried Nippel
0 521 38327 7 (hardback), 0 521 38749 3 (paperback)

Friendship in the classical world, by David Konstan
0 521 45402 6 (hardback), 0 521 45998 2 (paperback)

Sport and society in ancient Greece, by Mark Golden
0 521 49698 5 (hardback), 0 521 49790 6 (paperback)

Food and society in classical antiquity, by Peter Garnsey
0 521 64182 9 (hardback), 0 521 64588 3 (paperback)

Religions of the ancient Greeks, by Simon Price
0 521 38201 7 (hardback), 0 521 38867 8 (paperback)

BANKING AND BUSINESS IN THE ROMAN WORLD

JEAN ANDREAU

TRANSLATED BY

Janet Lloyd

CAMBRIDGE
UNIVERSITY PRESS

PUBLISHED BY THE PRESS SYNDICATE OF THE UNIVERSITY OF CAMBRIDGE
The Pitt Building, Trumpington Street, Cambridge CB2 1RP, United Kingdom

CAMBRIDGE UNIVERSITY PRESS
The Edinburgh Building, Cambridge CB2 2RU, UK http://www.cup.cam.ac.uk
40 West 20th Street, New York, NY 10011-4211, USA http://www.cup.org
10 Stamford Road, Oakleigh, Melbourne 3166, Australia

First published 1999

Typeset in 11/12¹/₂ Baskerville MT in QuarkXPress   [SE]

A catalogue record for this book is available from the British Library

Library of Congress Cataloguing in Publication data
Andreau, Jean.
[Vie financière dans le monde romain. English]
Banking and business in the Roman world / Jean Andreau;
translated by Janet Lloyd.
p.   cm. – (Key themes in ancient history)
Includes bibliographical references and index.
ISBN 0 521 38031 6 (hardback) – ISBN 0 521 38932 1 (paperback)
1. Finance – Rome – History.   2. Businesspeople – Rome – History.
1. Title.   11. Series.
HG186.R75A5313   1999
336.37 – dc21   98-48325   CIP

ISBN 0 521 38031 6 hardback
ISBN 0 521 38932 1 paperback

Transferred to digital printing 2004

Contents

Preface

In the last decades of the fourth century BC, between 318 and 310, professional bankers (*argentarii*) began doing business in Rome. They continued operating until the second half of the third century AD when, for the time being, their profession disappeared. This book is a study of all aspects of private finance throughout these six centuries, the central period of ancient Roman history. Financial life – loans, for example – existed before the beginning of this period and sprang up again in late antiquity, but these six centuries seem to me to constitute a unity for various reasons which will be explained in the course of the book.

I do not deal at all with public finances, with the income or outgoings either of Republican Rome or of the Principate. But I do examine the way in which Rome and the various cities of the Empire controlled and regulated banking and private business, and also the financial activities which were sometimes conducted by public authorities.

I try to indicate the state of current research, and to raise the main historical issues about banking and business. In keeping with the aims of the series to which it belongs, this book is intended for students who are looking for information about the social and economic history of ancient Rome. But I hope it will also be useful to more advanced readers, and especially to economic historians of mediaeval and early modern Europe. To date, there is no other synthesis of the whole range of financial activity, from the fourth century BC to the third century AD.

In a discussion of the respective interests of sociology and anthropology, Moses Finley wrote, 'We should create a third discipline, the comparative study of literate, post-primitive (if I may), historical societies (I include the attribute 'historical' because the larger and more complex societies, non-literate or literate, which anthropologists do study, are severely contaminated by their contact with the modern European world' (Finley, 1975: 119). I have looked at Roman banking and business from the viewpoint of this comparative discipline.

vii

I would like to express my very deep gratitude to Paul Cartledge and Peter Garnsey, who asked me to write this book in the 'Key Themes' series. This is an honour for me, and has given me the opportunity to write a synthesis on the topic I have studied for many years. I am sorry to have been so slow in writing it, and I thank them for having been so patient. I am very grateful, too, to Pauline Hire and Tamar Hodos, and to Dick Whittaker. Lastly, I express my gratitude towards Churchill College, Cambridge, of which I am very proud to be a fellow, and whose hospitality is always most welcome.

Acknowledgements

Translations of the Latin texts are from the Loeb Classical Library, London and Cambridge MA.

Cicero, *De imp. Cn. Pompei*, translated by H. Grose Hodge, 1966.
Pliny the Elder, *Nat. Hist.*, translated by H. Rackham, 1968.
Suetonius, *The Lives of the Caesars*, translated by J. C. Rolfe, 1965.
Tacitus, *Histories*, translated by Clifford H. Moore, 1962.

Abbreviations

AAN	Atti dell'Accademia di Scienze morali e politiche della Società nazionale di Scienze, Lettere ed Arti di Napoli
AE	Année Epigraphique
AIIN	Annali dell'Istituto Italiano di Numismatica
AJPh	American Journal of Philology
AncSoc	Ancient Society
Annales (ESC)	Annales Economies, Sociétés, Civilisations
ANRW	Aufstieg und Niedergang der römischen Welt
BA	Bollettino d'Arte
BAR	British Archaeological Reports
BSAF	Bulletin de la Société nationale des Antiquaires de France
CH	Cahiers d'Histoire
CIL	Corpus Inscriptionum Latinarum
Cod. Just.	Corpus Juris Civilis, Codex Justinianus
CR	Classical Review
Dig.	Corpus Juris Civilis, Digesta
Eph. Epigr.	Ephemeris Epigraphica
IG	Inscriptiones Graecae
JRA	Journal of Roman Archaeology
JRS	Journal of Roman Studies
MAAR	Memoirs of the American Academy in Rome
MAL	Memorie della Classe di Scienze morali e storiche dell'Accademia dei Lincei
MBAH	Münstersche Beiträge zur antiken Handelsgeschichte
MEFR	Mélanges de l'Ecole Française de Rome
MEFRA	Mélanges de l'Ecole Française de Rome, Antiquité
MH	Museum Helveticum
NC	Numismatic Chronicle
OGI	Orientis Graeci Inscriptiones Selectae
Pap. Tebt.	The Tebtunis Papyri

PBSR	*Papers of the British School at Rome*
PP	*Parola del Passato*
P.W., *RE*	Pauly-Wissowa, *Realencyclopädie der Altertumswissenschaft*
RAAN	*Rendiconti dell'Accademia di Archeologia, Lettere e Belle Arti di Napoli*
RAL	*Rendiconti della Classe di Scienze morali, storiche e filologiche dell'Accademia dei Lincei*
RBN	*Revue Belge de Numismatique*
RD	*Revue historique de Droit Français et étranger*
REA	*Revue des Etudes anciennes*
REJ	*Revue des Etudes Juives*
REL	*Revue des Etudes Latines*
RFIC	*Rivista di Filologia e di Istruzione classica*
RIDA	*Revue internationale des Droits de l'Antiquité*
RSI	*Rivista storica Italiana*
SDHI	*Studia et Documenta Historiae et Iuris*
TAPhA	*Transactions and Proceedings of the American Philological Association*
TP	*Tabulae Pompeianae*
TPSulp	*Tabulae pompeianae Sulpiciorum*
TZ	*Trierer Zeitschrift*
ZPE	*Zeitschrift für Papyrologie und Epigraphik*
ZRG	*Zeitschrift der Savigny-Stiftung für Rechtsgeschichte*

Glossary

Accensus (pl. *accensi*): see *Apparitores*.

Actio institoria (pl. *actiones*): through this, a third contracting party could take legal action against the master of the slave with whom he had done business.

Actor (pl. *actores*): slave who was empowered by his master to act for him; farm-manager.

Aerarius: bronze-worker.

Aes rude: bars of weighed bronze which were used as money.

Aes signatum: bronze bars which were marked but not minted.

Ager publicus: land belonging to the city.

Alimenta: loans organized by Nerva and Trajan; they were intended to assist in the upkeep and education of Italian children.

Amicitia: friendship.

Aneu tokou: interest-free loan (Greek words).

Apparitores (sing. *apparitor*): civil servants, such as lictors and heralds, who worked with the magistrates.

Arcarius (pl. *arcarii*): cashier, usually a slave.

Argentaria (pl. *argentariae*): deposit bank; deposit banking.

Argentarius: professional deposit banker in Italy and in the western part of the Roman Empire.

Argyramoibos (pl. *argyramoiboi*): professional money-changer and assayer (Greek word).

Argyrognomon (pl. *argyrognomones*): coin assayer (Greek word).

Atokos: interest-free loan (Greek word).

Augere rem: to increase one's own patrimony.

Augustalis: member of a municipal board devoted to the cult of the Emperor.

Centesimae usurae: annual interest-rate of 12 per cent (1 per cent per month).

Circumforaneus: travelling trader.

Coactor: professional money-receiver.

Coactor argentarius: professional deposit banker and money-receiver.

Codex: collection of wax tablets bound together.

Codex accepti et expensi: in the Republican period, traditional Roman register, held by the paterfamilias.

Cognomen: second individual name of Roman citizens.

Collectarius: deposit banker in late antiquity.

Commodare: to make an interest-free loan.

Consuetudo: custom, habit.

Curator: municipal magistrate in the western part of the Empire.

Daneistes: moneylender (Greek word).

Demosie trapeza: in Egypt, bank belonging to the State which played a role in tax-collection.

Dispensator: treasurer, usually a slave.

Divisor: intermediary whose function was to distribute money during the election campaigns.

Dominus: owner.

Emporos: wholesaler (Greek word).

Emptio venditio: sale.

Equites (sing. *Eques*): equestrians, knights, second status in the Roman elite (after the senators).

Euergetism: generosity (toward a city, for example).

Faber argentarius: silversmith.

Faber tignuarius: builder.

Fenerator: anyone who lends money at interest; specialist moneylender.

Feneratrix: female specialized moneylender.

Fenus nauticum: maritime loan.

Fenus publicum: interest-bearing loan given by the State.

Fenus unciarium: in the early Roman Republic, annual interest-rate of 100 per cent (8.5 per cent per month); in the first century BC, annual interest-rate of 12 per cent.

Fides: good faith, confidence.

Index nundinarius: list of towns in which periodic markets took place.

Inopia nummorum: deficiency of cash, lack of liquidity.

Institor: slave agent through whose mediation his master tried to make a profit.

Instrumentum domesticum: all the instruments and objects used in daily life.

Janus medius: arch or vaulted passageway near the forum, where moneylenders used to meet.

Kalendarium: personal register in which loans were inscribed.

Kapelos: retailer (Greek word).

Knight: see *Eques*.

Kollektarios: deposit banker in late antiquity (Greek word).

Kollybistike trapeza: bank for changing and assaying money; private bank (Greek word).

Lex praepositionis: document that established the terms and limits of the institor's action.

Liturgy: Greek institution by which members of the elite were compelled to pay public services (for instance, the equipment of a warship).

Locatio conductio: renting.

Mensarius: city magistrate who played the role of a public banker.

Mercator: wholesaler.

Mutuari: to give a loan.

Mutuum: loan.

Naukleros: shipowner (Greek word).

Negotia procurare: to take charge of the private affairs of other people.

Negotians (pl. *negotiantes*): wholesaler.

Negotiatio: a business deal, a concern.

Negotiator: in the second and first centuries B C, Italian businessman who was resident outside Italy; in the Principate, wholesaler.

Nomen: family name of Roman citizen.

Nummularius: professional money-changer and money-assayer; from the second century A D onwards, deposit banker.

Nundinae: periodic market.

Palliata: Roman comedy which was supposed to take place in a Greek context, such as Plautus' comedies.

Paterfamilias: the father, that is the oldest living male in the Roman family.

Patrician: in early Rome, member of the hereditary elite of the city.

Peculium: ownings taken out of the master's patrimony and entrusted to a slave.

Pecunia nautica: maritime loan.

Pecunia traiecticia: maritime loan.

Periculum: financial risk.

Permutatio: transfer of funds from one place to another without any material transportation.

Permutatio publica: transfer of public funds.

Philia: friendship (Greek word).

Plebeian: member of the plebs.

Plebs: Roman citizens who do not belong to the elite; free people living in the city of Rome.

Praeco: public crier, herald.

Praenomen: first name of Roman citizens.

Praetor: Roman magistrate in charge of Justice.

Probare: to assay coins or metals.

Procurator: a free man who agrees to take charge of the private affairs of others (but there are other meanings of the word *procurator*, especially in political and administrative matters).

Promagister: important manager of a *societas publicanorum*.

Propinqui: kith and kin.

Publicanus: lessee in public contracts (concluded with the Roman State).

Publicum: public contract.

Publicum agere: to run a public contract.

Publicus: regarding the State; regarding the whole city-State.

Quaestuosus: looking for profit and trying to get richer.

Ratio: financial account; bank account.

Ratiuncula: diminutive of *ratio*.

Receptum argentarii (pl. *recepta*): undertaking given by a banker to a creditor of his client.

Senatores: members of the elite who had held magistracies in the city of Rome; met in the Senate (*Senatus*).

Senatus: important political council in Rome, the members of which held or had held Roman magistracies.

Senatusconsultum: decision of the Senate.

Servus: slave.

Servus communis: slave belonging to several owners.

Servus vicarius: slave who is a part of another slave's *peculium*.

Sevir Augustalis: member of a municipal board devoted to the cult of the Emperor.

Societas danistaria: private company set up to lend money at interest.

Societas publicanorum (pl. *societates*): tax-collectors' company.

Socius: partner in a commercial company.

Spectare: to assay coins or metals.

Spectatio: the assaying of coins or metals.

Spectator: money-assayer.

Sumptuosus: spendthrift.

Tabulae auctionariae (or *auctionales*): registers sales by auction.

Tessera nummularia: small rod of bone or ivory which was attached to a sealed sack of coins.

Trapeza: deposit bank (Greek word).

Trapezites: professional deposit banker in the eastern part of the Roman Empire (Greek word).

Tria nomina: the three names of Roman citizens (*praenomen, nomen, cognomen*).

Triclinium: dining-room.

Trutina: pair of scales.

Usura: interest of a loan.

Vascularius argentarius: silversmith.

Vecturae periculum: risk involved in transporting goods, for example, by ship.

Vilicus: farm-manager, usually a slave.

Villa: large farm, rural estate.

Volumen: scroll.

Table of monetary equivalencies

As	bronze coin. Its weight was reduced between the third and first centuries BC from a Roman pound (libral as) to a twelfth of a pound (uncial as).
Dupondius	2 asses. Bronze coin
Sestertius	$2^{1}/_{2}$ asses in the third and second centuries BC; 4 asses from the second century BC onwards. Silver coin during the Republic, bronze coin in the Principate.
Denarius	10 asses in the third and second centuries BC; 16 asses from the second century BC onwards. Silver coin.
Aureus	25 denarii. Gold coin.
Drachma	silver coin of Greek tradition (in the Roman period, drachmas were minted by a number of Greek cities, in the eastern part of the Empire).
Didrachm	2 drachmas. Silver coin. Staters were usually worth two drachmas, as well.
Tetradrachm	4 drachmas. Silver coin.

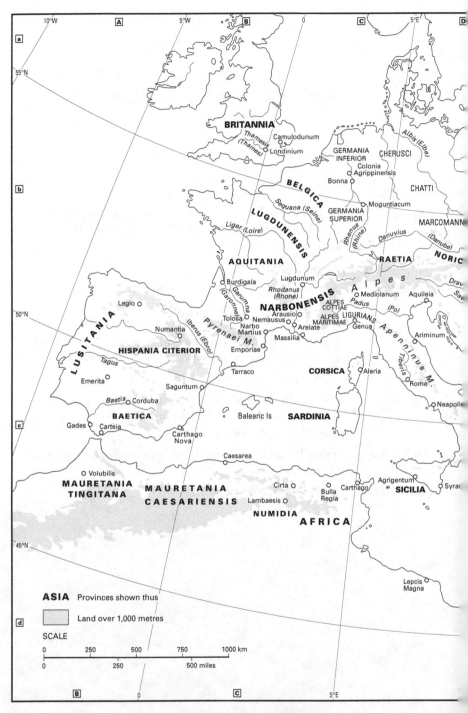

The Roman world in the first century AD

CHAPTER I

Introduction

What is to be understood by 'banking and business'? All operations involving money on its own, independent of trade, which consists of transactions involving merchandise.

Money provides a standard of value; it constitutes a means of exchange and payment, a means of storing value. Once it was issued, money rapidly became a point of reference in economic life and in the acquisition of private wealth. To be sure, the non-monetized sector did not disappear, and its social and economic importance was by no means negligible. But whatever its importance, it now had to be considered in relation to the monetary phenomenon.

In the course of history it has sometimes happened that monetary instruments other than metal coins and banknotes have been put into circulation. That has clearly been the case in the twentieth century, but also in the late Middle Ages and the early modern period. The best known and most important of these monetary instruments was the bill of exchange.

In the Roman world, virtually the only monetary instrument consisted of minted coins. That does not mean that the Romans always paid in cash, nor that they were always forced to move about with quantities of coins. But coins constituted the only organized system of monetary instruments. That is one very important difference between Graeco-Roman antiquity and modern Europe.

When money circulates freely between private individuals, it greatly affects the social balance. It constitutes an unavoidable reference-point for all the social groups that have recourse to it. Even if the poor and the rich do not use the same coins, money creates a common denominator for them.

If money gives rise to private transactions between individuals who may profit or lose thereby – transactions which are not regulated in advance by an unchangeable ritual and in which prices are not rigidly fixed – then it is inseparable from certain forms of market. That was the case in all pre-industrial societies. What kind of market? Not the perfect competitive market of the modern science of economics, nor the situations with which we have become familiar over the last century or two. These were markets that were geographically restricted, subject to strong fluctuations and very different from one another, depending upon what products were involved. They were, notwithstanding, places that operated in accordance with supply and demand. Through money's very existence, its effect was to widen social distances; it increased possibilities for both individuals and groups, accentuating the inequalities between them.

At the same time, however, in that money constituted an instrument common to all, it also reinforced not only social relations but also an intuitive awareness of the cohesion of the community, symbolized by the political authority that minted the money. Despite the greater social divisions, the effect of money was to maintain a community's consciousness of its existence.

Throughout antiquity, the rich (or some of them) and the elite (or some of them) would lend money at interest. At the end of the Roman Republic and under the Principate, many of the senators and knights were not above accepting this source of income on either an occasional or a regular basis. It was not prohibited, and they hardly bothered to disguise the fact that they were creditors, who held debt claims.

But banking was something quite different. Banking is a term to be applied only where a professional makes use of the money from the deposits that he receives. A deposit banker (in Greece a *trapezites*, in Rome an *argentarius* or a *coactor argentarius* or, later, from the second century AD on, a *nummularius*) did not limit himself to lending his own money or to playing the role of a broker. He exercised a commercial profession which consisted of receiving and holding deposits for an indefinite or for a fixed term and then lending the funds available to third parties, thereby acting as a creditor. The Latin legal texts distinguished between those who had the right to open an account (*ratio*), that is to say bankers, and those who did not have that right. They were wise to do so, for the existence of deposit banks had important implications, both economic and social.

Those who consider the knight Atticus and the senator Crassus to have been proper bankers do not have a clear idea either of how business operated in the ancient world or of the social and political roles played by the various kinds of financiers. Even C. T. Barlow, who distinguishes the *argentarii* and the *nummularii* from the non-professional moneylenders, fails to draw all the consequences from the heterogeneous nature of Roman financial circles. Although he stresses the differences that existed between the different kinds of financiers, he refers to a 'banking community' as a particular category of men which intervened in political life, in which it constituted a powerful pressure group.[1] On the contrary, all the evidence indicates that if the professional bankers influenced political life, it was neither in the same fashion nor with the same ends as the elite financiers.

The appearance of deposit banks (in mainland Greece in the fifth century B C, and in Rome at the end of the fourth century B C) is thus an event of considerable importance. It marks a turning point in the economic and social evolution of ancient societies.

But this division into two groups, the businessmen on one side, and the professional bankers on the other, is itself inadequate. The business world was extremely diverse socially, and the non-professional businessmen never constituted a unified group.

Not only were different groups of businessmen distinguished from one another by their technical specialities, their wealth and their legal status; they also went about their economic activities in different ways. The expression 'economic activities' should be seen as distinct from 'work', for the very concept of work, in the modern sense, is not strictly applicable to any of the activities (and in particular was totally alien to the way of thinking of the social elite). The phrase 'their economic activities' is intended to convey all the coordinated actions that they undertook in order to ensure a more or less regular return, an income in kind or money, on which they could survive in society.

I use the expression 'work status' to refer to the different ways in which men went about these activities. It is a concept that relates to the sociology of work and that lies somewhere between a legal status and a social class. An individual's work status is determined by his relation to economic activity at both an institutional and a symbolic level. It involves the material organization of that individual's working life, the mode of his remuneration, the manner of his choosing this work, and the way in which he conceives of it. It also involves his relationship, in his work, with the State.[2] The work status of a professional banker with his own work-

---

[1] Barlow 1978. I do not share the conclusions of Bürge 1987, in whose opinion 'there were no banks in Rome; the Roman bank is a modern fiction' (Bürge 1987: 508).

[2] Andreau 1982; 1985c; 1987a: 25–33.

shop was quite different from that of a member of the elite, such as C. Rabirius Postumus, and neither resembled those to be observed in the banks of today.

The professional bankers were small-scale entrepreneurs, defined by the name of their trade, and they did not belong to the privileged orders of society. They worked behind a counter or in a shop, and observed regular hours. They had learned their skills through an apprenticeship and they were obliged to respect the regulations that governed their trade. For the financiers from the social elite, in contrast, financial business represented a choice which they were free to revoke and which did not impinge upon their possession of their patrimony. Nobody would have suggested that they plied a particular trade or that they were affected by any professional regulations.

Furthermore, the various social groups did not regard money in the same way. The members of the elite saw money in relation to their patrimony. For them, it was either a substitute for a patrimony or else an income from it. Psychologically, then, it did not function as capital – even when, in the economic process, in effect it did operate precisely as that. The concept of money to the professional bankers and merchants is harder to pin down. And in between those two categories there were the 'entrepreneurs', to whom chapter 4 will be devoted. Quantitatively, the role that they played in the Roman economy was very limited, but they were the most 'modern' of those involved. It was their understanding of money that comes the closest to what we call capital. They were prepared to invest large sums of money in order to derive even larger profits, to sidestep the logic of the patrimony, at least for the time being, provided they could thereafter acquire an even greater patrimony for themselves.

From an economic point of view, there are compelling reasons to pay attention to these divisions. In almost all pre-industrial historical societies, non-agricultural activities are the major preoccupation of at least two different circles: on the one hand, the aristocracy, the social and political elite, most of whose members already possessed a patrimony in the form of real estate; on the other, men with urban trades, artisans, traders, and bankers.

This division of non-agricultural activities into two social blocks (on the one hand the elite, on the other the professionals), is pretty well constant. However, the organization of those two major groups, the relations between them, and the distribution of social functions and ranks varied from one period to another. In some cases tradesmen played a crucial political role within cities; elsewhere they remained dominated by the landowning aristocracy. We need to compare antiquity both to the Middle Ages and to the modern period. It could be that the respective economic roles of the aristocracy and the professional circles played a part in bringing about the Industrial Revolution. To confuse the bankers of the ancient world with the senators and knights who were also money-lenders would be to obstruct further reflection on these matters.

In the present work, I have tried to adopt two parallel and complementary lines of procedure: on the one hand, to distinguish between the various groups of financiers, and also between banking and other business affairs; on the other, to consider in general all financial activities, banking included, in order to see how they interacted or were complementary.

Chapters 2, 3, 4, and 5 will be devoted to the various categories of financiers, such as the members of the elite who were financiers, the money-changers/bankers, the 'entrepreneurs', and the businessmen in other categories, in particular dependants. Chapter 4 will also consider the financial links that existed between the various groups of businessmen. In the remainder of the book, chapters 8, 9, 10, 11, and 12 will study private financial affairs as a whole.

In classical Greece, the Hellenistic world and the world of Rome, there were city-states, kingdoms, and empires. At what point is it justifiable to speak of States? How should a State be defined? But those questions are not part of the present work's brief, and so cannot be tackled here.

The city of Rome, and the empire at large had a major influence on business. The public authorities promulgated rules (for example, on the interest rate). They regulated the various trades. They alone could mint coins or authorize the minting of coins by others (generally cities within the Empire). In the course of their exploitation of public property, known as *publica*, they became involved in vast business ventures, sometimes agricultural (the exploitation of the public land that was leased out), sometimes commercial (supplies for the armies) or 'industrial' (public building projects), and frequently financial (the collection of taxes, the transfer of funds, and foreign exchange operations).

However, the vast majority of businessmen, whether or not they were bankers, were private entrepreneurs, and the State and the cities did not intervene in their affairs. So it is important to study them independently from the State, the more so since Roman history tends all too often to be limited to the history of the public authorities. To be sure, the senators and knights derived, whether legally or illegally, considerable revenues from their political, administrative and military responsibilities. At the end of the Republic, the foremost knights were deeply involved in the farming of state taxes. But part of their wealth still came from their family patrimony and from the income derived from that patrimony.

On that account, the present work does not discuss public finances, that is to say public money or fiscal matters, as such. All the same, the city of Rome, and then the Empire, were very concerned to regulate private affairs and to check up on them. Chapter 9 will therefore be devoted to the action and influence of the State. Chapter 8 will also touch upon this, for it will be examining rates of interest.

Over the past century, or even the past two, historians have been divided over how to interpret the ancient economy. Two opposed tendencies have surfaced from time to time and continue to do so. The representatives of these are often labelled 'modernists' and 'primitivists'. Both terms are clearly pejorative, being both schematic and inaccurate.[3]

The modernists are certainly aware that the ancient economies were different from those of the nineteenth and twentieth centuries, but they are inclined to minimize the importance of those differences. They reduce them to a matter of quantities rather than structures. They are convinced that modernization and the Industrial Revolution could have come about in antiquity, although it is true that they did not. However, according to them, the reason why they failed to materialize is not to be sought in the nature and organization of the ancient economy itself. The failure was provoked by non-economic factors that cancelled out the strengths and advantages of the economic system. In the view of some 'modernists', the foremost of those factors were external pressures and invasions. For others, such as M. I. Rostovtzeff, for example, the reason was an internal social crisis within the Empire, which undermined the foundations of prosperity and growth.

The 'primitivists' (M. I. Finley, for example) think, on the contrary, that the ancient economy suffered from intrinsic limitations that made it impossible for it to produce any kind of industrial revolution.[4] Not only do they lay more emphasis than the 'modernists' on the wide gap separ-

---

[3] See Finley 1979; Andreau and Etienne 1984; Andreau 1995c.   [4] Especially Finley 1973.

ating antiquity from our own period,[5] but they reckon that antiquity could not possibly have achieved any better results than it did. If it eventually declined, this was not because it had somehow been assassinated, but because it had reached the limit of its possibilities. To that extent, even if certain aspects of antiquity testify to an energy and sophistication that were lacking in the Middle Ages, it nevertheless was more archaic, since the latter contained one or two seeds that were to germinate and flourish in later years.

This is not the place to analyse the various positions taken up in this altercation on the ancient economy, sometimes also referred to as the 'Bücher-Meyer controversy'.[6] Nevertheless, the present enquiry into financial life in antiquity relates directly to that age-old debate. According to the analyses of economic historians, banks and credit played an extremely important role in the development of industrial economies. What role did they play in the ancient world? Were they more or less 'modern'? I shall be attempting to answer those questions, particularly in chapter 12.

Where the early modern and modern periods are concerned, economic historians also pay great attention to the quantitative aspect of money transactions. Chapter 11 will be partly devoted to the attempts that have been made to quantify these for antiquity. They raise many problems, and my conclusion on this subject will be pessimistic. It is possible to detect a few tendencies or, for example, to estimate that credit was more developed in some regions than in others and in some periods than in others, but that is about all.[7]

In the case of antiquity, a 'qualitative' study (centred on the evolution of financial operations, professions, and enterprises, and taking into account both legal regulations and daily practice) is frequently more fruitful. Making the most of 'qualitative' indications, it is possible – at least up to a point – to grasp the evolution of business from one period to another.

Before the second century BC, there is virtually no evidence available for the financial life of Roman Italy, and I shall have very little to say about it. Late antiquity has clearly left us more sources. However, I shall not venture far into this period because to give a satisfactory account of its economic evolution, it would be necessary to continue to as late as the

---

[5] Finley (1973: 141) emphasizes, for example, that in Antiquity there existed neither paper money, nor bank money, nor commercial bills, nor bearer securities.   [6] Finley 1979.

[7] See Finley 1985: 27–46

sixth or seventh century. I shall be referring to late antiquity only for purposes of comparison on certain, specific points.

Was the financial life of Rome more or less modern, more or less rational than that of the Middle Ages and that of the early modern period? The manner in which the question is formulated (following Max Weber) shows that these problems cannot be usefully tackled unless, in one way or another, one adopts a comparative perspective. Where the economic history of antiquity is concerned, any research without a comparative dimension has conspicuous limitations.

This book is too short for me to develop wide-ranging comparisons between Roman antiquity, Greek antiquity and more recent periods in the history of Europe. All the same, I should like to show the need for and interest of comparison in two ways: on the one hand, on certain specific points that I consider to be important, by comparing the relevant Roman documentation to that of other historical periods; on the other, by presenting the practices and institutions of Rome in such a way as to facilitate comparison, albeit elsewhere and at some later date. For insensitivity to the importance of the comparativist perspective affects one's treatment of the documentation in a way that could discourage all comparison between different periods and different societies.

It is, of course, important to define what is being compared and the aim of the comparison. Comparative history should be problem-solving history. In the present work, the Industrial Revolution constitutes the distant point of comparison. Why did Max Weber compare the ancient town to the medieval town? Because he thought that, in one way or another, modern economic rationality stemmed from certain medieval structures and attitudes. Does such a continuity really exist between the Middle Ages and the economic and social evolution of the seventeenth and eighteenth centuries, in England, the Netherlands, and France? That is one question that is inevitably raised. I shall at any rate be considering certain observations that have been made about antiquity in the light of situations in the more recent history of Western Europe, and shall also venture a few partial conclusions on analogies and differences.

CHAPTER 2

The financial activities of the elite

Throughout its history, Roman society was dominated politically and socially by a minority the basis of whose patrimonies was initially real estate, and whose attitudes were aristocratic. This minority, at first limited to senators, later came to comprise two great privileged orders, the senators and the knights. It never numbered more than a few thousand heads of families, surrounded by their wives, their children, their relatives, and, of course, their dependants.

Alongside this minority however, there were other elite members who possessed patrimonies of a similar nature, sometimes just as great or almost, and who modelled their lifestyles on those of the senators and the knights. These elite members comprised first and foremost the most prestigious and prosperous of the aristocrats of various other cities that were part of the Empire. At the top of the Roman social pyramid, there was thus a relatively homogeneous elite, which constituted a veritable ruling social class. To differentiate between this and the Senate and the order of the knights, both of which belonged to it but represented only its most prestigious, most wealthy and most cultivated echelons, I shall use the term 'elite'. As for the Senate and the knights, I shall call them either 'the imperial elite' or 'the two great orders'.

It is not possible to determine precisely where the limits of the elite class were drawn. No doubt it did not include all the decurions and councillors of the various cities within the Empire. On the other hand, some wealthy men who had no place in the civic hierarchies, certain freedmen for example, may well have been included.

These landowning elite members derived large incomes (sometimes legally, sometimes illegally) from their political role in the city – a role for which, nevertheless, the cost was high. They also had other non-agricultural private interests. Over recent years there has been much discussion about the extent of these other interests, but there can be no doubt of their existence. Some stemmed from occasional, isolated operations

9

(P. Veyne has called these 'one-off' ventures or trading deals).[1] Others gave rise to regular, ongoing activities. Many of these interests were financial. This chapter will be devoted to them.

Our principal sources are literary texts. These contain many general reflections on the patrimonies of the rich, the senators and the knights, on their credits and their debts, and on their cupidity. They also contain many allusions to particular business ventures, and prosopographical information about particular members of the elite.

We possess particularly extensive information relating to the first century BC, thanks to the works of Cicero, in particular his correspondence, which is crammed with it (although it is not always very easy to interpret: the orator and his correspondents often make no more than rapid allusions to such matters or content themselves with gossipy winks and nudges, the meaning of which all too often escapes us).

Legal texts sometimes allude to the affairs of members of the elite, but no more than they do to those of any other Roman citizen. During the periods in which we are interested, they were subject to no specific regulations. That is one of the differences between members of the elite and the professional bankers (*argentarii* and *coactores argentarii*, later *nummularii*). The activities of the latter were certainly regulated by the beginnings of a law governing the profession. As for the technical treatises on agriculture, known as agronomic treatises, they have very little to say about the financial operations of the landowners whom they mention. Nevertheless, they too are valuable, as they help us to understand the strategies and rationality of these individuals.

Financial operations are never mentioned in inscriptions except if the elite member in question has lent money to some city or other.

When writing of the fifth and fourth centuries BC, the Greek and Latin historians frequently address the matter of debts and the political and social problems that these created. Some of their texts openly imply that the moneylenders included a number of patricians. Such was the case in 385 BC, when M. Manlius Capitolinus, represented as one of the first senators to be won over by the claims of the *plebs*, embraced the debtors' cause.[2] The plebeians were, without doubt, more encumbered with debts than the patricians, and some of their creditors were patricians. But we must be careful to avoid confusing moneylenders with

---

[1] Veyne 1976: 175, note 149.   [2] Liv. 6. 11–20.

patricians. Manlius is careful to distinguish between the ferocity of the moneylenders and the political arrogance of the patricians.[3] C. T. Barlow raises the question of whether, in that case, they should be called professional moneylenders. He concludes, rightly, that they should not.[4]

Even though the word *fenerator* could, in all periods, be applied to anyone who advanced interest-bearing loans, very early on it came to designate in particular men who specialized in lending money, or usurers. By the end of the Republic, certain members of the two great orders were deriving a proportion of their income from advancing interest-bearing loans which was by no means negligible. In Cicero's day that was certainly the case of Q. Considius, who was probably a senator. (At the time of Catiline's conspiracy, he was said to hold fifteen million sesterces' worth of debt-claims.)[5] But an elite member (let alone a senator) was never a professional. Throughout the history of Rome, whatever the period, the existence of a senator's patrimony of real estate, his social and political obligations, and his consciousness of his rank and dignity would prevent him from specializing in a single economic activity. Besides, in the early years of the Republic, moneylenders, whether patrician or not, certainly never reached such a degree of specialization.

Even the term 'moneylender' may not be apposite for the early fourth century. The city of Rome was not yet minting discoidal coins. Perhaps, as M. H. Crawford suggests, we should be thinking in terms of loans in kind.[6] There is certainly no reason why that idea should be excluded. But above all, we should recognize that currency was mostly a matter of metal bars, for these had been used as money for a long time already. The bars of weighed metal were known as *aes rude*; later, bronze bars that were marked but not minted (*aes signatum*) were brought into circulation. Servius Tullius never minted discoidal coins, or even bronze bars stamped with the forms of animals. Nevertheless, many scholars nowadays recognize that the bronze bars that are called 'bars with a *ramo secco*' date from his reign and that that is how we should understand Pliny the Elder's famous statement, 'King Servius was the first to mark bronze with a stamp'. Some, like Crawford, reckon that all he did was fix a weight-standard; but even that constituted an important innovation and

---

[3] Liv. 6. 14.3 and 15.10. [4] Barlow 1978: 16–17. See also Bürge 1987: 495–509.
[5] Val. Max. 4.8.3. There is nothing to prove that the fifteen million sesterces all belonged to Considius; he was probably a credit intermediary. [6] Crawford 1985: 22.

certainly does not rule out the possibility of bronze bars being used as a means of exchange.[7]

Between the Punic Wars and the Principate, the documentation relating to loans of money advanced by members of the elite increases century by century. In the third and second centuries B C known cases remain few and far between.[8] But the comedies of Plautus and Terence contain a number of allusions to the practice. In the *Asinaria*, for instance, the false manager Saurea claims he spent three days in the forum, looking for moneylenders for his master.[9]

In contrast, Shatzman lists twenty-five senators attested as money-lenders in the last century of the Republic,[10] and Nicolet lists seventeen knights.[11] That represents a very significant sample. From the first century AD on, moneylending is mentioned in all the general texts relating to the wealth and sources of income of the elite. Over and above land, livestock, houses, and properties that brought in rent, slaves and precious objects, a wealthy member of the elite, whether or not a senator or knight, also held debt-claims.[12]

In parallel, passages relating to the management required by such revenues also multiply. Even if the elite member would ordinarily be assisted by dependants or friends, he still had to check out the characters of his debtors and their solvency, to note when payments were due and the conditions of the loan, for instance how to intervene when legal action was unavoidable (an extreme recourse that appears seldom to have been used).[13] In Rome, creditors took to using the *columna Maenia* to publicize information relating to the solvency and goodwill of their debtors.[14] Sensible moneylenders would avail themselves of any such information before granting credit to anyone whom they did not know well.

Under the Principate, the vast majority of senators and knights were regularly lending money. The Emperor himself lent considerable sums. All these elite members who, in effect, in economic terms invested their money in this way, constituted a class of creditors who could count on

---

[7] Pliny, *Nat. Hist.* 33.43. See Crawford 1976; Ampolo 1974; Zehnacker 1979; Zehnacker 1990; Pedroni 1995.   [8] Shatzman 1975: 75 and Nicolet 1966: 368–9.

[9] Plautus, *Asin.* 428–30.   [10] Shatzman 1975: 76.   [11] Nicolet 1966: 372–3.

[12] Petr. *Satir.* 37.8–9; Sen. *ad Lucil.* 2.6 and 4.41.7; Plut. *Mor.* 101c and 795E and F; Tac. *Hist.* 1.20.3; Juv. *Sat.* 11.39–41; Apul. *Apol.* 20.3; Tert. *Cult. fem.* 1.9.3; etc.

[13] Saller 1982: 121 emphasizes the fact that before taking their debtors to court, creditors would have recourse to all other possible means.

[14] Cic. *pro Cluentio* 13, 38–9; see Andreau 1987b: 163–4.

an income from finance but whose patrimonies also included land and property, and who on that account were not professional financiers.

Was this already the situation during the last century of the Republic? Or by then were there fewer senators and knights who operated as moneylenders? It is hard to say. Cicero, at any rate, lent money often, and frequently large sums. One of his letters shows that he and Atticus both invested money in this fashion, himself through the intermediary Cluvius of Puteoli, Atticus through Vestorius.[15] Quite apart from the loans that he is known to have advanced and taken out within the aristocratic world,[16] Cicero – at least during some periods in his life – was thus receiving income from money lent through a businessman more specialized than himself.

The letter to which I referred above[17] is rather mysterious, almost encoded, but does not betray any desire to conceal these investments. It is just a joke, a piece of word-play prompted by a mention of the fourth century B C Greek geographer Dicaearchus. Although it was fashionable to deplore moneylending for interest, the Greek and Latin elite members do not – in these periods at least – appear to have been at great pains to conceal their investments, except when they were acting illegally (for example, when the rate of interest was classed as usurious). Under the Late Republic and the Principate, lending money for interest was not legally forbidden in Rome. Had it been the subject of a real moral and social taboo among members of the elite, fewer general reflections on it would have been forthcoming, and there would have been fewer open references to loans. In this respect, Roman antiquity is quite unlike the eleventh, twelfth and thirteenth centuries. In the Middle Ages, public opinion was fiercely hostile to lending for interest, and this cannot be explained purely by Church doctrine. Although it was practised, lending money for interest was utterly condemned.[18] That was definitely not the case in Rome.

It would be mistaken to think that moneylenders always sought to accumulate interest at the highest possible rates. Some loans carried no interest at all. In some cases this would be a manifestation of the generosity that was a feature of the aristocratic ideal of friendship and of links of kinship and clientship. In other cases, an interest-free loan would constitute an act of euergetism toward a particular city that the elite

---

[15] Andreau 1983a; for the letter, see *ad Att.* 6.2.3. On Vestorius, see also D'Arms 1981: 49–55.

[16] Früchtl 1912 and Shatzman 1975: 416–22; N. Rauh has shown that in 45 B C, the debit-notes held by Cicero amounted to an enormous sum, possibly several million sesterces (Rauh 1989: 60–9).

[17] Cic. *ad Att.* 6.2.   [18] See Giardina and Gurevic 1994: 71–80.

member in question was taking under his protection. And sometimes, particularly under the Late Republic, the gift or interest-free loan might have political significance. But such practices notwithstanding, a desire for gain and a taste for wealth were certainly spectacularly apparent.

In the life of aristocracies, politics, social matters, and culture are always closely intermingled with patrimonial and economic preoccupations. It is important to analyse precisely how these different levels interacted, but we should beware of isolating any particular one of them, with the mistaken idea that it is more important than the rest. By picking out one, no matter which, we would limit our understanding of it since, in isolating it, we should overlook the links that connected it with contemporary practices and attitudes as a whole, in fact all that goes to make up what might be called the anthropology of an ancient society.[19]

Alongside the practice of simply advancing interest-bearing loans, which all elite members tended to consider as a customary source of income, aristocratic finance included a whole series of operations that were more or less widespread, more or less specialized, but hard to classify as they were marked by great fluidity. They were less common than lending money for interest. Some required more attention and a higher level of financial and legal competence than others, and were monopolized by a specialist minority. It is significant that, with very few exceptions, women from the ruling classes did not undertake such operations – whereas they could advance interest-bearing loans just as men could, as part of their management of their own patrimonies.[20]

In the interests of clarity, I shall classify these operations in six categories. But the same men could well be involved in several categories at once. It is the operations that I am classifying, not the men, and it would be arbitrary to assign individuals to particular groups.

The first three categories comprised all specialized forms of moneylending, the intermediary role of credit, and the transfer of debt claims.

While many elite members invested their funds, some lent very much more than others, regarding this source of income as relatively more important than the rest of their patrimony. Such behaviour reflected a thirst for greater wealth and a desire to increase their patrimony, *augere rem*. These men were known as *feneratores*, specialist lenders for interest. At least, that was what others called them, but it was certainly not what

---

[19] See chapter 12.
[20] In the texts from the Republic and the Principate, the word *feneratrix* (female specialized moneylender or usurer) is used only twice; see Varro, *L.L.* 7.96 and Val. Max. 8.2.2.

they themselves claimed to be. For even if a senator or a knight acknowledged without embarrassment that he lent money for interest, *fenerat*,[21]
he would certainly not describe himself as a *fenerator*. As early as the time
of Cato the Elder,[22] or even earlier, *fenerator* had taken on a specialized
and pejorative sense. When Seneca writes of the loans advanced by rich
senators or knights, he applies that term only to specialized businessmen
who spent all their time in the forum.[23]

We know the names of a number of high-flying *feneratores*: Q.
Considius,[24] the knight Q. Caecilius, Atticus' uncle,[25] Octavius Ruso, a
certain Alfius, a freedman by the name of Cercopithecus Paneros,[26] and
the philosopher Seneca himself. It is hard to say whether those not
known to be senators or knights were members of the elite. For *feneratores*
could be found at every level in society. Some were 'entrepreneurs' (we
shall be considering these in chapter 4), and some came from the ranks
of the ordinary people. A number of other moneylenders of whom we
know no doubt deserved the description of *feneratores* but are not so called
in the texts that have come down to us. One case in point was probably
Cornelius Senecio, the extremely wealthy knight mentioned by
Seneca.[27]

Many *feneratores* from the aristocracy did not limit themselves to
lending their own funds; they also loaned sums entrusted to them by
other members of the elite. The documentation from Cicero's period
mentions several examples where a specialized advancer of interest-
bearing loans served as an intermediary between senators and knights
wishing to invest their money and those who would eventually borrow
it. Cluvius and Vestorius of Puteoli operated as intermediaries in this
way. But mention should also be made of M. Scaptius and P. Matinius,
who were residents of either Cilicia or Cyprus and who had loaned the
city of Salamis in Cyprus a large sum of money belonging to Brutus.[28]
These intermediaries included both knights and other members of the
elite (for example, municipal aristocrats). And then there were the 'entrepreneurs'. Very few senators can have played such a role. Nevertheless,
the senators who were described as *feneratores* no doubt did not limit
themselves to lending their own funds. Among the intermediaries who
were not senators were some, at the end of the Republic and the beginning of the Empire, who were resident in the provinces and therefore

---

[21] Pliny the Younger, *Epist.* 3.19.8.   [22] Cat. *de Agr.* pr. 1.
[23] Sen. *ad Lucil.* 41.7; 76.15; 81.2. See Bürge 1987: 495–509.
[24] Val. Max. 4.8.3.   [25] Sen. *ad Lucil.* 118.2; and Val. Max. 7.8.5.   [26] Suet. *Nero* 30.
[27] Sen. *ad Lucil.* 101.1–4; and Demougin 1988: 103.   [28] Andreau 1983a.

counted as *negotiatores*, in the sense of the word at that time. Their particular task, in those provinces, was to make the funds belonging to elite members in Italy, which they were handling, bring in a profit.[29]

In Rome, one of the spots most favoured by the financial system, where intermediaries such as the above, or their employees or dependants, would meet, was the *Janus medius*, an arch or vaulted passageway that was probably situated at one end of the facade of the *Basilica Aemilia*.[30] According to one of Horace's scholiasts, money matters were handled there by *feneratores* acting as intermediaries. Both creditors and lenders would be found there – that is to say both passive investors seeking to place their money and also intermediaries arranging credit, who were experts at investing money.[31]

At the end of the Republic, a number of large sums were lent to cities in the provinces, while others found their way into private commercial transactions in Italy or elsewhere. Whether or not such loans were contracted in Rome, the respective sums destined for those two purposes were probably for the most part handled by different sets of intermediaries. Credit for cities raised specific problems which senators, knights, and tax-collectors were better placed to tackle. It is worth noting, however, that Cluvius of Puteoli had lent money to cities in Asia but also committed funds to commercial operations in Puteoli. It would therefore be mistaken to conclude that strict specialization was inevitable.

Among the loans advanced to traders, maritime loans deserve a special mention. Two relatively recently published documents, a papyrus from Vienna and a tablet from Murecine, relate to such loans, and they have in consequence again become the focus of considerable interest. Far higher rates of interest were charged for these than for other loans, but the financial risk fell to the creditor, which was not the case with other kinds of loans.[32]

Could intermediaries providing credit receive unsealed deposits of money, which they were authorized to use provided they undertook to repay the equivalent to the man who had deposited the money with them? Did they, like professional bankers, provide the twofold service of both receiving deposits and advancing credit, which constitutes the basis

---

[29] Barlow 1978: 108, 111 and 116. Bürge 1987 is too inclined to confuse the two senses of the word *negotiator*, that of the late Republic and that of the Principate.

[30] Platner and Ashby 1929: 275–7 and Coarelli 1985: 180–9.

[31] Pseudo-Acron, *ad Hor. Sat.* 2.3.18–19; see also Cic. *de Off.* 2.87, and *ad Att.* 2.1.11.

[32] See Ankum 1978; Wolf 1979a; 1979b; Purpura 1984; 1987; Santoro 1985; Ankum 1988; Casson 1990.

of any deposit bank? Or was that service reserved for professional bankers, *argentarii, coactores argentarii*, and, later, *nummularii*?

I am now certain of the correct answer to that question (although in the past I have been in two minds about it). Non-sealed deposits of money were reserved for professional bankers. The service of both accepting deposits and advancing credit was linked with the notion of an account, *ratio*, and with that of a register in which the state of one's clients' accounts was recorded. No elite financier followed the same procedures as deposit-bankers. Wherever our sources indicate how money passed through the hands of one or several intermediaries, no non-sealed deposit was involved.

When Brutus' money was loaned to the people of Salamis in Cyprus through the intermediaries Scaptius and Matinius, these two were the sole official creditors. Until Brutus revealed his hand in the affair, neither the people of Salamis nor Cicero knew that the sums loaned belonged to him. And the reason for Brutus' approaching Cicero was that the sum of money did belong to him, and so it was he who was assuming the financial risk of the operation.[33] If Brutus had arranged a banked deposit with his intermediaries, the financial risk would have been theirs. Presumably there was a mandate contract, which made Scaptius and Matinius the sole official creditors, but to which was added a clause that relieved them of the responsibility of financial risk.

In other cases a loan would take the form of a company contract between an elite member and one or more professionals, with the former investing his money in the enterprise, while the latter was (or were) responsible for getting it to produce a good return. According to Cicero, that is how Crassus proceeded with his freedmen.[34] If the company was a *societas danistaria*, as in the tablet from Transylvania,[35] this represents another legal means for formalizing the financial relations between a sleeping partner who was the investor and an intermediary. In the case of that particular tablet, it is certain that neither of the two partners was a member of the elite. However, there was nothing to prevent an elite member from concluding a contract of this kind – nothing, that is, but moral and social pressures.

It is worth noting one other attested procedure for investing money through an intermediary. In the case of the sums that Cicero and Atticus invested through the mediation of Cluvius and Vestorius, debt-claims

---

[33] Cic. *ad Att.* 5.21.10–13; 6.1.3–8; 6.2.7–9; 6.3.5–6; see Andreau 1983a: 14.
[34] Cic. *Par. Stoic.* 6.46.   [35] Tabl. n° 13; see *CIL* III, 950–1.

were ceded. In the metaphor that Cicero elaborates in connection with Dicaearchus the geographer, the intermediary who advanced the credit held debt-claims over provincial debtors. If Cicero or Atticus wished to invest money, the intermediary would sell them some of these debt-claims, and the debt would be set on a new footing, with a change of creditor.[36]

This way of proceeding, which must have been quite common, explains how a senator or a knight would manage, without too much difficulty, to recoup the money he had loaned, or at least some of it. He would sell on his debt-claims either to the intermediary who had ceded them to him or to some other intermediary, and the intermediary would then cede them to someone else. The mechanism seized up as soon as a liquidity crisis or a debt crisis developed.

The three other categories of operations practised by elite financiers who (more or less) specialized in them were business management, operations involving coins (assaying and foreign exchange), and transfers of funds.

Senators and knights, who were frequently away from Rome and Italy, needed people to manage their patrimonies in their absence. In the cases known to us, a task so responsible would not be entrusted to a single individual. They would turn not only to their relatives and their direct dependants, but also to private managers ('procurators'), particularly to keep an eye on their rural properties. What was needed was somebody sufficiently highly placed to be capable of taking charge of financial matters – not, to be sure, the budget and lifestyle of the family and the household in general, but the management of lending and borrowing, and of large purchases and payments.[37] When a loan was needed, the manager would try to find moneylenders. If a debtor wished to pay off his debt by selling debt-claims, he would ascertain their value.

For Cicero, it was Atticus who filled this role – at least from the time when he returned to Italy in 65 BC. We do not know who managed the orator's affairs before that date. Lucius Egnatius Rufus, for his part, assisted Atticus as the *chargé d'affaires* of Quintus Cicero. But Atticus himself sometimes absented himself from Rome, to stay for a while in Epirus or elsewhere in Greece, for example, and when this happened a certain L. Cincius took charge of his interests. We must conclude that

---

[36] Cic. *ad Att.* 6.2.3. This is the metaphorical sense of the expression *itaque justum ego locum totidem verbis a Dicaearcho transtuli.* See Andreau 1983a: 12–13.   [37] Rauh 1989: 60–71.

there were many such *chargés d'affaires*, although very few of them are known to us.

Did they receive remuneration? There must certainly have been some agreement whereby they were rewarded for such time-consuming work, which could well prove harmful to their own interests. But in the cases known to us, there is no suggestion of any regular payment such as, for example, a percentage of the sums handled by them. Atticus and Cicero were very close friends, to be sure, but the patrimonial interests of the two men were never confused. Besides, men of this rank not only were responsible for their wives and children but were also the heads of large households full of slaves and freedmen; and they possessed numerous estates. They needed to keep a tight grip on the situation. We know from Cornelius Nepos that Atticus was extremely frugal in his daily life.[38] Despite all this, there is no indication that he presented any lists of expenses to Marcus or Quintus Cicero! Cornelius Nepos explains that he had chosen to *negotia procurare*, to take charge of the affairs of others, in order to prove that, even if he was not entrusted with the affairs of the State, this was not because he was lazy, but because he had made a deliberate choice. *Chargés d'affaires* such as he contributed indirectly to the smooth running of the State, by assisting those who held magistracies. So it was that Atticus took charge of the interests of the two Ciceros, of Cato, of Hortensius, of Aulus Torquatus, and of a fair number of Roman knights.[39] Even if Atticus did benefit from the responsibilities that he discharged (and it seems virtually certain that he did – at least indirectly), his attitude should be understood in the context of a whole series of overall choices made in accordance with the lifestyle to which he was accustomed. It cannot be reduced to a quest for profit at all costs. Atticus' way of life was not that of his uncle, the *fenerator* Q. Caecilius, nor was it that of the great Crassus, as described by Cicero.

Now let us move on to consider moneychanging and the assaying of coins. Apart from *tesserae nummulariae*, which pose problems of their own, the documentation available to us is almost exclusively devoted to the procedures adopted for the assaying of coins[40] and the activities of professional money-changers, that is to say, first and foremost, the *nummularii*. When the need arose, many members of the elite must have turned to professional *nummularii*, and their slave-financiers, *arcarii* (cashiers) and *dispensatores* (treasurers), were probably capable of handling day-to-day operations. But Crassus had slaves of his own, who were coin assayers

---

[38] Corn. Nep. *Att.* 13.6.   [39] Corn. Nep. *Att.* 15.3.   [40] Bogaert 1976.

(*argyrognomones*), and from funerary inscriptions, we know five slaves who
were *nummularii*, some of whom may have worked from their master's
house.[41] Other funerary inscriptions, dating from the reigns of Augustus
and the Julio-Claudians, testify to the fact that there were also slaves who
were *argentarii*, mainly belonging to the imperial family. But most of these
argentarii slaves were goldsmiths or silversmiths, not bankers or coin
assayers.[42]

Private individuals, like the State, sometimes needed to transport
cash, but, also like the State, they would endeavour where possible to
avoid having to transport the cash itself and to find other ways of
effecting a transfer.[43] To whom would an elite member, a senator say,
turn, to arrange such a transfer?

If it was a matter of sums belonging to the State, or of private funds
legally acquired in the exercise of public responsibilities, the companies
of tax-collectors (*publicani*) would arrange the transfer, thereby in a way
playing the role of a public bank. When Cicero went in 51 BC to Asia
Minor, where he was to serve as governor of Cilicia, he paused in
Laodicea to collect the money owed to him by the State. It was handed
over to him by tax-collectors. The operation was what Cicero called a
publica permutatio, a transfer of public funds.[44] Subsequently, he entrusted
to the tax-collectors the 2,200,000 sesterces that he had earned in the
course of his proconsulship in Cilicia. This shows that these public
agents would receive and hold funds belonging to private individuals,
but probably did so only if those individuals were senators on official
missions.

When the sums being transferred were nothing to do with the State
or with magistrates carrying out their official duties, no tax-collectors
would be involved. If this was the case, there was no set procedure regularly used by all. People had to make their own personal arrangements.

In 45 BC, Cicero's son, young Marcus, went to Athens to complete his
studies. Cicero, who was not in Rome at the time, appealed to Atticus to
find a way to transfer the money that his son would be needing. Atticus,
who had lived for a long time in Athens and had many contacts in
Greece, found a Greek who was prepared to advance money to the
young Marcus. The name of this Greek, who was an Epicurean, was
Xeno. There is nothing to suggest that he was a professional banker or

---

[41] Plut. *Crassus* 2.8; and Andreau 1987a: 199–202.   [42] Andreau 1987a: 93–104.
[43] On the physical transport of coins, see Howgego 1992. The risk involved in transporting coins,
by ship for example, was known as the *vecturae periculum* (Cic. *ad Att.* 12.24.1 and *ad Fam.* 2.17.4).
[44] Cic. *ad Fam.* 3.5.4.

even a financier. He owed money to Atticus. By providing Cicero's son with cash, he could pay off his debt. Cicero, for his part, had to make sure to pay over to Atticus the rents of the houses that he leased out in the Argilete and Aventine quarters of Rome.[45] The provision of credit for Marcus involved no professional banker. Atticus was reimbursed in Rome each time he arranged for money to be made available in Athens. The whole point of the operation was to transfer funds without having to transport coins from one spot to another.

Here is another example of a transfer of private funds. In 48 B C, following the battle of Pharsalus, Cicero, giving up the struggle against Caesar, again crossed the Adriatic, and lived for almost a year in Brindisi, until such time as Caesar should return from his campaigns and agree to be reconciled with him. In the course of this stay, he was in need of money several times. He obtained it from Tarentum, through a certain Minucius, to whom Atticus had turned.[46] There is no indication that this Minucius was a professional banker. At any rate, there was no operation involving credit, since Atticus, in Rome, arranged for the sale of some property belonging to Cicero and used the proceeds to reimburse the money provided by Minucius.

While in Brindisi, Cicero also obtained money from a certain Cn. Sallustius, who was a friend, or rather a client, of his. In 58 B C, when Cicero, on his way into exile, had travelled from Rome to Brindisi, he had been accompanied by a man named Sallustius, no doubt this same Cn. Sallustius. In 47 B C, Cn. Sallustius did not simply provide Cicero with 30,000 sesterces. Like Cicero, he, too, wished to obtain a pardon from Caesar, and at some point Cicero considered sending him to Caesar, along with his own son Marcus, to convey his requests. All of this indicates that Sallustius was not a professional banker.[47]

No more than in the previous examples was any operation for advancing credit involved on the part of either Cn. Sallustius or Atticus. Cicero immediately wrote to Atticus, instructing him to pay the money owed to Publius Sallustius, who was in Rome and was certainly a relative of Cnaeus.[48]

The tax-collectors (*publicani*) constituted a group recognized by the State, a veritable order within the city. Their financial activities, as tax-collectors, were pursued in the service of the State. They were also

---

[45] See Cic. *ad Att.* 12.24.1; 12.27.2; 12.32.2; 13.37.1; 14.7.2; 14.16.4; 14.20.3; 15.15.4; 15.17.1; 15.20.4; and 16.1.5. See Früchtl 1912: 25–7.   [46] Cic. *ad Att.* 11.14.3 and 11.15.2.

[47] Cic. *ad Att.* 1.3.3; 1.11.1; 11.11.2; 11.17.1; 11.20.2; *ad Fam.* 14.4.6 and 14.11; *ad Quint. fr.* 3.4.2–3 and 3.5.1; *de Divin.* 1.28.59.   [48] Cic. *ad Att.* 11.11.2.

involved in private financial activities, but these appear to have been of a varied nature and might have fallen into any of the six categories enumerated above; so there is no reason to treat them as a separate group in themselves.

The same goes for the *divisores*, who distributed funds within the framework of political life. They were responsible for handing over to the members of a particular tribe the gifts presented to them by the candidates for election who came from that tribe. Such distributions within each tribe were perfectly legal, which is why this body of men was officially recognized by the city, despite the fact that, in the last decades of the Republic, their activities degenerated into electoral corruption pure and simple. Their private financial affairs may have inclined them to the role of intermediaries providing credit, but we have no means of knowing.

The elite financiers possessed patrimonies that made it possible for them to live off the incomes that those patrimonies provided without working. Apart from the debt-claims that they held, mentioned above, they owned land, livestock, luxurious residences and urban properties, which brought in an income, slaves of every kind, precious objects, and liquid cash. Through the agencies that they entrusted to their slaves and the loans that they advanced to them, they also made profits from commerce and the production of goods in craftsmen's workshops.

The lives of most of them were dominated by their duty to take part in the running of the Empire or of the various cities within the Empire. It is true that a few freedmen acceded to the ranks of the elite, and also that many members of the elite never acceded to magistracies. Nevertheless, an elite member was defined first and foremost by his pre-eminent standing both socially and in politics.

The greater their political role, the better we know them. Most of our information relates to the senators and the knights. Where a financier did not belong to either of the great imperial orders, it is not easy to place him. Take Cluvius of Puteoli, for instance: was he a member of the municipal aristocracy of either Puteoli or elsewhere? Was he a trader, or a trader who had risen into the elite? And what about Vestorius? We are far less well informed about men such as these than about Atticus or the knight C. Rabirius Postumus.

Between a wealthy senator and a member of the municipal elite in comfortable circumstances, there were certainly considerable differences from the point of view of both financial means and social prestige. Some kinds of financial profit that were legally permissible to the one group were not permissible to the other. Senators did not have the right to be tax-collectors and were not free to set off for the provinces in the capacity of *negotiatores*. At the end of the Republic, certain posts in the companies of tax-collectors were reserved for knights. Clearly then, there were sharp differences between the various components of the elite class.

Nevertheless, over the past few decades historiography has tended, in my own view rightly, to underline all that made for the cohesion of the senators and the knights, both socially and economically, and to minimize all that divided them. Forty years ago, H. Hill was defending the untenable notion that the senators formed a class of landowners, while the knights constituted a bourgeoisie of businessmen.[49] Today, nobody would accept such an idea. Both the archaeological documentation and the epigraphy of the *instrumentum* (household inventories) reveal the extent to which the interests of the knights and the senators were comparable. The marks and inscriptions on amphoras, for example, indicate no differences between the behaviour of senators and that of knights.[50] It is therefore perfectly justifiable to regard them as two components of the same elite, of which, however, they were not the sole members.

The work status of the elite was characterized by a total absence of any notion of the need to work, by an absence of professionalism, and by a free choice of activities. There were no limits set upon the latter, or only in a negative sense: certain operations were, by virtue of some law or custom, deemed unworthy of such or such a category. But those apart, the elite members could exercise a free choice. They were bound by no fixed hours and would often engage in their chosen activities in their own homes.[51] For these members of the elite, as for others, economic activity may have been a means of making profits and ensuring an adequate income; however, in their eyes, there was no distinction between it and other aspects of their social life. A senator or a knight was never a professional man in the way that an *argentarius* was.

As for the concept of economic activity, the attitude of the elite was dominated by three main features. The first was that, except where agriculture was concerned, they thought not in terms of enterprise, but rather in terms of patrimony. Although the agronomic texts may reveal a way of thinking about the estate and the villa as a single unit, there is

---

[49] Hill 1952.   [50] Manacorda 1989: 451–3. See also D'Arms 1981 (Index, *s.v. Equites*).
[51] Vitr. *De arch.* 1.2.9 and 6.5.2.

never any sign of that kind of thinking where other activities are concerned.[52]

The second feature was that the elite always started off with a collection of properties already in their possession, and all their economic
strategies were founded upon the management of those possessions.
Money was thus never regarded as capital, a value introduced into the
economic process in order to create new wealth, but rather was seen
either as a component of their patrimony, a substitute for land, houses,
and slaves, or as an income provided by the patrimony. It was certainly
not by chance that Cicero referred to the overall private affairs of the
elite using the expression *emptio venditio locatio conductio*, or buying, selling,
and leasing.

Of course that is not to say that elite members never acted as entrepreneurs or as the managers of businesses. But they drew no clear distinction between the role of an entrepreneur and that of a man living
off his private income, firstly because they regarded themselves basically
as the latter, and secondly because they would often delegate the function of an entrepreneur, whenever it was in principle theirs, to dependants, either slaves or freedmen. This brings us to the third feature by
which their attitude was characterized: for them, the important thing
was to be clear whether they were delegating or were themselves responsible for the management of the enterprise. Even in the agricultural
domain, that was so. The great distinction that they drew between personal management and delegated management led them to overlook
other differences, for example that between leasing out a farm and
exploiting it directly.

In his study of the economic attitudes of the elite, P. Veyne has drawn
a distinction between two strategies: the strategy of security, which was
designed to cope with possible setbacks and was centred on real estate,
because 'the land ensured a minimum of economic security, which in
turn preserved one's social standing', and the strategy of profit.[53] I think
that to these two strategies a third should be added, the strategy of provident management, in which monetary transactions, liquid money, and
financial activity counted for a great deal.

It was land, not moneylending, that offered security. Faced with
financial affairs, the elite could choose between two main ways of proceeding. The first went hand in hand with the strategy of provident man-

---

[52] On this subject I do not agree with Di Porto 1984 and Petrucci 1991 who, in my opinion, ascribe
to the Latin texts a far too 'modern' concept of enterprise. See further chapter 5.
[53] Veyne 1991: 131–62.

agement. What should one do in order to have at one's disposal the ready cash required for the aristocratic life? And in what financial business should one engage in order to preserve one's patrimony without diminishing its value, or even moderately to increase it (so as to be sure of its not decreasing)? The second way of proceeding fitted the strategy of profit: how could one make money in order to increase one's patrimony greatly, even if that involved taking greater risks?

The first of those two ways of proceeding was that of those elite members who limited themselves to investing their money. In doing so, what did they hope for? Certainly to recoup interest from their money, which might enable them to expand their patrimony, but also to diversify their sources of income, since the price of real estate and the income from it might fall. And they could hope also to gain access to liquid cash: not all the income from real estate was paid in cash, and furthermore such income materialized (more or less) only once a year, sometimes not even then. If one did not wish to keep one's liquid cash shut up in a strongbox, the best thing to do was to invest it – always providing one could find reliable ways of doing so.

The second way of proceeding was that adopted by most professional moneylenders. The point for them was to make as much money as possible. Where the desire for profit was not the manifestation of a passion pursued on its own account, the ultimate objective would be to increase one's fortune massively, either so as to be able to lead a more extravagant life, or else so as to climb further up the social ladder. If we are to believe Cicero, in the case of Crassus the passion for financial profit (he was *quaestuosus*) was a response to his desire to lead an ever more luxurious life (he was *sumptuosus*). In the case of Vespasian, the quest for profit stemmed from the far more 'rational' desire to strengthen his patrimony, the better to assure his position in the senatorial order.

Because the patrimonies of the elite had increased greatly in a more or less regular fashion,[54] between the third century BC and the time of the Julio-Claudians, in the second and first centuries BC, many senators and knights, through fear of not being able to maintain their rank, had tended to launch themselves into as many ventures as possible, both private and public.

It is not surprising that such an economic attitude and such a work status should have affected the nature of the financial techniques used by the elite and also the structure of their business ventures. In the

[54] Jaczynowska 1962; Amsden 1986: 55–70.

domain of financial techniques, they help to explain the absence of codified and formalized credit procedures, for example the absence of a bill of exchange. As to business ventures, historians of the ancient economy have long been surprised at their fragility and at the constraints that hampered them. Even M. Rostovtzeff, who was convinced of the existence of an ancient capitalism, regarded the position of (financial and other) business ventures and the legislation by which they were governed as the major weaknesses of the Roman economy. He wrote as follows: 'Roman laws never mention the types of companies that are so familiar in modern times, clearly because such companies did not exist. The Roman *societates* were mere groups of individuals who were but slightly limited by the existence of the company.'[55] As goes almost without saying, all scholars less convinced than he of the modernity of the ancient economy have always stressed the limits of private enterprise in Rome.[56]

How did the specializing elite financiers manage their affairs? How were the offices of moneylenders such as Q. Caecilius structured? How many collaborators did they have? If we had an exhaustive list of the staff of the important elite members operating in this domain, it would, like that of the managing personnel for State business, without a doubt strike us as being very restricted. It does not take long to account for the slaves and freedmen who managed the business affairs of Atticus and Cicero. But, except in the case of the tax-collectors, the financial affairs of the elite were not organized by a firm, a financial organization quite separate from the rest of their patrimony. The loans advanced by Q. Caecilius constituted a series of operations that were an integral part of his patrimonial interests as a whole.

The likelihood is that the range of possible relations was extensive, and that an elite member specializing in finance would thus be surrounded by a whole network of dependants and associates. We should think in terms of networks rather than commercial companies.[57] I shall now enumerate six possible kinds of relations, but the list is by no means comprehensive:

(a) businesses that were managed directly, with the collaboration of

---

[55] Rostovtzeff 1957: 171.
[56] For example Brunt 1965: 125–6. E. E. Cohen has recently stressed the very simple and strictly personal nature of the Athenian banks (Cohen 1992: 61–6). A. Di Porto (1984) and A. Petrucci (1991) take an opposite view from this general consensus. In chapter 5, I shall be returning to consider their conclusions, but I should state here and now that they do not convince me. Their vision of ancient enterprise is far too modern.   [57] Andreau 1995b.

actores, dispensatores (treasurers), and *arcarii* (cashiers), all of whom were slaves;

(b) businesses managed by procurators, who would frequently be domiciled far away from the *dominus*;

(c) loans advanced to freedmen, above all to one's own;[58]

(d) businesses managed by slaves who worked as agents;

(e) debt-claims bought from intermediaries and loans made to intermediaries. In such cases most of the work involved fell to the intermediary (or intermediaries, if there were more than one). The investor would receive a proportion of the income. When Cluvius held debt-claims on a number of cities in Asia or on individuals living in Asia, it is to be supposed that at least some of them must have been acquired through intermediaries (even if Cluvius did maintain a wide network of associates in Asia Minor);[59]

(f) finally, sleeping partnerships, which – to judge from the comments on Crassus – for a senator represented one of the most reprehensible forms of relations, although non-senators could resort to them without compunction.

The clienteles of elite financiers, whether the latter were specialists or not, were composed of two groups. On the one hand, the elite as a whole constituted their overall clientele for all the services that they provided. The elite financiers truly were 'the financiers of the aristocracy' in both senses of the expression. They themselves were part of the aristocracy, and it was, furthermore, for an elite clientele that they acted as financiers.

On the other hand, particularly where their money-lending operations were concerned, the elite financiers also attracted clients from all the other strata of society, but in those cases the sums involved were usually more modest and the operations less concentrated, since these other social circles were less wealthy and, besides, for them, other sources of finance were available: 'entrepreneurs', professional bankers, and certain traders who were also moneylenders. When the elite members loaned money outside their own circle, it was probably in two very different types of situation: on the one hand, they financed well-to-do people in need of loans, in some cases in order to pursue their own economic activities ('entrepreneurs', for example, who were close to the elite

---

[58] D'Arms 1981: 103–4.

[59] Cicero's letters of recommendation show that it was common to have procurators and various correspondents in the provincial towns, for example in Asia (Deniaux 1993).

both culturally and socially); on the other hand, they advanced loans to dependants in need, who could not make ends meet, year in year out, without running up debts. This second kind of situation must have been common in the countryside, but there is little evidence to show for it. When small-scale landowners offered their land as security, this speeded up the process which led ultimately to the concentration of real estate in the hands of the elite.

I will conclude with three observations on the social and economic functions of this financial activity. First, it encouraged monetization in all the social circles in which the elite financiers moved, but above all within the elite itself. An aristocracy whose wealth remains constant flourishes with all the more brilliance when it has the means of procuring liquid cash – liquid cash which, in its turn, stimulates purchases and, as a result, encourages the commercialization of merchandise. The reason why the two great orders flourished with such brilliance, particularly in the first century BC and the first century AD, is that they managed to balance the annual character of their agricultural income, part of which would be paid in kind, with the considerable cost of daily living expenses and the relatively exceptional occasions when their members, for political or social reasons, found themselves obliged to pay out even greater sums all at once. The elite managed to do this all the better because it was itself able to provide the financial services that it needed. This self-sufficiency of the elite as a group helped to ensure its success and its longevity. Nevertheless, the very flexibility of the elite, its ability to control everything and profit from everything, was no doubt also the very thing that imposed limits upon the Roman economy.

Secondly, this financial life encouraged commercialization and the circulation of patrimonies. Although the very notion of the patrimony was central to the thinking and behaviour of the members of the elite, and those patrimonies were hereditary, their components (land, buildings, and slaves) were easily bought and sold, above all in Italy and the more prosperous and advanced provinces. Professional bankers certainly played a role in this mobility of patrimonial possessions, but so did the elite financiers, as N. Rauh has recently shown.[60]

Finally, the elite financiers provided credit for all those in need of money. Was that credit destined above all to finance production and trade? No, it was not. However it did finance some production and trade, just as it financed everything else: that is to say consumption, particularly

---

[60] Rauh 1989.

conspicuous consumption, the needs of foreign cities that were liable to be plundered by provincial governors and tax-collectors, and so on. The Romans made no distinction between a productive loan, that is to say a loan destined for economic activity, and any other kind of loan. However, that certainly does not mean to say that none of their loans was productive.

CHAPTER 3

Banks and bankers

The first bankers to receive deposits from their clients and to use some of that money to make loans made their appearance in Athens during the second half of the fifth century B C. They were known as 'trapezites' and the word used to denote their business was *trapeza* (literally 'table').[1] Similar professionals first installed themselves in the Forum in Rome between 318 and 310 B C.[2]

Were they Greeks? There is nothing to indicate that they were. It is true that Plautus gives his bankers Greek names and sometimes calls them 'trapezites', but he was writing *palliatae* ('cloaked') comedies, which were set in Greece. And the only banker from the third century whose name is known to us was called Lucius Fulvius, a thoroughly Latin name![3]

Did they start off as assayers/money-changers, and later become money-changers/bankers? Given that deposit banks had already existed in the Greek world for at least a century, I incline to think, rather, that the *argentarii* received deposits right from the start.[4] In Plautus' works, at any rate, they were money-changers, assayers and deposit bankers, all at once.[5]

There is absolutely nothing to suggest that the first *argentarii* were silversmiths. Up until the beginning of the fourth century AD, there are no signs at all of any *argentarii* working as silversmiths. Silversmiths were sometimes called *fabri argentarii* or *vascularii argentarii*, etc., but never simply *argentarii*.[6]

In the course of the last century of the Republic, several important innovations are noticeable. In the second half of the second century B C

---

[1] Bogaert 1966: 137–44; 1968: 61–3 and 305–7.
[2] Andreau 1987a: 337–40. See Livy 9.40.16.   [3] Pliny, *Nat. Hist.* 21.8.
[4] Andreau 1987a: 344–6.   [5] Andreau 1987a: 333–56.
[6] See Gummerus 1915–18, still a fundamental work.

the *argentarii*, still deposit-bankers, took to regularly attending auction sales, so as to advance credit to buyers.[7]

In the same period, the presence of *nummularii* is attested for the first time, in the sanctuary area of Praeneste.[8] They appear in Rome, in the early years of Augustus' reign. Up until the first half of the second century A D, the *nummularii* limited themselves to assaying coins and changing money. Subsequently, they became deposit-bankers, like the *argentarii*, but never took part in auctions.[9]

From the time of Cato the Elder's *De agricultura* until about the mid-second century A D, a third professional group was also active, the *coactores*. They were not bankers but private receivers, who took a commission on the amounts that they held for their clients.

Finally, a fourth profession made its appearance during the first century B C, that of the *coactores argentarii*, who were receivers and money-changers/bankers. I have in the past dated their appearance to the third quarter of the first century B C, for I thought that the first one known to us was Vespasian's grandfather, Titus Flavius Petro.[10] However, G. Maselli and A. Petrucci are convinced that in the very early first century, Lucius Munius of Reate was already a *coactor argentarius* (a deposit banker) and not simply a *coactor* as I had believed. If they are right, the *coactores argentarii* must have appeared earlier than I suggested.[11] But that modification would not affect the distinction between *coactores* and *coactores argentarii*.

We know of no woman banker. According to Callistratus, the profession of *argentarius* was officially banned to women.[12]

The Greek world of the Roman period also had its professional assayers, money-changers, and deposit-bankers. But it is worth noting two differences between it and Italy and the Latin-speaking provinces. The first relates to auctions. In the Greek world, professional bankers never took part on a regular basis. Auctions certainly took place, and the buyers were certainly free to borrow money to pay the vendors for their purchases. But trapezites, as such, did not take part in those sales.

---

[7] N. Rauh (1989: 45–54) thinks that, as early as the Second Punic War, the *argentarii* were providing credit at auctions. However, his arguments do not seem decisive to me.

[8] Degrassi 1957–63: 106a (the last decades of the second century B C).

[9] *Dig.* 2.13.9.2; 2.14.47.1; 14.3.20; 16.3.7.2.

[10] Suet. *Vesp.* 1.2; and Andreau 1987a: 139–67 and 293.

[11] *CIL* I, 2.632; see Maselli 1986: 49–50; Andreau 1987a: 147 and 152; Petrucci 1991: 298–9. They emphasize the use of the words *usura* and *ratio*. But Petrucci is wrong to call this receiver Mummius; his name was Munius.   [12] *Dig.* 2.13.12.

The second difference relates to the geographical distribution of these professions. Whereas the Latin-speaking world as a whole adopted Italian customs and seems to have been very homogeneous in this respect, in the Greek part of the Empire, regional peculiarities are noticeable, particularly in Egypt and Palestine.

In Egypt, among the private banks one comes across *kollybistikai trapezai*, 'exchange banks', which first appeared at the end of the Ptolemaic period and subsequently spread, particularly from the time of Augustus on. These banks, which at first limited themselves to foreign exchange, subsequently became deposit banks, just like other *trapezai*.[13] Their history appears to run parallel to that of the *nummularii* in the Latin-speaking part of the Empire. In the second and third centuries AD, there were private banks that were leased out and that do not appear to have enjoyed a monopoly,[14] but such establishments also existed in the same period in certain cities in the Greek half of the Empire. Finally, in Egypt there were also public banks, *demosiai trapezai*, which were the heirs to the royal banks.[15] These public banks had no equivalent in the Graeco-Roman world, for they were State institutions, responsible for the payment and collection of sums due from the State or to the State, and they played a fiscal role.[16]

In Jewish Palestine, so long as the Temple existed, the Jews were annually required to pay a half-shekel tax, to be paid in certain predetermined coins (staters and half-staters). Temple money-changers, accorded some kind of official standing, were responsible for changing into the required currency other coins that were delivered to the Temple.[17]

Without doubt, in the course of the second half of the third century AD, the banking professions went through some very hard times. What is known as 'the third-century crisis' resulted in a serious interruption in their history, particularly in the Latin-speaking part of the Empire. It was occasioned partly by a depreciation in the value of metal coins and by a rise in prices, but the first signs of the situation were already detectable in the second century: after the early years of the second century, no *argentarii* are attested in Italy outside Rome and the major ports (Ostia, Portus, and Aquileia), and the *coactores* also disappear from our documentation. In the course of the third century, the *coactores argentarii* likewise disappeared.

[13] Bogaert 1994: 10–12. On the private bankers of Roman Egypt, see also Rathbone 1991, who calls them 'freelance professionals' (390). [14] Bogaert 1994: 8–10 and 77–93.
[15] Bogaert 1994: 13–18 and 133–52. [16] Bogaert 1968: 403–8.
[17] Lambert 1906: 24–7.

We know of no banking *argentarius* between 260 and the last third of the fourth century A D. The word *argentarius*, used on its own and to designate a profession, is not attested for about seventy years. Then, in about 330–340, it reappears. At this time, however, it was applied to silversmiths, not to money-changers, whereas in the past, *argentarius*, used on its own, had never designated a metalworker.

The explanation is that the profession of an *argentarius*, a money-changer/banker who provided credit at auctions, disappeared during the second half of the third century. The word *argentarius*, used on its own, was, as it were, liberated by that disappearance and came to be used for a different profession, that of silversmiths. Subsequently, these silversmiths known as *argentarii* in their turn took to effecting money-changing and banking operations, as is attested by, for example, several passages from Saint Augustine.

Between the second half of the third century and the first half of the fifth, the noun *argentarius* was thus used to designate a profession in three different ways, each for a fairly short period:

(1) at the beginning of the second half of the third century A D the profession of an *argentarius*, in the sense of a money-changer/banker, disappeared (as did the credit that used to be available at auctions, which was never to become available again). The word *argentarius*, used on its own to designate a profession, is thereafter not attested for a good half-century;

(2) from the 330–40s, it is again attested, but now used to designate silversmiths;[18]

(3) towards the end of the century, these silversmiths began, in their turn, to accept deposits and became money-changers/deposit-bankers. Thus once again there existed *argentarii* who were deposit-bankers, but they did not play any part in auctions, and they also practised as silversmiths. These *argentarii* are still well attested in the sixth century, in the reign of Justinian, and even at the end of the century, in the works of Gregory the Great.

The destiny of the word *argentarius* proves that by the time of the Tetrarchy the *argentarii* and the *coactores argentarii* of the Early Empire had disappeared. Had the *nummularii* also disappeared? That is hard to confirm, but none is mentioned during the first half of the fourth century. And what of the trapezites of the Greek part of the Empire?

---

[18] For example Firm. Mat., *Math.* 3.3.14; 4.21.6; 7.26.10; *Cod. Theod.* 13.4.2 and 12.1.37. See Andreau 1986.

Outside Egypt, none is attested in the first half of the century, but that does not prove that they had in effect disappeared. In Egypt where, thanks to the papyri, the documentation is more abundant, we know for sure that some banks, both public and private, continued to function. Private bankers are well attested in Alexandria around the middle of the fourth century (in the works of Saint Basil) and also at Oxyrhynchus (in a dozen or so papyri).[19] For the subsequent period, there is once again documentation on banking professions outside Egypt.[20]

A number of literary texts, both Greek and Latin, allude fleetingly to the banking professions and to financiers, and a few, such as Plautus' *Curculio* and Cicero's *Pro Caecina*, refer to them at greater length. In general, however, professional bankers, money-changers, and receivers are as much neglected by the ancient authors as are other shopkeepers, artisans, and traders. Information of a prosopographic nature about such individuals, which is abundant on the subject of senators and knights, is extremely rare. However, other types of documentation on them are available.

First, there are the texts of the jurists. The affairs of elite financiers came under the provisions of the law applying to all Roman citizens and, with very few exceptions, were never subject to any special regulations; but the banking professions, for their part, were affected by the beginnings of a professional code of law. The jurists were therefore more prone to write about these. The *Digest* provides a few fragments from their texts, but they are very selective. The aspects of the profession that were still of concern to the contemporaries of Justinian, such as the production of documentation in a court of law, do crop up from time to time, whereas there is virtually no mention of the credit that was provided at auctions.

Then, there are funerary inscriptions. At no time did artisans and shopkeepers have their professions mentioned as a matter of course in their funerary inscriptions. But right at the end of the Republic and under the Principate, some did have this done. Why some but not others, we do not know. Customs certainly varied from one region to another. In Italy, Gaul, and Germany, professions were mentioned more frequently than in North Africa or in the Danube area. Thus, we have in our possession over a hundred inscriptions relating to professional businessmen dating from between the time of Cicero and the third century AD.

---

[19] Bogaert 1994.
[20] One also comes across *collectarii* or *kollektarioi*; see Andreau 1983b and Bogaert 1994 (in particular 121–31).

Over half the professionals who are mentioned practised in Rome, and 20 per cent practised outside Italy, in the western provinces.[21] These percentages are surprising (between 10 and 20 per cent of all the pagan inscriptions in Latin were found in Rome, and probably a good third in Italy, Rome included). Should we conclude that bankers in the provinces were more likely not to have the name of their profession mentioned in their funerary inscriptions? It does not seem an adequate explanation. In the case of the wholesalers the percentages are very different. Under the Early Empire only one quarter of the *negotiatores* or *negotiantes* are attested in Rome, and one quarter in the rest of Italy, but one half elsewhere in the western provinces. Thus, although the banking and financial professions certainly were represented in the provinces, they constituted a phenomenon that was overwhelmingly Italian, and many of them operated in Rome itself.

We are in possession of many more inscriptions dating from the period of Augustus and the first century AD than from the following two centuries.[22] However, the reason for this is hard to interpret. We should bear in mind the overall number of funerary inscriptions (which increased greatly between the first century AD and the mid-third century) and also epigraphical customs (references to professions, particularly in Rome, dwindled considerably). One thing, however, is sure: in Italy, outside Rome and the major ports, from the beginning of the second century AD onwards, the banking professions were tending to disappear.

Two batches of wax-covered writing tablets found in Italy and both dating from the first century AD refer to the businesses of professional bankers. One consists of the 153 tablets found in Pompeii in the house of L. Caecilius Jucundus.[23] Jucundus was an *argentarius* or a *coactor argentarius* who exercised his profession between the reigns of Tiberius and Nero. At auctions, he would pay the sellers the price of the objects sold and would extend credit to the buyers. When he paid the sums due to the sellers, they would give him receipts, which he would keep. The vast majority of the tablets discovered in his house are receipts of that type. But about fifteen of them relate instead to tax allocations agreed between the colony of Pompeii and Jucundus.[24] Unlike the others, these tablets therefore do not relate, strictly speaking, to L. Caecilius' profession. Professional bankers were no more likely to become city tax

---

[21] Andreau 1987a: 313–29.   [22] Andreau 1987a: 257–311.
[23] *CIL* IV, 3340; see Andreau 1974a and Jongman 1988.   [24] Andreau 1974a: 53–71.

farmers than any other citizen. However, outside their profession they were allowed to engage in any operations that they wished to, provided these were legal.

Other tablets were found more recently (in 1959) in Murecine, close to Pompeii. They date from the same time as those of Jucundus and relate to business conducted in Puteoli, not in Pompeii. Several of them concern the interventions of bankers in auctions. I shall return to these in chapter 6.

Some of the operations in which these bankers engaged within the framework of their profession were also conducted by others who, professionally, had nothing to do with banking. That was certainly the case where coin-assaying and money-changing were concerned. Plato cites among those who would change money, as well as *argyramoiboi* (professional money-changers and assayers), shipowners (*naukleroi*), wholesalers (*emporoi*), and retailers (*kapeloi*).[25] The same went for the collection of payments. On his departure for Egypt, the knight C. Rabirius Postumus was instructed to recover the credits owing to Gabinius, yet Rabirius Postumus was not a professional *coactor*. Cicero compares him to a professional money-receiver simply because, in this instance, Rabirius, although not a *coactor*, did collect money.[26] Anyone was free to collect money on account from a third party, whether or not he made a charge for doing so.

Let me now describe the various operations carried out within the framework of the profession by professional bankers, money-changers, and cashiers: the assaying of coins; foreign exchange; the advancing of credit and the collection of money at auctions; the reception of deposits and the payments that money-changers/bankers effected, which constituted the basis of bank accounts; the advancing of loans; and all the other operations that arose out of the above.

Trapezites, *nummularii*, and *argentarii* all acted as assayers of coins. To verify the value of coins, particularly gold coins, the ancients could use a touchstone. Professional assayers also relied on a series of more empirical techniques. By looking at a coin, feeling it, and tapping it to make it ring, they could check its worth and ascertain that it was not filled with some other substance, or not 'sauced' (that is to say that the outer layer of silver did not conceal a 'soul' of copper). They would check its dimen-

---

[25] Plato, *Polit.* 289c; see Bogaert 1968: 329, note 143.
[26] Cic. *Rab. Post.* 11.30; and D'Arms 1981: 27–8, 30 and 80–1.

sions and its type, perhaps by comparing it to samples or to representations of various coins. They would check that it had been minted by an officially authorized workshop. Finally, they would weigh the coin on a *trutina*. This was a small pair of scales with arms of equal length, designed to be held, not set down, and equipped with two plates, curved to form bowls. In this way they could make sure the coin had not been worn or scratched away and that, with use, it had not lost too much weight.

There is very little documentation available on the subject of foreign exchange, which is not really surprising since, given the extent of Roman domination, there must have been much less need for money-changing than in classical Greece. At the time of the independent Greek cities, over a thousand cities and hundreds of sovereign polities issued currencies.[27] A unified Mediterranean clearly gave rise to fewer foreign exchange operations. The services of trapezites, *nummularii*, and *argentarii* were more in demand for changing high-value coins into smaller ones (changing gold into silver or bronze), for changing ingots of precious metals, and for changing various categories of money in circulation in the Empire into other categories. For many cities were authorized by the Emperor to mint bronze or even silver coins, particularly in the eastern part of the Empire. Not all the coins minted officially in the imperial workshops constituted valid currency throughout the Empire.[28] These various currencies that circulated concurrently in different parts of the Empire sometimes needed to be changed.

But the most informative documents about the changing of money are the inscriptions written in Greek that relate to changing high-value coins into small-value ones. The assayers/money-changers were entitled to charge a commission (of about 5 per cent) on such operations, and they appear to have derived substantial profits from this. In some cities, for example Pergamum, Mylasa, and Sparta under the Empire (the documents that have come down to us date from the second and third centuries AD), all money-changing of this type had to pass through an individual money-changer or a company of money-changers/bankers who or which had been granted a money-changing monopoly. The city would levy part of the money-changer's commission, by way of a municipal tax. In Pergamum, under the reign of Hadrian, this led to ill-feeling between the money-changers and the shopkeepers, with the latter accusing the former of having made illegal profits at their

[27] Bogaert 1968: 308–31.   [28] Grant 1956: 102–12.

expense.[29] The fact that a tax was levied helps to explain why cities were so keen to mint money, even if it only took the form of bronze coins.[30] The changing of money into smaller-value coins was thus more than simply a modest daily occupation, for as A. Gara has convincingly argued, it was an integral part of the Empire's fiscal policy.[31]

These professional money-changers worked in little shops or out of doors, at trestle tables. They were independent small-scale entrepreneurs and their activities usually involved a manual exchange of coins.[32] We do not know how their relations with the State were conducted at a practical level. How did they manage their money-changing operations, that is to say how did they dispose of the coins received from clients for which they had no use? Did they sell them back to the Public Treasury or Mint? If a monetary reform led to certain coins being withdrawn from circulation, were they responsible for collecting them and restoring them to the State? We do not know.

Now let us move on to the auction sales that frequently took place in Graeco-Roman antiquity, particularly in Italy.[33] Merchandise was sold by auction in ports, in fairs, and in wholesale and retail markets, as were harvests, property, slaves, etc. Announcing an auction was a good way of advertising a sale. It would be particularly profitable when, following a death, the heirs decided to get rid of all or part of the patrimony of which they had become co-proprietors. Auctions also played an important role where loans were concerned, for if a debtor had provided security and was unable to pay off his debt, whatever he had pledged could be sold at auction at the insistence of his creditor. Cicero's correspondence cites several examples of auctions held following a death in the family,[34] and the tablets of Agro Murecine refer to several examples of auctions held for the sale of pledges.[35]

It was the public crier, the *praeco*, who presided over such auctions and awarded the objects to the highest bidders. At the time of Plautus and Cato, money-receivers (*coactores*) would be present at auctions; they did not forward loans but charged a commission for receiving money from the buyers and then passing it on to the sellers. The services of a receiver would be all the more indispensable where both the seller and the buyer were constantly on the move (as in the cases of itinerant traders and

---

[29] See the inscription *OGI* 484 + II, 552; Bogaert 1968: 231–4 and 401–3; and Gara 1976 115–24.
[30] Gara 1986: 107.   [31] Gara 1976; 1979; 1988.
[32] Bogaert 1976 and Andreau 1987a: 521–5.
[33] See in particular Talamanca 1954; Thielmann 1961; Thomas 1957; Andreau 1974a; 1987a; 583–97 and passim.   [34] Rauh 1989.   [35] Bove 1984d: 75–138.

absentee landlords). A receiver was officially responsible for keeping detailed registers relating to these auctions (*tabulae auctionariae* or *auctionales*), in which he would note down dates, detailed descriptions of the objects sold, prices, and the names of the sellers and buyers.

From the second half of the second century B C on, the *argentarii* regularly took part in auctions, paying over the purchase price to the sellers and advancing a short-term loan to the buyers (for a period of a few months or a year at the most). The buyer and the seller would themselves conclude the contract of sale.[36] The presence of the money-changer/banker did not rule out that of a *coactor*, whose job it would be to receive money and to transmit it to those to whom it was owed (the *argentarius* and the seller). Does this mean that the receiver was an employee of the *argentarius*, as is suggested by a scholium on Horace?[37] Possibly, in some cases. However, the rest of our documentation indicates, rather, that the receivers tended to be independent, working autonomously. On the other hand, where an *argentarius* was present at an auction, it would be he who kept a register of the sales.

The first century B C (either the early years, if it is true that L. Munius of Reate was one, or – if not – the mid-century) saw the appearance of *coactores argentarii*, who were at once receivers and money-changers/bankers.

Did some auctions take place without money-changers/bankers being present? Probably, but we cannot be sure. The presence of the public crier, the *praeco*, at any rate, was indispensable, for it was he who allocated the articles sold to the highest bidders.[38]

The credit from auction sales was very important to the *argentarii*, but in the eyes of the jurists it did not constitute the heart or hard core of the concept of a bank, an *argentaria*. As they saw it, what characterized a bank was the twofold service that it provided: receiving deposits and advancing credit. The banker lent, not his own money, but at least some of the money that he had received from his clients. A bank was also characterized by the bond that linked the banker and his client.[39] The client had deposited his money with the banker; he could either leave it on deposit or withdraw it whenever he wished, or else he could ask his banker to make payments with it.[40] This link was thus manifested by a

---

[36] Thomas 1957: 45–59.   [37] Pseudo-Acron, *ad Hor. Sat.* 1.6.86; see Andreau 1987a: 717–20.
[38] Thomas 1957: 60–1 and Thielmann 1961: 54–5.   [39] Plautus, *Curc.* 71–9.
[40] Paulus writes, describing bankers: *(. . .) rationes conficiunt, (. . .) et accipiunt pecuniam et erogant per partes* (*Dig.* 2.13.9.2).

series of operations conducted by the banker and by the records of those operations that were entered on the register. All those operations put together constituted the deposit account of his client, his *ratio*. I am therefore convinced, along with E.E. Cohen, that ancient bankers truly were deposit bankers, and not merely pawnbrokers.[41]

The jurists' view of a deposit bank (*argentaria*) was at once very rigid and very flexible. The definition of the kernel of a bank was rigid: for them, a bank was based on the concept of a deposit account, and anything unconnected with the account was, strictly speaking, no concern of the bank's. However, it was flexible as to the details of the operations that a bank made possible: an account was neither more nor less than that series of operations.

A few remarks seem called for on the subject of sealed deposits, also known, in legal parlance, as regular deposits. These deposits, in the form sometimes of coins, sometimes of objects or documents, had to be restored to their owners untouched by whoever accepted them as deposits. Whether or not he was a banker made no difference either to the purpose of a regular deposit or to the rules governing it. The person with whom it was deposited had no right to use the sum of money or object, or to make it bring a return by investing it. Such a deposit would be kept in a closed sack. When a text mentions handing over to some individual the money contained in a sack (*in sacculo dare*), it usually means that a sealed deposit is being consigned.

But such sealed deposits were clearly not the major feature of a bank, for that was constituted by the non-sealed deposit, which the banker had the right to invest, provided he would subsequently restore an equivalent sum to its owner. However, a study of bank deposits in Rome is complicated by the legal problems to which they gave rise. The point is that while there can be no doubt that *argentarii*, *coactores argentarii*, and (later) *nummularii* were accepting non-sealed deposits, it is not at all certain that jurists were recognizing the existence of an irregular deposit contract to accompany this financial practice. Many legal historians believe that at the time of what they call 'the classical period of law' (the second and third centuries AD) no such contract existed and that a banked deposit was legally regarded as a loan. However, in all probability, only interest-bearing deposits would legally be considered as loans, whereas others, those that brought in no interest to the depositors, were for their part

---

[41] Cohen 1992: 8–10 and 22–5.

regarded as true deposits, regular deposits. According to Roman law, a deposit could not bring in a profit to the depositor.[42]

As in classical Athens, the deposits received by bankers thus fell into two distinct categories: some produced interest for the depositors; others did not. In the eyes of the jurists, only the latter were true deposits. However, it is difficult to draw the line between the interest-bearing deposits and the others. By and large, non-remunerated deposits probably corresponded to what we would call payment deposits (deposits principally intended for making payments or for withdrawals), while others corresponded to what we call investment deposits (from which the depositor wished to make a profit and which, in some cases, he would agree not to withdraw before some pre-fixed date).

But what should we make of this? M. I. Finley argued that the situation testified to the primitive nature of ancient banking. W. E. Thompson, on the other hand, believes (wrongly, in my own view) that in classical Greece no deposits were remunerated, but (in contrast to Finley) he interprets this as a sign of modernity.[43] He reckons that if a banker had paid out substantial interest on his deposits, he would have had to charge his borrowers far too high interest rates, as a result of which he would have been not so much making loans to businessmen, as simply practising usury. If, on the other hand, the banker paid no interest on any of the deposits that he held, his room for manoeuvre would have been far greater.

I am convinced that neither Finley nor Thompson is right. Whether payment deposits were or were not remunerated is not in itself a clear indication of either archaism or modernity. The debate on the archaism of the ancient economy is certainly a central one; we cannot get around it. But what is so difficult to determine is which phenomena truly are symptomatic of either modernity or archaism. To my mind, remuneration for payment deposits cannot be included among those phenomena.

For if remuneration for payment deposits guaranteed the depositors a profit, it meanwhile made the position of the bankers more fragile, and it might well have turned businessmen seeking loans away from them. Yet on the opposite hypothesis, would not an absence of interest likewise have turned those same businessmen away, discouraging them from depositing their money in the bank? The success of a deposit bank surely depended on the number of its deposits and depositors. And anyway, is

---

[42] Andreau 1987a: 533–44.   [43] Finley 1973: 141 and Thompson 1979.

the interest of the banker more indicative of modernity than that of the client?[44]

Nowadays, banks distinguish between short-term deposits (upon which the depositor can draw whenever he wishes to) and long-term or fixed-term deposits (which the banker does not have to restore to the depositor until the predetermined date). The latter deposits are remunerated. In principle, it is recognized that the former also deserve some kind of recompense. But that recompense does not always take the form of interest. Instead, the banker offers the depositor a number of services, and those 'banking services' are considered sufficient remuneration.[45] Clients appreciate the banking services more than they would interest paid on short-term deposits.

All that can be said for sure, then, is that certain deposits carried no interest, while others (regarded as loans by the Roman jurists) were remunerated. As for the interest rate involved, we have no way of knowing what it was; but obviously it must have been lower than the interest rate that bankers could expect to obtain by making loans of the money placed on deposit.

A client could either withdraw the deposited money all at once, or little by little. He might also visit the bank with one of his creditors and ask the banker to pay him, or – in certain circumstances – he might send his creditor to the bank on his own. In the latter case, the client would give the banker a payment order and the creditor, if unknown to the banker, would present himself bearing some kind of token by which he could be recognized.

A cheque is a written note by which a client of a bank orders it to pay a specific sum to the beneficiary of the cheque. But a cheque is given to the beneficiary, whereas other payment orders are given to the banker. In antiquity there were no cheques that were transmissible by endorsement. Were non-transmissible cheques used? In the Latin-speaking world there is no trace of them. In the eastern Mediterranean, the use of cheques is attested in at least two regions, in Canaan, following rulings made by Mosaic law on the payment of wages,[46] and in Egypt, where cheques from the end of the Hellenistic period have recently been found and published, along with the records relating to the cheques, which were given to the banker. Such cheques continued to be used in Egypt

[44] Andreau 1980: 423–5; 1987a: 532.
[45] See for example Hamel 1966: 206–9 and Ferronnière and de Chillaz 1976: 47.
[46] Ejges 1930: 83–4 and Bogaert 1968: 340, note 206.

after the Roman conquest.[47] Yet the regions in question do not seem to have enjoyed an economic life much more prosperous or highly developed than other regions. The existence of these non-transmissible cheques was not as important historically as that of the transmissible cheques which came into use later, in modern Europe.

As for transfers, these could be made between clients of the same bank, as seems to be attested by two passages, one in Plautus, the other in Terence.[48] There was no system of institutionalized compensation between banks of the same city, but that did not prevent transfers from taking place, as is attested by a number of papyri. To facilitate such transfers, a banker sometimes held an account in the bank or banks of one or several of his colleagues.[49] Such an arrangement, though not impossible, was no doubt much more rare between banks in different cities, and must have depended on the personal relations of the individual bankers concerned. Professional bankers, unlike elite financiers, were local financiers who specialized in operations on the spot.[50] The body of documentation available on them suggests that they seldom arranged long-distance transfers or foreign exchange operations.

The service that a banker provided by making payments for his clients was connected with the *receptum argentarii*. The *receptum* was reserved for *argentarii* (up until the second or third century AD, when it was extended to the *nummularii*). It was the undertaking that the banker gave to a third party, when he promised to pay him the money that a client of his owed him.[51] The *receptum* involved three people (the banker, his client, and the third party), but it was binding upon only two of them, the banker and the third party. Legally, thanks to the *receptum*, the client needed neither to express his agreement nor to be present. Clearly, however, in one form or another an agreement also existed between him and his banker on the payment of the debt in question on a predetermined date.

The *receptum* existed and was used from the second century BC down to the third century AD (after which it lapsed), but the literary and legal texts seldom mention it. In the *Digest*, a number of fragments relating to the *receptum* were, as O. Lenel shows, inserted there at the time of Justinian and were applied to the *constitutum*, which was then to some

---

[47] Bagnall and Bogaert 1975; Bogaert 1994: 20–4 and 245–52.
[48] Plautus, *Asin.* 436–40 and Ter. *Phormio* 921–3.
[49] Bogaert 1994: 102, note 43 and 250–2.
[50] In the Heroninos archive, in Egypt, the role of bankers is primarily local (Rathbone 1991).
[51] Kaser 1971–75: I, 585; Bürge 1987: 527–36; Andreau 1987a: 597–602.

extent replacing the *receptum* but was not limited to bankers.[52] Given the silence of the literary texts, it is not possible to determine how frequently it was used or in what financial or commercial circumstances. Presumably it facilitated operations relating to the banked deposit (as the client was not required to withdraw the money from the bank in order to hand it over to his creditor). It also constituted a pledge, a guarantee of payment to a third party who was about to lend money to the banker's client.

A banker would advance loans and these would figure in the deposit accounts. But although several texts testify to the existence of such loans, very few specific cases are known to us outside Egypt. However, the tablets of Lucius Caecilius Jucundus, in Pompeii, record seventeen cases of loans advanced by the banker Jucundus to buyers at auction sales. Virtually all we know about these loans is when their repayments fell due. They were very short-term, just for a few months or at the most a year. When a banker is lending not his own funds but those of the bank, he has to lend for short periods. This helps to moderate the overall size of the credits, for in economic terms a successful banker is one who lends 'long-term' after borrowing 'short-term'. The scanty evidence available to us suggests that such was not the case with Roman bankers.

The various operations conducted by an *argentaria*, that is to say stemming from the concept of a deposit bank and from the profession of money-changer/banker, were all recorded for each client in a deposit account, known as a *ratio* in the singular, or in certain stylistic contexts (colloquial language, comedies, etc.) as *ratiuncula*. Other expressions sometimes used were *ratio accepti et expensi* ('an account of deposits and payments') and *ratio implicita propter accepta et data* ('a complex account including both deposits and payments').[53] Ulpian, citing the famous jurist Labeo, provides the following definition: 'Labeo says that an account is made up of mutual affairs which consist in paying out, collecting payments, lending, obliging, and paying off one's debts.'[54] It was not quite what we would today call a current account: the obligations recorded in the account were not renewed or reviewed, and the various articles included in the account were so disparate that the banker's client was not expected to calculate his compensation. The banker, however, did have to calculate that compensation, taking into consideration all the debts and deposits of that client. If Titius owed him 20 and had deposited 10, the *argentarius* could claim only the outstanding difference, 10,

[52] Lenel 1881: 62–71.   [53] *Dig.* 2.14.47.1.   [54] *Dig.* 2.13.6.3.

and moreover had to be careful to make no errors in his calculation of that difference.[55]

Several passages in Plautus' plays, one of which occurs in the *Aulularia*, show that a banker did not keep an up-to-date record that allowed him to know instantly how the account of each client stood, and also that he did not send his clients periodical updates. If a client wished to know how he stood without paying a visit to the banker, he had to tot up the deposits and withdrawals for himself.[56] Sometimes the banker allowed an overdraft; at least, that is exactly what happens in the *Aulularia*.[57] So long as an account remained open, the debtor, whether the banker or the client, was not obliged to pay off what he owed. But when the account was closed (by the unilateral decision of either of the parties), the client had either to withdraw his balance or to reimburse the banker.

All the operations effected on an account were entered in a register kept by the banker, the *rationes*, and this constituted the tangible reality of his clients' accounts. Up until the end of the Principate, this register was, in the Latin world, undoubtedly a *codex* (a collection of pages bound together at one edge), never a *volumen* (a scroll). We have no way of knowing precisely how such a register would be organized. Some historians think that the articles were classified according to clients, and that each client's account was kept on a separate page or set of pages. Others, myself included, believe that, on the contrary, articles were entered chronologically in the order in which operations were conducted on a day-to-day basis.[58] As for the bankers of classical Greece in the fourth century BC, R. Bogaert thinks they may have kept their records in a book classified according to clients, but we have no proof of this.[59]

Of two points we may be certain. First, this register should not in any way be confused with the *codex accepti et expensi*, the old traditional Roman register kept by all those with a patrimony. The *codex accepti et expensi*, which was never linked with any particular profession, seems, in fact, to have fallen out of use in the course of the Early Empire.[60] It too was kept on a day-to-day basis. Bankers may well have kept such registers, of course, but in order to manage their own affairs as a whole, not simply within the framework of their professional activities. One of the features that distinguishes these bankers from elite financiers is that the bankers

---

[55] Gaius, *Inst.* 4.64–8; see Kaser 1966, 248; 1971–75: I, 644–7 and II, 447–8.
[56] Plautus, *Aulul.* 526–31, *Capt.* 192–3 and *Curc.* 371–4.
[57] Plautus, *Aulul.* 526–31. In the Heroninos archive, overdraft facilities do not seem at all usual (Rathbone 1991: 328–9).   [58] Andreau 1987a: 615–26; Bürge 1987: 509–19; 1995.
[59] Bogaert 1968: 378–80.   [60] Thilo 1980.

would regard their professional field as utterly distinct from the rest of their activities, even where (as must frequently have been the case) all their activities were oriented toward profit and the acquisition of wealth.

Secondly, a banker's register of accounts was required by law to be produced whenever a client was involved in a law-suit, even if this did not involve the banker personally. The register was not considered to provide absolute proof, but it was deemed to be reliable, particularly where it constituted the only record of whatever had taken place. The banker was required to produce (*edere*) only the information relating to the account of the particular client involved; either he produced a copy of it or he allowed the original to be consulted, but he would make available only the records that related to the client's own account, for these records were considered to be the property of the client. Production of the register or of a copy of it did not imply that the account was closed.

Professional bankers might also engage in other financial activities, some of which would constitute a direct prolongation of their major professional operations, while others, on the contrary, would be simply part of the potential financial life of any man or woman with money to dispose of. First and foremost amongst these activities was certainly money-lending: bankers were clearly not averse to lending, over and above a proportion of the funds deposited by their clients, funds of their own or funds entrusted to them as credit intermediaries but quite separate from bank deposits.[61] As Q. Cervidius Scaevola points out, they also sometimes managed property for their clients (*rationes administrare, rem gerere*) by virtue of a special mandate.[62] As they were the holders of written documents, they were in a position to help their clients to prove what their expenses truly amounted to. So bankers tended to be used as witnesses.

Two points should be emphasized. On the one hand, professional bankers were part of the professional world and so were ranked socially far below the aristocracy. On the other hand, they alone were entrusted with banking responsibilities, and the ancients recognized that this made their position exceptional, as is shown by the texts of the jurists. Inevitably, this unique situation affected their daily lives and the services that they rendered.

From the point of view of their social rank, they must be emphatically distinguished from the elite financiers. Admittedly, we know no details of

[61] In *Dig.* 16.3.7.2 (Ulpian), this is money lent *per mensam, per nummularios*; see Andreau 1987a: 541.
[62] *Dig.* 34.3.28.9 (Scaev.).

the composition of their patrimonies, but it is noticeable that no banker is attested as having been either a knight or a senator. The father of Octavian (later Augustus), Caius Octavius, is no exception to that rule, since, according to Suetonius, it was – precisely – unthinkable that this senator could also have been an *argentarius*, even when starting out on his career.[63] As for the municipal aristocracies, we know of no banker who was ever a member of one, either in the East or the West. Furthermore, from the reign of Tiberius on, freedmen could not legally become either municipal magistrates or decurions.

In this respect, the situation of bankers was the same as that of any other professional groups, apart, that is, from the wholesalers of the Early Empire, the *negotiatores* and the *negotiantes*. Several (freeborn) wholesalers known to us were municipal aristocrats;[64] one was even a member of the equestrian order.[65] But these inscriptions relating to wholesalers are more frequently provincial than those relating to bankers, and also mostly of a later date. (In commerce and banking, freedmen are more numerous in Italy than in the provinces, and in the first century AD than in the second and third.)

The token of wealth and social standing represented by membership of one of the privileged orders, whether imperial or merely municipal, shows that professional bankers and financiers were not on as high a social level as wholesalers, although their standing was certainly comparable to that of the members of other professions.

The second point to make is that there is very little perceptible difference between bankers in the strict sense of the term, on the one hand, and receivers and assayers/money-changers, on the other. Yet one would have thought that deposit bankers, who could lend money and charge interest on it, had a greater chance of becoming wealthy. Nevertheless, the available documentation does not bear that out.

Between the time of Caesar and the first half of the second century AD, many of the professional bankers and financiers were freedmen. Half the *coactores* and half the *argentarii* known to us are explicitly stated to be freedmen; and half the known *coactores argentarii* and *nummularii* were definitely or almost definitely freedmen. As at least a minority of them had an elite member as their patron and had themselves personally acquired a certain position in their city, it is not surprising that, outside Rome, some are to be found among the *Augustales* and the *seviri*

---

[63] Suet. *Aug.* 3. 1; see Andreau 1987a: 430–8.
[64] *CIL* III, 2086; VI, 33 887; X, 5585; XIII, 257; XIII, 1954; XIII, 2448; XIII, 11 179; *AE* 1900; 203, etc.
[65] *CIL* VI, 29 722.

Augustales (the priests dedicated to the Emperor's cult), and, in Rome, among the *apparitores* (magistrates' attendants).

The freedman Caius Papius Apelles, an *argentarius* buried in Capua, was the *accensus* of a consul, probably under Augustus. An *accensus*, the attendant of a magistrate, who himself appointed him, was not a permanent employee. His functions ceased when the magistracy did. A *coactor*, Ti. Claudius Secundus, who was a freedman either of Claudius or of Nero, was also an *accensus* and at the same time a scribe.[66] Four *coactores argentarii*, one *nummularius*, and five *argentarii* known to us were *Augustales* or *seviri Augustales* in cities in Italy.[67]

Right at the end of the Republic and up until the first half of the second century AD, many professional financiers, mostly in Italy, thus belonged to the elite of the freedmen, while others were free-born plebeians of a certain social standing. Although they themselves could not enter the Senate or the equestrian order, it occasionally happened that a few of them (no doubt only a very few) managed to get their sons or grandsons accepted by those orders. The father of Horace (who himself was a knight) was a freedman who had at one time exercised the profession of a *coactor*. The poet's allusions to his father help us to understand how the latter had purchased real estate and had provided his son with an education of a kind to facilitate his accession to the aristocracy.[68] The *coactor argentarius* T. Flavius Petro, who had exercised his profession in Reate at the time of Caesar and the triumvirate, was the grandfather of the future Emperor Vespasian.[69] Finally, the *coactor* Ti. Claudius Secundus Philippianus' son, Ti. Claudius Secundinus, was a knight at an extremely tender age, for he was nine when he died.[70] Such cases of social promotion must have been rare. But they did exist and are signs of an undeniable mobility that was available, for example, to men exercising urban professions as bankers or businessmen.[71]

From the second century to the last decades of the Republic, the number of freedmen among the professional bankers seems to have been considerably lower. We know of several free-born *argentarii* at the time of Cicero, first and foremost M. Fulcinius, who is mentioned in the *Pro Caecina*. These free-born bankers must have enjoyed more prestige and greater standing than the freedmen of the beginning of the imperial period. They did not belong to the aristocracy any more than the

---

[66] *CIL* x, 3877. see also *CIL* vi 1605, 1859 and 1860.
[67] Andreau 1987a: 367–8, 375–6, 387, and 406.   [68] Andreau 1985b; 1987a: 370–1.
[69] Suet. *Vesp.* 1.2.   [70] *CIL* vi, 1605, 1859, and 1860, and Andreau 1985b.
[71] On this social mobility through business, see Andreau 1985b and 1992a; see also D'Arms 1981, *passim*.

freedmen did, and we know virtually nothing of their patrimonies. But the documentation relating to euergetism illuminates some of the differences between them and their colleagues of the early years of the Empire.

In the second century B C and at the beginning of the first century, particularly in Delos and the rest of the Greek world, but also in Italy and in Rome itself, certain trapezites and *argentarii* were in possession of considerable fortunes, which sometimes allowed them to make a great show of their generosity. Consider the banker M. Minatius, installed in Delos around the mid-second century B C; he was offered a statue and a crown by the association of the Poseidoniasts (worshippers of Poseidon) of Berytos.[72] Then there was L. Aufidius, also a trapezite in Delos, whose son very probably acquired the status of a knight, following the Social War.[73] Above all, we should not forget Philostratus, a native of Ascalon, who was a trapezite in Delos and subsequently became a citizen of Naples. In Delos, he was among those who subscribed towards the building of a theatre at the Syrian sanctuary. He offered two altars in the sanctuary of the gods at Ascalon, and dedicated the northern portico in the agora of the Italians and also the adjoining *exedra*. He was honoured with at least four statues.[74] In Italy, the banker of Scipio Aemilianus rates a mention. In the course of 162 B C or at the beginning of 161, he paid out the impressive sum of 1,200,000 sesterces, all in one go;[75] and L. Munius, a receiver (or possibly a receiver/banker), dedicated a very large sum of money to Heracles.[76]

The bankers and financiers of the subsequent period do not appear to have been able to make such ostentatious financial gestures. But that does not necessarily mean that they were less important economically and socially. Operating on a smaller scale, they contributed to the diffusion of monetary transactions and of deposit and credit facilities, in circles and cities where these had not hitherto been widely available. Bogaert underlines the somewhat 'democratic' nature of banking in Hellenistic and Roman Egypt, and the values of the cheques and payment orders there bear this out.[77] The situation was similar in the Latin-speaking part of the Empire. This was banking for people of no more than average means, but it certainly made an impact on the affairs of members of the elite (in particular through the part that bankers played in auctions).

[72] *IG* 1520. See Bogaert 1968: 187–8.
[73] Bogaert 1968: 190; Barlow 1978: 104–7; Etienne 1990: 136–43.
[74] Bogaert 1968: 188–9 and Mancinetti 1982.   [75] Polybius 31.27.
[76] Bodei 1978: 53–4; Verzar 1985; Andreau 1987a: 690.   [77] Bogaert 1985: 82–3.

CHAPTER 4

Other categories of financiers

As well as the elite financiers and the professionals, there were other categories of financiers. I shall pick out one intermediate category in particular. Although difficult to pin down and numerically relatively small, nevertheless it seems to me an important group: the bigger businessmen, whom C. Howgego suggests calling 'entrepreneurs'.[1]

There are two main reasons for singling out this group, which the Latin writers themselves did not distinguish as such and for which they had no specific word. The first has to do with the documentation that is available. Among the financiers whom we come across, there are some who were neither professional bankers, *argentarii*, nor *nummularii*. Their activities, financial means, and social relations had far more in common with those of the members of the elite. But they did not belong either to the Senate or to the equestrian order. Their life-style, their business affairs, and their patrimonies also seem to have differentiated them from the elite. They include a number of *negotiatores* who, in the second and first centuries B C, established themselves outside Italy to run their businesses. One was Publius Sittius of Nuceria, a member of the elite of his city who, through his taste for business deals, had allowed himself to run into debt in Italy and had thereby lost a considerable proportion of his real-estate patrimony. He went off to invest his money in the provinces, and even lent some to the king of Mauretania.[2] Such a figure had little in common with a professional banker but held a very marginal position in relation to the life of the imperial elite (even if such men as he did have occasion to mingle with senators and knights).

The second reason, which is of a more general nature, is connected with my comparative approach. As I observed in my Introduction, in almost all pre-industrial historical societies, non-agricultural activities involve two separate groups: on the one hand, the aristocracy, whose

---

[1] Andreau 1985c: 380–2 and Howgego 1992: 14.   [2] Cic. *pro Sulla* 20.56–9.

members possess from the outset a patrimony in the form of real estate; and on the other, professional men, town-dwellers with a specialized trade, such as artisans, traders, and bankers. But in many societies, in between these two groups there are intermediate groups or strata composed of businessmen, merchants, and bankers. Their members engage in bigger business deals than those of the professional men, and they enjoy greater social and political prestige. The consistency and success of these circles situated on the margins of the aristocratic elite vary enormously from one society to another. In the course of the last centuries of the Middle Ages, they acquired a dominant position, above all in Italy.[3] It was they who ran important international affairs and controlled the commercial networks, wielding bills of exchange.[4]

Non-agricultural activities are thus usually divided not between two social groups (the elite and the professional men), but between three. And the least stable and most mobile of the three, and the group that varies the most from one society to another, is definitely the intermediate one, that of the 'entrepreneurs' (or 'bigger businessmen'). In some cases, it is very homogeneous and constitutes a veritable bourgeoisie; in others it comprises a number of isolated figures who are very different from one another. The origins of its members vary enormously, as do their political roles. In any comparison between the social and economic structures of different pre-industrial societies, these intermediate circles need to be brought to the fore, and we need to reflect upon their composition and role: that is my purpose with regard to the Roman world.

The first part of this chapter is composed of four very unequal sections. The first is devoted to the 'entrepreneurs'. The second tackles two categories of financiers about which we know very little: the usurers and high-interest moneylenders, and the merchant-financiers. Next, I shall have a few remarks to make about maritime loans, for which the creditors were probably in many cases 'entrepreneurs' or merchant-financiers. The last section of this chapter will be devoted to the business relations between financiers from different categories, and to the possible ways of moving from one category to another.

First, the 'entrepreneurs'. One has been named above: Publius Sittius. Let us consider another example. I shall then attempt to pick out a few of their salient characteristics.

T. Flavius Petro, Vespasian's grandfather, was a professional banker.

---

[3] Giardina and Gurevic 1994: 89–99.   [4] Boyer-Xambeu 1986.

But Vespasian's father, T. Flavius Sabinus, who also conducted financial business, was not. He began his career as a tax-collector in Asia, then practised money-lending at interest among the Helvetii.[5] Was he a knight? Apparently not, but he married a knight's daughter, Vespasia Polla.[6] It is hard to determine precisely what his functions were in Asia. He was probably not the *promagister* of the company responsible for collecting taxes, but the description *publicum agere* shows that he held quite a high position in the hierarchy of the company of tax-collectors. Such posts implied the possession of a patrimony. He strove to increase that patrimony by advancing interest-bearing loans to the Helvetii. And he must have been successful, for his sons did accede to the equestrian order and subsequently to the senatorial order.

The literary texts provide less information on these 'entrepreneurs' than on the members of the elite, and it is not possible to identify them from funerary inscriptions, unlike *argentarii*, since they generally practised no profession. Furthermore, this was a quite limited circle and it comprised very different types of individuals. So it is hard to define its limits, and one comes across many doubtful cases. All the same, it does seem to me that it is possible to distinguish two main characteristics:

(1) The social position of 'entrepreneurs' was always more or less the same. They had not yet made it as far as the Senate or the equestrian order, or else the position that they had acquired in the equestrian order did not satisfy their aspirations. Yet they were quite close to acceding to the imperial elite. In order to 'arrive', they pinned their hopes on their economic activities and the acquisition of greater wealth. The circle of 'entrepreneurs' thus constituted a major phenomenon of mobility and social advancement.

(2) Not only were they very mobile socially, they were equally so in a technical and professional sense. Their financial position and cultural background enabled them to eschew any profession apart from those of large-scale wholesaler or shipowner. Their active lives were therefore infinitely more flexible and multi-faceted than those of the professional bankers. To achieve success in their businesses, they were perfectly prepared to sell their land, if they had any, or to leave not only their native city but Italy itself. Some of them possessed a patrimony composed partly of real estate and partly of movable chattels. In their lives, political and cultural activities, and euergetism and ostentatious consumerism, held a

---

[5] Suet. *Vesp.* 1.2.
[6] Demougin 1992: 171–2; I would like to thank S. Demougin for the information that she provided about T. Flavius Sabinus.

less important place than in the lives of the senators and knights, while business held a far greater place. B. W. Frier claims that Roman investors were keener on finding reliable investments than on making very high profits.[7] In respect of the vast majority of senators and knights, who sought the best means to manage their patrimonies, he is undoubtedly right. This is exactly what Veyne calls the security strategy and what I have referred to above as the strategy of provident management.[8] However, such strategies are not consistent with the behaviour of the 'entrepreneurs'. They, for their part, adopted above all a profit strategy, and would certainly take risks in order to succeed in their speculations.

In the field of private finance, they clearly practised money-lending, using their own funds as well as those of their friends and connections. They would advance loans to private individuals, to cities, to vassal rulers and foreign sovereigns. They are to be counted accordingly among the largest-scale *negotiatores* of the Late Republic, particularly those Italians who had settled outside Italy in order to advance their private affairs. They acted as intermediaries in all kinds of operations involving credit and payment. Some had many connections in commercial circles, others fewer. Some served as tax-collectors (*publicani*), and were to be found among those who held important responsibilities in their companies, without being part of the topmost elite of tax-collectors (which was composed solely of knights).

Apart from the slaves who operated as businessmen, about whom I shall have something to say in chapter 5, it is possible to distinguish two other separate circles of financiers, about both of which very little is known.

We know virtually nothing about the urban and rural usury, the lending of money at very high interest rates, which strangled the poor and was a regular feature of all pre-industrial societies. Four graffiti appear to testify to its existence in Pompeii, but they constitute very limited and isolated evidence.[9] Even in Egypt, very little is known about these high-interest loans. Many of the loans studied by D. Foraboschi and A. Gara are not of this type.[10]

In any city it was common knowledge who were the professional bankers, which members of the elite would advance interest-bearing loans, who made high-interest loans, and who were borrowing. At least, so Dio Chrysostom informs us.[11] However, the documentation that has

---

[7] Frier 1980: 22 and note 5.   [8] Veyne 1991: 131–62, and above, 24–5.
[9] Andreau 1974a: 119–22.   [10] Foraboschi and Gara 1981; 1982.
[11] Dio Chrys. *Speech* 46.8.

come down to us, if any, concerns only the upper social strata. For the ordinary people, invariably, we have much less information. Apuleius' *Metamorphoses* tells us of a rich moneylender who took security in Hypata, and a *nummularius* in Thebes, but this work tells us nothing about high-interest moneylenders.[12]

The second category, unconnected with the above, comprised the merchant financiers. These operated as both wholesalers and financiers (and would, for example, advance loans to other traders). Demosthenes refers to one such individual in fourth-century Athens.[13] But in Rome, they elude us totally, although there can be no doubt that they existed. Perhaps the Sulpicii of Puteoli, to whom the tablets of Murecine belonged, fell into this category. However, we cannot be certain. We shall be returning to them in chapter 6.

Maritime loans were known in Latin as *pecunia traiecticia*, 'money that travelled', or sometimes as *pecunia nautica* (the expression *fenus nauticum* is not attested until the time of Diocletian).[14] A loan of this kind would be arranged between a moneylender and a wholesaler (or a shipowner) to finance a one-way or a return journey. The subject of the contract was a sum of money for which the security was the ship, the cargo (frequently purchased with the money loaned),[15] and other merchandise or land belonging to the borrower. The money would be repaid, along with very high interest rates, only if the ship reached its destination safely. If the vessel or its cargo was lost through no fault of the borrower, the latter remained under no obligation to his creditor. The moneylender alone bore all the risks attendant upon sea-voyages. Those risks justified the very high rate of interest (*pretium periculi*).

It is somewhat surprising that most pagan authors deplored contracts such as these, which were based on the risk involved, whereas, later, the Fathers of the Church considered them to constitute the only acceptable form of interest-bearing loans.[16]

Did maritime loans alter much between the fourth century BC or the

---

[12] Apul. *Metam.* 1.21.6 and 1.22.2; 4.8–21; 10.9.3. See Andreau 1987a: 185, 364, 393–5, 664.

[13] Dem. *Against Apat. (Speech 33)*, 4–5; see also Dem. *Speech 34*, 51–2, and Vélissaropoulos 1980: 42–5.

[14] See Biscardi 1974; Casson 1980; 1986; 1990; De Salvo 1992: 336–43; Purpura 1987; Rougé 1966: 345–60; 1980; 1985; de Ste. Croix 1974; Tchernia 1986b; 1995; Vélissaropoulos 1980: 301–11. On the Murecine tablet 13 (and also on tablet 34, which is not concerned with a maritime loan), see Ankum 1978; 1988; Bove 1984d; Purpura 1984; Santoro 1985.

[15] This is almost certainly the case in, for example, *P. Vindob.* G 40 822; see Casson 1990: 202.

[16] Vélissaropoulos 1980: 302.

Hellenistic period and the Principate? That is a question often asked and to which many answers have been offered. For my own part, I believe that there was a strong measure of economic and social continuity, even if the demands of Roman law made a few legal adjustments necessary.

It used to be believed, for example, that, in the Roman period, the ship and its cargo never served as security for the loan. However, the papyrus Vindob. G 19 792 shows that that idea was incorrect.[17] Another question concerns the way in which interest rates were calculated. According to the corpus of Demosthenes' speeches, the interest would be expressed as a fixed sum, the size of which would depend upon the length of the voyage and whether it would be only one-way or a return journey. And in Rome? There, the interest may have been a proportional levy, such as one third of the sum loaned. But quite possibly within a single period several different kinds of calculations were used, depending on the circumstances.[18] Continuity is not incompatible with the existence of several variations.

It has often been said that maritime loans corresponded to the small-scale individual commercial activities that were characteristic of the period preceding the Roman conquest. It has been suggested that, in Rome, from the second century BC onward, commercial companies were organized and therefore rendered the practice of the *pecunia traiecticia* unnecessary.[19]

Roman commerce certainly progressed between the third century BC and the beginning of the Empire. But whatever the nature of that progress, is there any proof that maritime loans became too archaic for the conditions of trade? I think not. The fact that we possess very little documentation on maritime loans does not constitute a clinching argument. The truth is that we are sadly lacking in documentation on commercial transactions as a whole (documents relating to commercial companies are likewise very rare).

Several pointers undermine the notion that maritime loans were used only for small-scale commercial activities. The first is the presence of a maritime loan in the archive of the Sulpicii, who lived in Puteoli and whose business affairs were anything but small-scale. The second is provided by the Vindob. papyrus G 40 822: if an extremely large cargo transported from Muziris in India to Alexandria occasioned a maritime loan, how can the practice be said to be reserved for

---

[17] Casson 1986: 16.
[18] Rougé 1985: 164–5. The Murecine tablet *TP* 34 is concerned with the interest of a third, but this is not a maritime loan; see Santoro 1985. [19] Rougé 1980 and De Salvo 1992: 343.

small-scale operations?[20] In any case, there is nothing to prove that maritime loans were incompatible with the existence of company contracts. The example of Cato the Censor would seem to indicate precisely the contrary, if the contracts concluded by his freedman Quintio are to be interpreted as types of maritime loans.[21] The Berlin papyrus refers to five borrowers,[22] the Vindob. G 19 792 papyrus to four.[23] Had these merchants or shipowners who were contracting together for a maritime loan not drawn up a company contract between them? The fact that the documentation on the subject happens to be slight has led to a belief that maritime loans were used in the Roman world far less than during the classical Greek period, but in my opinion that belief is erroneous.

To make bottomry (maritime) loans, you had to be acquainted with the circles of maritime commerce and you needed business contacts in other Mediterranean ports. You had to be prepared to make risky investments. It is a small wonder that the professional bankers, who specialized in local affairs, do not seem to have made bottomry loans, at least not within the framework of their profession.[24] Nevertheless, they did sometimes play a role in the arrangement of maritime loans, as the creditors' payment agents, as intermediaries, as witnesses of the agreement, or as the receivers of contracts that were deposited with them for safekeeping. The actual lenders were likely to be 'entrepreneurs', merchant financiers, or elite financiers. In the Vindob. G 19 792 papyrus, it is a banker who makes the payments, while the lender appears to be a member of the elite in Theadelphia.[25] Some elite members probably advanced bottomry loans using as intermediaries financiers who were closer to maritime circles.

If it is discovered one day that bankers did make bottomry loans, I shall willingly accept the fact, but, in my view, that will not make much difference to the nature of the ancient economy.

What can be said about the business relations between the financiers from the various categories distinguished above? Because my own research into the financial life of the ancient world has concentrated (as a reaction to the earlier bibliography) on what separated the bankers from the elite financiers and the 'entrepreneurs', I have been criticized for neglecting the inevitable financial relations that existed between the members of those various categories, or even for denying that they

---

[20] Casson 1990.   [21] I am following Rougé's interpretation here (see Rougé 1980: 292–3).
[22] Bogaert 1994: 210–16.   [23] Bogaert 1994: 216–18.
[24] Bogaert 1968: 372–4 and 411–13; 1994: 217–18; Andreau 1987a: 603–4 and 668.
[25] Casson 1986.

existed, and thereby overlooking the mobility and fluidity that characterize all business deals involving money.

As I see it, those criticisms are ill-founded. I have, on the one hand, been struck by the complexity of Roman financial life, and I am unwilling to belittle that complexity. There is no reason why economic historians should not take the logical and typological precautions that are commonly adopted in political and administrative history. If it is worthwhile drawing a distinction between an ordinary consul and a suffect consul, how can it be justifiable to muddle everything up when it comes to economic history? Recent research on the metal ingots and oil amphoras of Baetica has demonstrated the interest of a detailed and probing study of the organization of production and commerce.[26] In the financial domain, such a study leads to drawing distinctions between the functions and methods of the various categories of businessmen.

At the same time, I was anxious to show that in a highly hierarchized society such as Rome, several levels of financial activity existed, linked to the multiple strata of statuses and circles. I have been amazed that Marxist colleagues, who speak constantly of class societies, should have regarded money as a 'no-man's land' that eluded all social constraints and represented an island of absolute liberty for all those who set out to grow rich!

To insist on the complexity of financial life and on the existence of social hierarchies is not necessarily to regard the Roman economy as archaic. For this classification of categories draws attention to the very concept of a deposit bank – a concept which was altogether new and an advance on the idea of interest-bearing loans pure and simple. The notion of the deposit bank also helps us to form a better idea of the financial activities of the senators and knights who, although not professional bankers, nevertheless handled far larger sums of money.

Let me now make a few supplementary remarks on the relations between financiers, considering, one by one, three types of business deals: those between professional bankers; those between financiers in other categories; and, finally, those between bankers and any other kinds of financiers.

Compensation, in the sense of an institutionalized mechanism (to regulate operations between different banks), did not exist. There was no system of compensation even between banks in the same city, let alone banks in different cities.

---

[26] See, for example, Domergue 1994 and Liou and Tchernia 1994.

However, the absence of any such system does not mean that there was no cooperation at all between bankers. Those who operated in the same town would obviously know one another. Their premises would frequently be situated in the same neighbourhood. A number of texts show that they worked together in the context of auction sales, and that they would sometimes borrow money from one another. In the Curculio of Plautus, Lycon goes to see his colleagues to ask for their help.[27] Quintilian, writing about a law that was probably imaginary, also mentions a banker who borrows from one of his colleagues.[28] A gloss to the Code of Justinian refers to *recepta* agreed among bankers.[29]

The tablets of L. Caecilius Jucundus provide further evidence of business relations between professional bankers. Two of the names that recur most frequently are M. Fabius Agathinus and P. Terentius Primus. One or the other, or both, may have been bankers. If M. Fabius Agathinus was one, tablet 151 attests the existence of a *receptum* according to which Jucundus undertook to pay Agathinus' debt to the city.[30]

Thanks to a number of papyri, we know that transfers were sometimes made from one bank to another, and we are beginning to gain a better understanding of the techniques used. A papyrus dating from the second century BC refers to a banker in Egypt with an account at one or several of his colleagues' banks. Similar examples are known in the first century BC and the first century AD.[31] However, those relations were not institutionalized or even general; they depended solely on the personal networks of individual bankers.

What financial relations existed between other categories of financiers? Credit intermediaries, who put borrowers in contact with moneylenders, were not established in every town. Whereas more or less specialized moneylenders were to be found virtually everywhere, in Italy such intermediaries were mainly concentrated in Rome and in the major ports. At the end of the Republic there were a few credit intermediaries amongst the Italian *negotiatores* settled in the provinces. For the Early Empire, the documentation is much more sparse. However, when Plutarch writes that in Greece, in his day, the major financial towns were Corinth, Patras, and Athens, one implication is certainly that intermediaries were to be found in these towns.[32] Some of these intermediaries – C. Rabirius Postumus and L. Egnatius Rufus, for example – were

---

[27] Plautus, *Curc.*, 5.3.682.   [28] Quintilian, *Inst. Orat.* 5.10.105.
[29] *Glossa ad Cod. IV, 18, 1, recepticia, gl. indefense*, col. 839.   [30] Andreau 1974a: 62–7.
[31] Bogaert 1994: 102, note 43 and 250–2.   [32] Plutarch, *Moralia* 831A.

knights.[33] Some were dependants of members of the elite, others were 'entrepreneurs', still others wholesalers.

Their precise financial functions varied as much as their social standing. In Puteoli, it was a matter of bringing together moneylenders and commerce, in particular to provide the monetary means for maritime loans. In the provinces, the interlocutors were sometimes private individuals, sometimes cities overburdened with taxes or spending beyond their means. In Rome, intermediaries might fulfil a number of functions. Some of the financiers whose names Cicero and Atticus mention probably gave priority to loans among the elite.

We should not imagine that specialization was highly developed. Cluvius of Puteoli had lent money to a number of cities in Asia, but was also advancing funds for commercial operations in Puteoli.

A professional banker, too, could operate as an intermediary. Of course, as a banker, he had particular responsibilities and engaged in particular operations. But there was no reason for his profession to exclude other forms of mediation. For example, an *argentarius* could, alongside his professional duties, operate as a credit intermediary, as Cluvius and Vestorius did.[34]

It is hard to be any more precise in an analysis of the relations that obtained between different types of financiers. Two rules seem detectable, however: money to be invested passed from less specialized hands into more specialized ones, from those less expert technically to those more so; and, very often, from the wealthy to the slightly less wealthy.

Finally, it is worth noting that in all these relations, and particularly where senators or knights were involved, several domains that were logically quite distinct became confused, even when certain financiers were more expert in one than in the others. The domains were:

(a) the economic domain, in particular, operations connected with commerce;

(b) the political domain, with all the profits and advantages that magistrates derived from their posts and also all the expenses to which their political careers committed them;

(c) the social domain, with its benefactions and all the transactions occasioned by family ties, links of patronage, etc.

And how could a man move from one category to another? In the first place, the boundaries between some categories were relatively ill-

---

[33] Andreau 1983a: 14–15. [34] Andreau 1983a: 16–20.

defined. The boundary between the members of the elite and the professional bankers was clear enough, whatever some modern scholars may think. But the boundaries between elite members and 'entrepreneurs' and between merchant financiers and 'entrepreneurs' were much vaguer. This classification into several different categories helps us to gain a better understanding of ancient financial life. But we should not form too rigid a view. Some financiers belonged to several categories at the same time. But not one was at once a professional banker and an elite member. For those two categories were separated by an important social barrier: to cross it meant abandoning the world of professions and shops.[35]

A man could belong successively to a number of different categories. This happened when he gained promotion up the social ladder, for the condition of a member of the elite was regarded as superior to that of a merchant or a professional man.[36] Horace's father, who began as a professional man, eventually led the life of a member of the elite. He never became a knight or a senator, but his lifestyle and his work status changed, and he was determined to provide his son with an education fit for the elite.[37] Horace's father thus had two successive lives (although we do not know whether he engaged in any financial activities in the second). According to Veyne's interpretation (with which I broadly agree), the fictional Trimalchio of Petronius was at some point an 'entrepreneur', then became an elite member, one who, for his part, certainly did not consider financial activities beneath him.[38]

From one generation to another, one's financial category might change, but in some cases those concerned gave up financial activities altogether. For Romans were all the more keen to inherit from an activity if it accorded with the norms of aristocratic life, that is to say all the keener if it related to a patrimony consisting of immovable property. Because financial activities required a certain degree of wealth, but did not really depend on the possession of a patrimony consisting of immovable property, and as they tended to be detrimental to one's rank and dignity, they were less often continued by the next generation than were activities such as agriculture, or the exploitation of quarries or mines, and so on.

Professions and activities that made it possible for those who practised

---

[35] On this 'social threshold', see Andreau 1987a: 370–2 and 379–82.
[36] On social mobility, see Andreau 1985b; 1990; 1992a.   [37] Andreau 1987a: 370–1.
[38] Veyne 1961; D'Arms 1981: 97–120; Andreau 1985c: 382. If one follows D'Arms, such remarks about Trimalchio are, on the contrary, invalidated.

them to move up the social ladder would later be abandoned if they were not suitable for the rank of the group into which the social climber and his heirs were trying to integrate themselves. Or, if not abandoned, they would at least cease to be the centre of the social climber's preoccupations, and would become simply one source of income among others.

The fact that a senator's grandfather had been a merchant thus does not constitute proof of the Roman aristocracy's general commercial vocation. What it does prove is that commerce could lead to wealth, which in turn led to a higher social rank. But it is also a sign that a descendant of traders would, if he wished to integrate himself into the aristocracy, cease to be a trader himself.

The professions of bankers and money-changers were thus sometimes passed on to freedmen, but seldom to a son or an heir. Neither M. Fulcinius, nor Horace's father, nor T. Flavius Petro (Vespasian's grandfather) passed on to their sons the profession of *argentarius* or *coactor*.[39] Titus Flavius Sabinus engaged in financial activities like his father before him, but he was not a banker. He was a tax-collector (or an important employee of tax-collectors) in Asia, and he engaged in lending money at interest to the Helvetii.[40] From Petro down to Vespasian, the Flavii preserved their taste for money and financial activities, and we know that, even as emperor, Vespasian continued 'quite openly carrying on traffic which would be shameful even for a man in private life'.[41] However, the taste for financial activities that was passed down from one generation to the next took different forms in different cases, as the family's social standing rose. In some cases, that of Horace, for example, the taste for financial affairs does not appear to have been transmitted at all.

A number of fragments from Q. Cervidius Scaevola, Paul, and Ulpian, reproduced in the *Digest*, suggest that an heir to an *argentarius* would, as a matter of course, not himself practise his father's profession.[42]

The documentation conveys an impression of harmony and smooth running. Taken as a whole, these various categories of financiers saw to it that money circulated from one extreme of the world of wealth and ease to the other: from senators and knights down to landowners of average means in the colonies, the municipalities or the outlying cities, and also down to traders and the proprietors of workshops, not to mention all the parasites who lived off the elite.

---

[39] Hor. *Sat.* 1.6.86; Cic. *pro Caec.* 4.10–11; Suet. *Vesp.* 1.2.   [40] Suet. *Vesp.* 1.2.
[41] Suet. *Vesp.* 16.2.
[42] *Dig.* 2.13.6 (Ulpian); 2.13.9.1 (Paulus); 14.3.20 (Scaev.); 40.7.40.8 (Scaev.).

Impressed by this harmony, I wrote in 1985 as follows: 'The diversification of the statuses of financiers led to a relative division of tasks which did not interrupt the smooth running of the economic apparatus . . . Where private financial activity was concerned, there was no flagrant mismatch between the statuses in play and the demands of economic life.'[43]

All the same, we should recognize that our existing documentation gives us access to only a limited section of the networks of the imperial elite. Even the business deals attested by the Murecine tablets are connected with the elite, since several imperial freedmen or slaves are involved. There can be no doubt that we know of only a small section of the networks of the elite. But that is not particularly grave, since it does allow us to form some idea of the whole. The most important question is how far those networks extended and what existed beyond them. What were the limits of this seemingly flourishing financial life of the first centuries BC and AD, which is known to us mostly in Italy? What existed beyond it?

It seems to me that two groups of financiers are likely to have engaged in local business without establishing any more far-flung relations. On the one hand are the usurers and moneylenders who were more or less wealthy but operated within narrow geographical limits. Such usurers and moneylenders must have existed throughout the Empire. On the other hand are the professional bankers, whose activities were more developed and more strictly controlled by the law, but they did not exist everywhere. In fact far from it.[44] We should remember that practically all the professional bankers known in the Roman West were Roman citizens, which means that, in the first century of the Empire at least, there can have been very few of them in the regions populated by 'peregrines'.[45] Where they did exist, their presence testified to a more highly organized financial life than where they did not, for their presence implied the existence of auction sales, and hence also of transactions involving patrimonies and security for unpaid debts.

In the Hellenistic period, particularly at the end of the second century BC, some *argentarii* and trapezites had reached a level of business and wealth that must have brought them into contact with members of the elite and with the wealthiest wholesalers and *negotiatores*. We have already come across Philostratus of Ascalon. However, their

---

[43] Andreau 1985c: 402, 403, and 404.　　[44] Andreau 1987a: 313–29.
[45] Andreau 1987a: 359–441.

successors, from the mid-first century B C on, never attained the same degree of affluence.

From that time on, every aspect of the activities of the professional bankers and of the operations that they conducted suggests that these were local affairs. In general, it seems to me that they did not include members of the imperial elite among their clients, either as borrowers or as depositors. Even a banker such as Jucundus, established in an average-sized but extremely prosperous town not very far from Rome, seems to me not to have penetrated the wider networks to which the bigger businessmen and elite financiers belonged. The existence of these professional bankers of relatively modest means and operating within a limited locality certainly helped to expand the sphere of monetization and credit. But it is hard to form a clear picture of the world that remained outside it.

CHAPTER 5

Dependants

Some slaves and freedmen worked in agriculture, others in commerce and manufacturing, yet others in banks or financial business. The nature of their statuses inevitably affected how these economic sectors were organized.

As is well known, a freedman had a particular legal status, and the social (and financial) links that he (frequently?) maintained with his patron also set him apart from men who were born free. Yet all the activities upon which free men engaged were also open to him. As from a particular date, he could work as an agent, *institor*, in the same way as a man born free. A free-born man (possibly his patron) could enter into a sleeping partnership with him; he could be lent money, and could be used as an intermediary to lend money.[1]

As for slaves, their status set them so far apart from free men and women that their activities, whatever they were, were never altogether confused with those of the latter.

In manufacturing, commerce, and business, slaves might find themselves in one of three situations. Either they worked directly in the service of their master; or they worked as their master's agent in a shop or a workshop, as *institores*; or else they were put in charge of a *peculium*.[2]

The financial slaves who worked directly in the service of their master were *actores*, *dispensatores*, or *arcarii*. In many cases these three words corresponded to different functions, but not always. For in some establishments or enterprises only one or two of those posts existed. The few references to professional banks that we possess refer only to *actores*. On the other hand, amongst the elite (whether financiers or not), all three posts could co-exist.

An *arcarius* was a cashier. He looked after a strongbox; he was also probably qualified to operate as an assayer of coins or a money-changer. But of the three, the *arcarius* was the least deeply involved in financial

---

[1] D'Arms 1981: 103–4. [2] Juglar 1894: 16.

operations and transactions and was the least well-placed to make any personal profit (over and above anything he might receive from his master in return for his services).

In contrast, an *actor* or a *dispensator* was certainly in a position to run some personal business in parallel to that of his master and, with luck, to make some money by so doing. A *dispensator* was not in charge of a shop or a workshop. He would be responsible for running his master's household, and in particular for administering the expenses; it would be he who paid the bills and kept the accounts.[3] *Dispensatores* are also to be found in the imperial administration and the administration of the Emperor's personal possessions.

Suetonius relates that Otho received 1,000,000 sesterces from one of Galba's slaves for having managed to get him taken on as a *dispensator* for the Emperor.[4] And a slave of Nero's, who had been his *dispensator*, was able to pay 13,000,000 sesterces at the time of his manumission.[5] Clearly a *dispensator* had opportunities for earning money. What were they? First, there were the sums given to him by his grateful master; secondly, there was fraud (Tiberius insisted on himself being present whenever payments were being made, because he reckoned that, under Augustus, too much money had been finding its way into the pockets of the *dispensatores*).[6]

However, the wealth of a *dispensator* neither surprised nor shocked anyone, so he must have had other sources of profit apart from fraud. If he had received a *peculium*, he was certainly in a position to do business for himself as well as for his master. His situation depended on his own financial skills, the connections of his master, and his own connections. He might, for example, advance interest-bearing loans.

The same went for an *actor*. An *actor* was empowered by his master to act for him. In some cases, he was responsible for the financial management of an estate or a workshop; in others, he might be the manager of his master's fortune. Not much is known about all his various functions.[7] But he surely had as many opportunities to make money as a *dispensator*.

A master could receive a proportion of the personal profits of his *actor* or his *dispensator* at three times: possibly while he was still a slave, if some agreement existed between the two, which I believe happened very seldom; next, when he came to be manumitted; and finally, at the death of the slave or freedman.

[3] Gaius, *Inst.* 1.122. See Liebenam 1903; Vulic 1923; Coello 1989; Carlsen 1992.
[4] Suet. *Otho*, 5, 2.   [5] Pliny, *Nat. Hist.* 7.129; see Millar 1977: 136.   [6] Dio Cass. 57.10. 4.
[7] Juglar 1894: 27–30; Andreau 1987a: 612; Aubert 1993.

There were invariably two points at which a master might receive a proportion of the profits realized by his slave: at the latter's manumission, if the slave ever became a freedman; and at the death of the slave or freedman. (We know that the law on the inheritance of freedmen changed under the Empire, becoming much more favourable to the master, and that it all depended on how many children the freedman had.)

The second category of slave-businessmen comprised the agents (*institores*).[8] The use of agents led to the *actio institoria*, through which a third party could take legal action against a slave's patron; this was probably introduced in the second half of the second century B C.[9] As Ulpian tells us,[10] in the second and third centuries A D, an agent might equally well also be a free individual, in theory either a man or a woman – although, as it happens, there are no women to be found in active financial life. Four legal texts relate to the *institores* of professional bankers.[11] They were not entrepreneurs, but managers through whose mediation the master made a profit. The equipment used, the money invested in the business, and the gains that it produced belonged directly to the patron, who was the entrepreneur. According to several texts in the *Digest*, the slave *institor* would often get a salary, a *merces*, in return for his work (*operae*). But, in some cases, he did not receive any direct reward. In such a case, his *operae* were free, *gratuitae*, but he probably had other benefits (for instance, some better opportunity to run his *peculium*). The money sunk in the business was not part of the *peculium* of the slave-agent. But that does not mean that the slave did not also possess a *peculium*, so that in practice a certain confusion could sometimes arise over which sums were entrusted to the slave as part of his *peculium* and which were those that he managed in his capacity as agent.

The slave-agent stood in for his master and acted for him *in solidum*, but only within the limits defined by the *lex praepositionis*, the document that established the terms of his post as agent. In the same way as a *servus actor*, the slave-agent was required to produce accounts of his management. A final account was presented when he was about to be manumitted. At that point, he had to return any profits produced by his management that he had kept in his own hands.

Slaves could be used as agents for moneylending, or even for borrow-

---

[8] Juglar 1894; D'Arms 1981: 143; Di Porto 1984; Kirschenbaum 1987: 89–121; Aubert 1993; 1994.
[9] Aubert 1994: 70–91.   [10] *Dig.* 14.3.7.1.
[11] *Dig.* 14.3.5.3 (Ulpian); 14.3.19.1 (Papinian); 14.3.20 (Scaev.); *Cod. Just.* 4.25.3.

ing money, in businesses other than banks.[12] Any financier could use agents. But the literary texts and inscriptions do not provide any certain examples. Most of them tell us no details about the nature of the relationship between the master and the slave.

The third category of slaves who engaged in business comprised those who held a *peculium*.[13] They had received from their master a portion of the master's patrimony, which the master could, in principle, reappropriate whenever he wished to. They used this *peculium* for financial deals, acting, for example, as professional bankers or as moneylenders. Two texts, by Paulus and Ulpian, both included in the *Digest*, relate to such slave *argentarii*.[14] Juglar calls them slave entrepreneurs, to distinguish them from agents, and he is right to do so. For it was truly they who exploited the shop, which they had themselves bought and equipped. Where third parties were concerned, the master was no longer responsible for the entire fortune of investments made by the slave. He limited his losses to the *peculium* that he had advanced. As J.-J. Aubert has remarked, 'even though a slave with a *peculium* was legally dependent, his economic activities were practically kept separate from his master's . . . A slave with *peculium* was not acting as business manager on behalf of a principal.'[15] Economically speaking, the *peculium* thus constituted a sort of long-term credit. That being so, the master became a kind of sleeping partner.[16]

The future pope Callistus, whom Hippolytus of Rome tried to discredit, was a slave in his youth, under the reign of Commodus. Callistus' master, Carpophorus, an imperial freedman, had entrusted him with a sum of money (as a *peculium*?). With this money, Callistus founded a bank, promising to make profits for Carpophorus. But later he found he was unable to return his clients' deposits. Why? Imprudence? Dishonesty? A liquidity crisis? He himself claimed that he had lent money to other clients who refused to repay him. At any rate, the depositors turned to his master, who was liable for whatever the *peculium* amounted to.[17] The story shows that the master had not made it his business to keep himself informed of how the bank was prospering: when Callistus' clients sought out Carpophorus, the latter knew nothing of the difficulties of his slave.

---

[12] *Dig.* 14.3.13 pr. (Ulpian) and 14.3.19 pr. (Papinian). Admittedly, in this second text, the agent is a *procurator*, but in this case Papinian guarantees an action *ad exemplum institoriae;* see Andreau 1987a: 703–4 and Aubert 1994: 109.

[13] Juglar 1894; Buti 1976; Di Porto 1984; Kirschenbaum 1987: 31–88.

[14] *Dig.* 2.13.4.3 (Ulpian) and 2.13.9.1 (Paulus).   [15] Aubert 1994: 4.   [16] Juglar 1894: 15.

[17] Hipp. *Refut. omn. haer.* 9.12.1–12; see Andreau 1987a: 615–16 and 631–2.

But several fragments in the *Digest* show that masters were sometimes equally ignorant of how their agents were handling their affairs.

When he was manumitted, the slave did not retain the entire *peculium* but returned part of it to his master. After his manumission, depending on the size of the *peculium*, a pension might be paid, at least for a few months or years, either to the freedman, if his means were not enough to live on, or to the master.[18] The master does not seem to have received any regular reimbursement before the slave was manumitted.

There is relative agreement on the principal features of the use of agents and the law governing the *peculium*, but many divergent opinions have been expressed as to the historical interpretation of these phenomena as a whole. In recent years, the importance of the role played by slaves in commerce and financial life has been emphasized by both A. Bürge and A. Di Porto, but whereas the former regarded it as a sign of archaism, the latter, on the contrary, has insisted on the modernity of such institutions.[19]

Di Porto tries to show that, although the nature of company contracts may have greatly limited the potential of Roman businesses, other structures existed which possessed all the economic advantages of the businesses of modern Europe, so that the Romans were indirectly familiar with a form of limited company. According to him, one of the instruments of these structures was the slave who belonged to several masters, the *servus communis*. Using him as an intermediary, the masters found themselves to be economic associates, even if they had concluded no company contract. A second instrument was the slave who was dependent on another slave, the *servus vicarius*. If a common slave had several *vicarii*, this led to an organization that was far more complex, a 'two-tier' system, further complicated by the fact that each slave and each *vicarius* could engage in several types of operations, several *negotiationes* at once. The third element in play here, and perhaps the most important, was the *peculium*, for where there was a *peculium* the master was only responsible in a limited fashion, and so what was in effect a limited company would be set up. Even a *vicarius*, a slave dependent on another slave, might have a *peculium*, a separate fraction of the *peculium* of the slave upon whom he depended.

Di Porto is right to underline the importance of the role played by slaves and freedmen in business affairs. He is also right to consider the features of Roman business in relation to the legal and social effects of

---

[18] Juglar 1894: 19, note 1 and 38–9.   [19] Di Porto 1984; Bürge 1987; 1988; Chiusi 1991.

slavery. Stressing the fact that Roman business was not founded upon kinship and that it remained within modest proportions, I have myself in the past drawn attention to the positive aspects of Di Porto's analyses.[20]

Nevertheless, I remain unconvinced by many of his theses. All his analyses are centred upon the shared slave who belonged to several masters and upon the existence of the *vicarii*. To be sure, there were shared slaves and slaves who were dependent upon other slaves. But how many? His book gives the impression that these were extremely widespread phenomena, whereas very few texts or inscriptions even allude to such circumstances. Furthermore, as A. Bürge has pointed out, the common slaves were workers, not 'managers'.[21]

Besides, a shared slave would belong to no more than two or three masters. He might have one or two *vicarii* working under him, seldom more. So these remained very small-scale businesses.

Did the existence of common slaves and *vicarii* make it possible to 'dispense with the company (*societas*)? I doubt it. It makes no difference, Di Porto claims, since there was also the institution of the *peculium*, which was the basis of a limited company. However, the real focus of his book is the common slave, not the *peculium*. The work's originality stems from the notion of the common slave.

Di Porto also tries to prove the existence of an abstract concept of business, the funds for which were kept separate from the rest of its proprietor's patrimony. He repeatedly emphasizes that the *peculium*, which was detached from the master's patrimony, constituted the funds for the business exploited by the slave. But that is not correct. The *peculium* was, certainly, separate from the master's patrimony (up to a point, and solely on the decision of the master), but what it constituted was a 'quasi-patrimony' for the slave, not capital for the business. The fact that part of the master's patrimony was transferred to the slave was not enough to create capital for the business. The concept of the patrimony remained central, even if it was only a fictitious patrimony, and even if a *vicarius* then, in his turn, received a fraction of that 'quasi-patrimony'.

Finally, it is true that the master of a slave with a *peculium* was responsible only for that sum. So, strictly speaking, his responsibility was indeed 'limited'. But I do not consider that that was enough to set up a 'limited company' in the modern sense of the expression. The context of management was completely different. An ancient business, as described by Di Porto, was characterized by a mismatch between the property, the

---

[20] Andreau 1990. [21] Bürge 1988: 860.

role of the management, and the profits. The proprietor took a large proportion of the profits, but played no part in the management. His limited responsibility did not make him an entrepreneur. The *peculium* was a kind of long-term credit; the master became a sleeping partner (and one who risked losing twice the sum invested since, if the slave lost it, the master also had to reimburse the other creditors).

The slave who managed the business likewise lacked the means to become a true entrepreneur. For his master's prestige and financial means exceeded his own by far. Admittedly, the master frequently abstained from supervising the business, but in principle he had the right to intervene at any moment, and even to withdraw the *peculium*. In two-tier businesses (that is to say, those in which slaves dependent upon other slaves also worked), the situation was even worse, as the *vicarius* was subject to a double threat and double supervision.

A slave or freedman could not hand on to his heirs all the money he had made. Such a state of affairs ruled out the formation of financial, industrial, or commercial dynasties. It prevented any accumulation of funds within the business, and also any capitalization on experience and trust. It negated the very concept of an entrepreneur or of the spirit of free enterprise, in the modern sense of those expressions. Thanks to the *peculium*, responsibility was, it is true, limited, but the businesses in question were deprived of both independent entrepreneurs and also a bourgeoisie.

The role played by slaves in commerce and financial life shows, as I have remarked elsewhere, that 'the hierarchy of orders and statuses was not a shackle that impeded the circulation of money and checked economic life'.[22] For centuries, economic life profited from the existence of slavery, and the Romans managed to adapt slavery to the needs of their economic life. The same goes for manumission. Here, they were far more successful than the Greek city-states. But concrete economic life was thus moulded by the existing equilibrium of statuses and social prestige. The growth of production and commercialization in no way upset the social order but was, on the contrary, adapted to that order. That represents an impressive achievement. But it also imposed limitations on the Roman world. All this was a very far cry from the 'structure of changing structures' that led to the Industrial Revolution.

---

[22] Andreau 1985c: 405.

CHAPTER 6

The tablets of Murecine

In 1959, while the autostrada linking Naples and Salerno was under construction, a building was discovered about 600 metres to the south of the Stabiae Gate of Pompeii, and was partially excavated. The part of the building that was dug out was composed of part of a peristyle and a number of rooms alongside it; on the northern side were three adjoining *triclinia* (dining rooms) (called A, B, and C), and on the eastern side at least two more *triclinia*.[1]

A number of objects found in the *triclinia* show that in AD 79 the building, which had been severely damaged in the earthquake of AD 62, was still being repaired. In *triclinium* A, *tesserae* of mosaic were discovered along with some earthenware plaques and a fragment of marble. In the next *triclinium* (B) were the remains of a boat, an iron anchor, and some oars, as well as a wicker basket containing lacquer-covered writing tablets. All these objects had been stored provisionally in the *triclinia* for the duration of the repairs to the building.

The writing tablets discovered in this way constitute the third major batch of tablets discovered in the towns of the Vesuvius area. The first batch consisted of tablets belonging to the banker Lucius Caecilius Jucundus, discovered in 1875 in a house in Pompeii (Region 5, Ins. 1, no. 16) and published by K. Zangemeister.[2] The second batch was made up of several groups of tablets discovered in Herculaneum and published by G. Pugliese Carratelli and V. Arangio Ruiz.[3]

This third batch of tablets was initially dubbed 'The New Tablets of Pompeii.' But as they relate to business conducted in Puteoli, not in Pompeii, that name was subsequently abandoned. They are now known either as the tablets of Agro Murecine, or of Murecine (the name of the spot where they were found), or as the Sulpicii archive, as they had been preserved by the Sulpicii, a group of businessmen from Puteoli.

[1] Elia 1960; 1961; see also Andreau 1994a.
[2] *CIL* IV Suppl. 1, 3340; see Andreau 1974a and Jongman 1988.
[3] Pugliese Carratelli 1948; 1953; Arangio Ruiz and Pugliese Carratelli 1946; Arangio Ruiz 1948.

The story of the conservation and publication of these tablets is a complicated one.[4] Suffice it to say that their first partial publication, by C. Giordano and F. Sbordone, was catastrophic and of very poor quality.[5]

It was G. Camodeca who made the greatest progress in studying the archive. He undertook a systematic reading of all the tablets, both those that had already been published and the rest. Noticing that some had been presented separately despite their all relating to the same operation, and that other fragments had by mistake been published several times over, under different numbers, he renumbered them all from scratch, preceding the figures by the letters *TPSulp, Tabulae Pompeianae Sulpiciorum*. He has devoted several articles to the tablets.[6] Then, in 1992, he produced an authoritative publication of many of them,[7] and is currently preparing to publish the rest of the batch. As well as his research, it is worth mentioning that of L. Bove, J.G. Wolf and J. Crook.[8]

Let me first describe the financial contents of the tablets of Murecine and try to draw a few economic and social conclusions from them. Then I shall tackle one specific problem recently raised by G. Camodeca: how should the activities, or the profession, of the Sulpicii be described?

The dates of the tablets of Murecine range from AD 26 (or 29)[9] to AD 61. They are all earlier than the earthquake of AD 62. They belonged to the Sulpicii, a group of businessmen from Puteoli. Although they were found in a building probably located close to the river port of Pompeii, they do not concern business conducted in that city. Nearly all were written in Puteoli, none in Pompeii. Yet they were taken there; why, we do not know.

That question is linked to the problem posed by the building in which they were found. What was its function? According to M. Pagano, it was either the headquarters of a business association (as the abundance of *triclinia* is reminiscent of the 'House of *triclinia*' in Ostia, recognized to be

[4] See Andreau 1994a.
[5] Giordano 1966; 1970; 1971; 1972; Sbordone and Giordano 1968; Sbordone 1971; 1972; 1976; 1977; 1978. On Giordano 1966, see Degrassi 1969. Tablets cited as *TP, Tabulae Pompeianae*, follow the numeration of Giordano and Sbordone.
[6] Camodeca 1982–9. Other articles by Camodeca are cited in Camodeca 1992:7, note 19.
[7] Camodeca 1992.
[8] Bove 1971; 1973; 1975; 1979; 1984a (G. Camodeca has largely reinterpreted the tablets concerning this Euplia; see Camodeca 1992: 199–235); 1984b; 1984c; 1984d; Wolf 1979a; 1979b; 1985; Wolf and Crook 1989.
[9] The dating of *TPSulp* 42 is not certain; if it dates from AD 26, it is the most ancient tablet in the archive (Camodeca 1992: 155–8).

the headquarters of the *fabri tignuarii*), or else an inn. If it was an inn, the likelihood is that one (or more) of the Sulpicii was its landlord, and that the archive belonged to him. If it was the headquarters of a business association, it is hard to explain the presence of these private commercial documents. The tablets were definitely not part of a business association archive itself, as such.[10]

The Caii Sulpicii mentioned in the archive were in all likelihood four in number: Faustus, Cinnamus, Eutychus, and Onirus.

Faustus and Cinnamus are mentioned more frequently than the other two. This was a circle of freedmen, as is suggested by the names of these men. We know from one of the tablets that Cinnamus was Faustus' freedman.[11] As for Onirus, G. Camodeca located an inscription in the *Ephemeris Epigraphica* that shows that he was free-born. He was the son of a freedman called Caius Sulpicius Heraclida, who is not named in the archive.[12]

The Sulpicii were the freedmen of freedmen, or the sons of freedmen, but not the freedmen of senators or knights. Nor do they appear to have been the freedmen of members of the elite of Puteoli.[13]

One of the tablets shows that Cinnamus was the agent (*procurator*) of his patron Faustus. It is also clear that Eutychus acted as Cinnamus' agent.[14] As we know, a private agent (*procurator*) had to be a free man. His job was business management and legal representation.[15]

One or other of the Sulpicii, usually Faustus or Cinnamus, figures in most of the tablets, whether their nature be legal (the *vadimonia*, for example) or financial (acknowledgement of debts, receipts, etc.). However, among the tablets already published, there are at least twelve in which none of them is named.[16] Also, it sometimes happens that the name of Caius Sulpicius Faustus appears as the creditor of a debt in association with another name.

In some cases the Sulpicii thus undertook either to look after documents belonging to their clients or their business contacts, or to keep some of their debt-claims safe in a strongbox; or else they themselves

---

[10] Pagano 1983. Might not this building in Murecine have been the headquarters of a commercial company? Unfortunately, we know of no other company headquarters to which to compare this building. M. Pagano does not favour such a hypothesis.

[11] *TPSulp* 72, which dates from AD 47; see Camodeca 1992: 23–9.

[12] *Eph. Epigr.*, VIII, 451 (Camodeca 1992: 26–7).

[13] Camodeca wonders whether they might have been attached to freedmen of one of the Sulpicii Galbae who, at the end of the Republic, owned slaves at Minturnae (Camodeca 1992: 27–9).

[14] *TPSulp* 39 and 72 (= *TP* 30). [15] Cic. *pro Caec.* 20.57.

[16] They are the tablets *TPSulp* 12, 15, 43, 51, 52, 55, 60, 64, 70, and *TP* 7 and 13.

acted as creditors in conjunction with others. The three hypotheses are certainly not mutually exclusive. The Sulpicii may have played one or another of those roles, or they may even have played all three at once.

In the tablets relating to the debts of a peregrine by the name of Euplia of Milo, for example, the main creditor was called Titinia Anthracis, or possibly Titinia Bacchis. Like Titinia, Cinnamus had also lent money to this Euplia.[17] He kept his own debt-claim carefully, in a strongbox, along with those of Titinia.[18]

Three economic observations are prompted at this point. The first is that these tablets without doubt constitute examples of commercial credit given in connection with activities in the port of Puteoli. For once, we have direct evidence of loans being advanced to traders, operations precise examples of which are never found in the literary texts, with the result that some historians have even denied their existence, wrongly concluding that in antiquity credit amounted to no more than consumption loans. Whether the Sulpicii were bankers, or moneylenders but not bankers (a question to which we shall be returning), there can be no doubt of the commercial nature of some of the loans that they advanced. Peregrines (Euplia of Milo, Tryphon of Alexandria, and Zeno of Tyre) are mentioned in the tablets. So are wholesalers such as Caius Novius Eunus and L. Marius Jucundus.[19] Wheat and dry legumes are cited as security in their cases. Finally, one of the Sulpicii is involved as an intermediary in a maritime loan. The evidence is strong enough to dispel all doubts.

Secondly, the tablets of Murecine indicate that members of the entourage of the Emperor and of the entourages of a number of senators were investing money through the financiers of Puteoli. In the preceding century, at the end of the Republic, such investments are implied by certain remarks of Cicero's, which, however, are no more than allusive.[20] In the Sulpicii archive, in contrast, these investments are made explicit. Several imperial slaves or freedmen are cited as lending money either to the Sulpicii or to traders operating in Puteoli. The Sulpicii borrowed a large sum of money, 94,000 sesterces, from an imperial slave by the name of Phosphorus Elpidianus, and another sum (the amount of which is not mentioned) from Marcus Lollius Philippus, who was probably one of Lollia Saturnina's freedmen.[21] They also acted as intermediaries in a debt of 13,000 sesterces contracted by the

---

[17] *TPSulp* 61; Camodeca 1992: 213–14.   [18] *TPSulp* 60 and 62.
[19] See Boulvert 1973; Macqueron 1979; Casson 1980; Wolf and Crook 1989.
[20] Andreau 1983a.   [21] *TPSulp* 73 (= *TP* 68); see Camodeca 1992: 248–57.

trader Caius Novius Eunus, in the reign of Caligula. The tablets of Murecine provide information on the role played by warehouses in which the security for such loans would be kept, and also on the private trade in cereals.

Such loans of money do not necessarily imply that the Emperor, or these senators and knights, had particular commercial interests. They were simply interest-bearing loans, arranged by intermediaries. No particular business venture would be involved, no ownership of ships. Furthermore, the loans agreed in this way were simply investments, involving no specialized activity of moneylending for interest. Even if the intermediaries (the imperial slaves or freedmen, and the Sulpicii) were specialist financiers, the Emperor or senator from whom the money came took no interest at all in how that money was managed. They certainly picked up the profits though, or at least part of the profits.

My third remark concerns the security for loans and the legal modalities of providing it. In the Sulpicii archive, the guarantees are, for the most part, material (that is to say they involved possessions, objects) and they always take the form of movable goods and chattels (slaves, precious objects, wheat, dry vegetables), not buildings. To be sure, we do know of private loans for which the security was land, particularly in the world of the knights and the senators. But the pledges used by the protagonists of the tablets of Murecine were of a quite different nature.

The modalities for providing security confirm the importance of auction-sales for financial life and loans. If the money loaned was not repaid, the creditor could put on sale the goods provided as security or as pledges, and would recover his outlay from the prices paid in the sale. If the proceeds of the sale were higher than the sum owed, he would pass the excess over to the debtor. The contract for the loan would include the possibility of an auction, and this would ensure plenty of publicity for the sale. The creditor could not legally avoid this. He was bound to put up a number of posters informing the city's inhabitants of the sale. It was clearly in the debtor's interest that the proceeds from the sale should be as great as possible, for if they fell short of the debt, he would himself be obliged to make up the difference.[22]

One of the Sulpicii was involved in a maritime loan as an intermediary.[23] In several other operations they acted either as sellers or as buyers.

[22] See the tablet *TP* 27, and also Bove 1975; 1984c.
[23] *TP* 13; see Ankum 1978; 1988; Wolf 1979a; Purpura 1984 (but *TP* 34 is definitely not a maritime loan; see Santoro 1985).

What picture of their activities can be formed from all these scraps of information?

There are three possible hypotheses between which, for the moment, no definitive choice can be made. According to the first, the one favoured by G. Camodeca, the Sulpicii were *argentarii*, professional bankers (or at least one of them, Cinnamus, was a professional banker). According to the second, they were traders who would also lend money and provide financial services. The third hypothesis, which is my preference, is that they were moneylenders (*feneratores*), but not traders (either never traders, or traders no longer, having decided to devote themselves solely to moneylending).[24]

There are a number of indications that favour each of those hypotheses. Let me mention them briefly, referring the reader to an article in which they are studied in greater detail.[25] Four points seem to favour G. Camodeca's hypothesis, but none seems to me to be conclusive. They are:

(1) in tablet *TPSulp* 82, the formula *ex interrogatione facta tabellarum signatarum* is used. The correct interpretation of this formula, not mentioned in any text and unknown except through a few tablets, is hard to determine. To Camodeca's mind, it shows that Cinnamus was a banker who provided credit at sales by auction. I, on the other hand, do not believe it necessarily applies to a sale by auction.[26]

(2) in tablet *TPSulp* 61 Cinnamus is presented as a creditor of Euplia and Epichares, just as Titinia is. Was he delegated to act by Titinia, by virtue of his role as a banker? I am convinced that he was not, and even if he was her delegate, that would in no way prove that he was a professional banker. For although bankers would sometimes be delegated to conduct such operations, not all those who accepted such delegations were bankers.[27]

(3) the third indication relates to the use of the expression *in rationem*.[28] There is a *ratio* between Priscilla and C. Sulpicius Faustus. Was this a deposit account, opened by Priscilla in Faustus' bank? That is possible but not certain, for the word *ratio* was also used in accounting that had nothing to do with the banking profession.[29]

---

[24] Andreau 1987a: 519, 658 and 706–7.   [25] Andreau 1994a: 49–55.
[26] Camodeca 1992: 29–36 and Andreau 1994a: 50–3.
[27] Camodeca 1992: 213–14 and Andreau 1994a: 53–4.
[28] *TPSulp* 58 = *TP* 59; see Camodeca 1992: 196–7.
[29] Camodeca 1992: 197 and note 87.

(4) Finally, the archive contains two fragments of large tablets in which payments of money are mentioned. But these cannot be parts of banking registers.[30] The formulaic expressions do not correspond to what we know about such registers. They are very different from the formulae used in the only banking register to have come down to us from antiquity.[31] Camodeca believes, rightly I think, that it is a register of loans (probably a *kalendarium*); such registers were kept by all those who lent money, not just by *argentarii*.

In opposition to Camodeca's hypothesis, it should be noted that in the tablets so far published there is no indication of any operations typical of *argentarii*. The tablets contain no clear allusions to the provision of credit at sales by auction, or to unsealed deposits or bank accounts. The Sulpicii appear in auctions selling off pledges, but as sellers, not as bankers providing credit. The operations upon which the Sulpicii engaged were certainly not incompatible with the activities of professional bankers. But neither were they characteristic of them.

The second hypothesis, according to which the Sulpicii were both traders and financiers, is also supported by various indications, but these are not totally convincing either.

F. Sbordone thought he had made out the word *mator*, and then had the temerity to interpret it as an abbreviation of *m(erc)ator*. From this he concluded that the Sulpicii were wholesalers. Unfortunately, *mator* was an erroneous reading of *Maior*, the elder. Nine or ten tablets do concern a purchase or a sale. But on two or three of these, the Sulpicii do not figure at all. Two or three others fail to constitute proof that the goods in question were being bought or sold within the framework of professional commerce. The purchase or sale could equally well have been of an item for personal use. As for the four remaining tablets, they relate to the sale by auction of pledges used as security for loans. Clearly, such sales do not prove that the creditors were traders.

The third hypothesis, finally, is based upon the uncertainties that surround the other two. If the Sulpicii were neither professional bankers nor wholesalers, they must have specialized in moneylending: they must have been *feneratores*.

The conclusion that must be drawn is that it is very difficult to define exactly what activities financiers such as the Sulpicii actually engaged in. We must wait for Camodeca to read and publish the tablets that remain

[30] Camodeca 1992: 207 and note 18, *TPSulp* 94 and 95.
[31] *Pap. Tebt.* III, 2, 1938, number 890.

to be studied or that have so far been misinterpreted, and hope that they will provide clinching arguments.

Whether the Sulpicii were *argentarii* or moneylenders makes no difference to the question of whether their business was 'primitive' or 'modern'. Distinguishing between one category and another does not imply any *a priori* concept of the ancient economy. But if Camodeca turns out to be right, their case would incline me to modify or qualify some of the ideas that I have been developing on professional bankers.[32]

The fact that they intervened in commercial business is in no way surprising, as we already know of other cases where *argentarii* did exactly that. Nor is the fact that some of their operations are not typical of professional bankers. There was nothing to prevent professional bankers from engaging in a wide range of operations, even if some of these had nothing to do with deposit accounts.

However, I should have to qualify my remarks on the financial means of professional bankers – qualify, not correct them, for even if the business ventures of the Sulpicii are considerably larger scale than those of L. Caecilius Jucundus, the sums that they handled are far from comparable with those that Cicero and Pliny the Younger mention in their correspondence. It is hardly surprising that a banker of Puteoli should be wealthier than his colleagues in Pompeii. However, it would become necessary to place more emphasis on the existence of different levels of wealth within the group of bankers as a whole.

Finally, it would become necessary to correct my remarks somewhat about the relations between professional bankers and the elite. The Sulpicii did enter into business relations with imperial slaves or freedmen and with the slaves or freedmen of men close to the imperial family. (I even believe that they helped them to invest their money, acting as intermediaries between them and the world of commerce.) To be sure, neither Caligula nor Lollia Saturnina appears in person in the tablets of Murecine, only their freedmen and their slaves do. All the same, if the Sulpicii were *argentarii*, figures from the elite would have been lending money, through the intermediary of the dependants, to professional bankers. In that case, we should have to conclude that some professional bankers (and some who were, furthermore, freedmen or the freedmen of freedmen) did have financial relations with elite networks.

Some people would find this very satisfying and consider that Roman banking was at last having its full dignity and modernity acknowledged.

[32] See Andreau 1994a.

Yet it would mean that the hand of the senatorial and equestrian elite weighed even more heavily upon Roman financial life than I had suspected. To my mind, the evolution of the banking professions in the second and first centuries B C indicates that professional bankers had won slightly greater autonomy in relation to the aristocratic financial world. If the Sulpicii were, after all, *argentarii*, the tablets of Murecine would indicate the opposite. Is an economy that is entirely controlled by the social and political elite really more 'modern' than one that is not?

CHAPTER 7

The tesserae nummulariae

Among the ancient objects customarily called *tesserae* are small rods of bone or ivory a few centimetres long, some thick, some less so, some of which carry inscriptions either on one or two of their surfaces or on all four of them.

Among these bone or ivory rods, one particular group has long been distinguished. We do not know the Latin name for these rods, but since the research work of R. Herzog,[1] they have been known as the *tesserae nummulariae*. These little rods, between 3 and 10 cm long and between 7 and 12 mm wide, are almost as high as they are wide. They consist of a rectangular parallelepiped body and a head the shape of which varies from one period to another. A hole is pierced either through the head or through the neck that links it to the body of the *tessera*.

With very few exceptions, the four long surfaces of these *tesserae nummulariae* carry inscriptions. Two of these, traditionally known as sides 1 and 2, carry proper names. In most cases the name of a slave, in the nominative (on side 1) is followed by the family name of his master, in the genitive (on side 2). The names thus read as Pilotimus Hostili, Pilargurus Lucili, Flaccus Rabiri,[2] etc. In seven or eight cases, the family name of the master is followed by the initial of his first name and the first letter of the word *s(ervus)*: e.g. *Pamphilus Servili M(arci) s(ervus)*.[3] Occasionally the master may be a woman, but the slave is always a man. In three or four cases, the master seems to be designated by his surname, not his family name. Thus one appears as *Metel(lus?)*.[4] On three of the *tesserae*, slaves belonging to *socii* are named: *Pamphil(us) sociorum, Piloxen(us) soc(iorum) fer(rariarum), Primus sociorum*.[5] As we shall see, these unnamed 'associates' may be identified as companies of tax-collectors.

---

[1] Herzog 1919; 1937.
[2] R. Herzog (1937: 1421–34) drew up a list of the *tesserae nummulariae* then known; the *CIL* references are given there. I shall refer to the *tesserae* by the numbers given to them in that list. The four referred to at this point are the *tesserae* 28, 29, 32, and 39. [3] *Tessera* 71. [4] *Tessera* 79.
[5] *Tesserae* 10, 15, and 102.

Ten *tesserae* carry not a slave's name followed by the family name of his master in the genitive, but the name of a free citizen in the nominative. Three of these ten free men have *tria nomina* (for example, M. Pilius Phoenix).[6] One, C. Octavius[7] has a *praenomen* and a *nomen*, and the six others have a *nomen* and a *cognomen* (for example, Valerius Priscus).[8] Finally, one *tessera* bears on its first side a single Greek name (but written in Latin letters), Hermia, who was possibly a peregrine.[9]

With very few exceptions, the third side bears the perfect form *spectavit*, 'has examined', but always written in an abbreviated form: either as *sp(ectavit)* or as *spec(tavit)*. On the rest of the third side and on the fourth, there is usually a date. The day and the month are followed by the name of the year's consuls, also written in an abbreviated form.

For palaeographic or epigraphic reasons, some of these rods are of doubtful authenticity. In the seventeenth and eighteenth centuries, these *tesserae* were known to the curious and to collectors, and some of those that have come down to us were probably manufactured in Italy during that period. Others are genuinely ancient, but it is uncertain whether they should be classed among the *tesserae nummulariae*. Discounting these doubtful cases, we know of about 160 *tesserae nummulariae*.

Almost all were found in Rome or elsewhere in Italy. Only six were found outside Italy (in Agrigentum, Ephesus, Hadrumentum, Arles, Vieille-Toulouse, and Virunum).

139 *tesserae* still bear a date. Some never carried a date, and on others the date is no longer legible. None of those with a date is earlier than 96 BC or later than AD 85 or 86. The periods for which the greatest numbers of *tesserae* have been preserved are the years between 79 and 40 BC (56 *tesserae* are attested for those four decades) and the years between 9 BC and AD 20 (31 *tesserae*).

From the seventeenth to the nineteenth centuries, all those who wrote about the *tesserae* agreed that they related to gladiators, who wore them round their necks on a cord or a little chain. The *tessera* was believed to testify that the gladiator had won his release, and so represented a mark of honour for him. The verb *spectare* was often used in connection with gladiators, in particular by Horace.

In the nineteenth century, that old interpretation was brought into question, when other possible functions for the *tesserae* were imagined. R. Herzog had the idea of connecting them with the assaying of coins. Showing that *spectare*, like *probare*, could mean to assay coins, that is to say

---

[6] *Tessera* 91.   [7] *Tessera* 61.   [8] *Tessera* 114.   [9] *Tessera* 70.

to verify their weight, their quality, and their type, he concluded that the little rods had been attached by means of a string to sealed sacks of coins, and that they guaranteed their authenticity and quality.

If the *tesserae* related to the assaying of coins, whose were the names that they bore? Herzog's answer was that these were the names of slaves who specialized in the assaying of coins, that is to say who were *nummularii*. The free men whose names appear on their own on a few of the *tesserae* were, he thought, also *nummularii*. He accordingly devoted most of his article *Nummularius*, in the *RE*, to a study of the *tesserae*.[10]

It was Herzog who invented the expression 'tesserae nummulariae'. Previously, people had spoken of 'gladiators' *tesserae*' or 'consulary *tesserae*'.

Who were the slaves' masters? He pointed out that some of the family names were those of monetary magistrates, others were those of 'big capitalists' ('Grosskapitalisten') who were members of either the Senate or the equestrian order, while others were those of Italian businessmen working in Delos, and yet others those of professional bankers (*argentarii*). Furthermore, he thought that Tyrannus Tiberi, whose name appears on a *tessera* dated AD 13, was one of Emperor Tiberius' slaves, and on another *tessera* he thought he recognized the name of the Empress Livia.[11] He concluded that these sacks of coins, assayed and labelled, emanated from a relatively broad circle of financiers with a wide variety of social and legal statuses (senators and knights, professional bankers, *negotiatores*, tax-collectors, and so on).

In what situations were these *tesserae* employed? Herzog pointed out that the materials used (bone, ivory, and possibly, in exceptional cases, steatite or bronze) were extremely durable. He concluded that the sacks of coins were intended to remain sealed for a long time. Did they circulate, and into whose hands did they fall? Did they remain deposited in the coffers of a bank, in the treasure-store of a temple, or in the State strongboxes? Herzog ruled out the possibility of the *tesserae* being used by the public authorities or issued by the Mint. According to him, they were produced by private financial establishments. The sacks to which they were attached circulated from hand to hand within the circle of financiers. Herzog did not believe that the sacks could have circulated among the wider public. When it was a matter of moving a sum of money or transferring it from one financier to another, the docket hanging from the sealed sack attested that its contents had been checked.

---

[10] Herzog 1937.   [11] *Tesserae* 109 and 78.

The *tesserae* were also used for sealed deposits placed in the coffers of a bank, serving a similar purpose.

All credit must go to Herzog for reflecting on the function of the *tesserae*, starting from scratch; and it seems to me that his intuition was correct. His little book and his article in the Pauly-Wissowa encyclopaedia furthermore contain many stimulating ideas and suggestions.

However, what he writes is not always coherent, nor was he a trustworthy specialist in Latin epigraphy. His identification of Tiberius and Livia, for example, does not seem admissible. And here is another example: on *tessera* 5 in his list, the name of a slave, Philodamus, is followed by the abbreviations *RV SAB*. The expanded rendering of this that Herzog suggested, namely *Philo(damus) Ru(briae) Sab(idiae servus)* (with two family names of women) is untenable. His research work enjoyed an astonishing success, with even the strictest of epigraphists displaying toward his research an indulgence that is hard to explain, for while some of his conclusions are valid, others are certainly not.

Herzog's central intuition does remain altogether valid: the *tesserae nummulariae* were tied to sacks of coins, and they attested that the contents had been verified. The four following points support his claims:

(1) The days and months indicated on the *tesserae* are extremely diverse; but the days that appear most frequently are ides and kalends. Of the 133 *tesserae* where the date is legible, 53 mention kalends and 25 mention ides. Now, it is known that payments (the repayments of debts, for example) usually took place on those days. (Yet, it must be said, at least a dozen of the *tesserae* are dated the kalends of January; if payments were suspended on the first day of the year, how is it that this date figures so frequently on the *tesserae?*)

(2) In several texts, *spectare* has the meaning of assaying coins or non-minted metals.[12] Similarly, *spectatio* and *spectator* are sometimes used in connection with the assaying of coins or metals.[13]

(3) It was customary to keep sums of money in sacks that were sealed up so that nobody could touch them.

(4) The *tessera* found in Arles, which unfortunately has been lost but the text of which has been recorded, displayed the abbreviations *spectat(. . .?) num(mos?)* or *spectavit num(mos?)*.[14] If the word *nummi* figured on this *tessera*,

---

[12] Plautus, *Persa* 3.3.437; Ovid, *Tristia* 1.5.25; Donatus, *ad Ter. Phorm.* 53; *Corp. Gloss.* 5.151.48. See Bogaert 1976: 7, note 7, and 15.

[13] Ter. *Eunuch* 3.5.565; Cic.2 *Verr.* 3.181; Donatus, *ad Ter. Eun.* 565; Symm. *Epist.* 3.11.2.

[14] *Tessera* Herzog 36. See Herzog 1919: 1–4; 1937: 1442.

its connection with the assaying of coins cannot be doubted (but admittedly, because of the ligatures, *num* could also be read as *mun*).

It seems to me that Herzog had two other good ideas, from which, however, he failed to draw all the consequences. The first was that the *tesserae* were not used every time coins were assayed, but were kept for situations in which the sacks would be changing hands or, in some cases, moved from one place to another. I think it is important to emphasize that the sacks of coins supplied with *tesserae* were supposed to change hands without being opened, since the receiver of coins trusted the guarantee that the *tessera* represented.

The assaying of coins was common practice, and many people engaged in it, some being highly specialist, others much less so.[15] A couple of passages, one from Epictetus, the other from Tertullian, show, for example, that shopkeepers and traders often needed to check coins for themselves.[16]

But, as Herzog himself realized without recognizing all the implications, a *tessera* was not used invariably every time coins were assayed. If a creditor such as Dordales, in Plautus' *Persa*, received coins from a debtor of his, accompanied him to the *nummularius* to have them assayed, and then kept them, what need would there be for a *tessera*?[17]

Consider another type of situation: a creditor about to receive money from a debtor would ask him to leave the sum with an assayer for as long as it took the latter to examine the coins. The sack would be sealed (*signatus*), but by the signet ring of either the debtor or the creditor (depending on the circumstances), who would thus leave his own personal imprint upon the wax. There would be no need for a *tessera*. Such a case is described in a passage of Africanus.[18] Petrucci has tried to prove that it is not incompatible with the use of a *tessera*, but some of his assertions are untenable. He seems to assume that the *nummularius* in this text, which – *via* Africanus – goes back to the jurist Mela, is a deposit banker.[19] But *nummularii* did not become deposit bankers until some time in the first half of the second century AD.[20]

Furthermore, whatever Herzog and Petrucci may think, I do not believe, either, that the action taken by M. Marius Gratidianus during his praetorship explains the use of *tesserae*.[21]

[15] Bogaert 1976; Andreau 1987a: 506–25.   [16] Epictetus, *Conv.* 3.3.3; Tertullian, *de paen.* 6.5.
[17] Plautus, *Persa* 3.3.437.   [18] *Dig.* 46.3.39 (Africanus).   [19] Petrucci 1991: 264–5.
[20] Petrucci 1991: 289–93.
[21] Andreau 1987a: 505 and Petrucci 1991: 258–63. On Marius Gratidianus, see now Verboven 1994, where the earlier bibliography may be found.

Tesserae had a useful function only if those receiving the sealed sacks would not be going to the bother of opening them. Herzog provides an altogether comparable example of a modern institution.[22] In Frankfurt, before the unification of Germany (before 1866), sealed sacks of coins would circulate from bank to bank, equipped with a label that indicated the total sum, the total weight, the name of the bank delivering the money, and that of the employee who had checked the coins. This practice, which was founded on trust, operated only in Frankfurt itself. After the unification of Germany it disappeared, because the circle of financiers concerned was no longer sufficiently limited.

The sacks of coins equipped with *tesserae* did not circulate among the wider public. They were necessarily restricted to a small group of financiers between whom mutual trust could be maintained. That is another point to bear in mind, and it is also one originally made by Herzog, who illustrated it with the example of Frankfurt. But as he proceeded with his research, he forgot it, and his conclusions ended up in contradiction to the idea.

The *tessera* did not supply the name of an institution recognizable to all and sundry which might in itself have inspired confidence in a wide public. The only sign of identification that it bore was the name of an assayer, who was almost always a slave. The name of the slave-assayer was followed by the family name of his master, which was officially also part of the slave's name.[23] So it was not the business of the master that was mentioned on the *tessera*, simply the name of the slave. It was therefore necessary that the person receiving the sealed sack without bothering to open it should know the slave (at least by name) and the business or department of administration in which he worked – or else that he should possess a list of all the practising assayers. The shape of the heads of the *tesserae*, which were all identical in any given period, also indicates that their use was limited to a restricted and coherent group of those who produced and used *tesserae*. Besides, had the sealed sacks circulated among the wider public, more of them would have been found, and the literary and legal texts would probably have contained a number of allusions to them.

But after recognizing that point, Herzog mistakenly over-extended the circle of the 'happy few' who had access to *tesserae*. He refers to large-scale private financiers, monetary magistrates (using them for their private affairs), 'big capitalists' (by which he probably meant members

[22] Herzog 1919: 31–3.   [23] Andreau 1987a: 500–1.

of the imperial elite), *negotiatores* in the provinces, professional bankers and money-changers, and tax-collectors, quite apart from the collaborators of all these people. The entire senatorial and equestrian elite would thus, according to him, have had access to *tesserae*, not to mention a number of other categories, which were widely dispersed spatially, and socially far less distinguished. This is a far cry from his example of Frankfurt! So keen was Herzog to make his discovery as significant as possible that he ended up in opposition to his point of departure.

In the absence of texts, we must reason on the basis of the probabilities and logic of the institution. The probabilities point strongly to a restricted circle of people, all with a roughly analogous social status. The problem is whom did this circle comprise?

We must adopt a process of elimination. Can they have been *negotiatores*, established in the provinces for the sake of their business ventures? No, for they were too distant from one another, and too different; they did not maintain close enough contacts. It is often claimed that the *tesserae* were connected with the businesses of Delos. But that is a myth created by Herzog and Cary, and founded upon a comparison between a few family names (as rare as Fulvius or Pomponius!).[24] The number of family names common to the businessmen of Delos and the masters named on the *tesserae* is not statistically significant, particularly as many of them were extremely commonplace. No *tesserae* have ever been found on Delos. Indeed, not many have been found outside Italy at all. Besides, the heyday of Delos was earlier than the period of the *tesserae*.

Can these sums of money have belonged to the State and been despatched by State offices to supply the needs of the administration, or the army, or public works, mainly in Italy? That might have been an attractive hypothesis, but it too must be eliminated, since in the imperial period there are no traces of any imperial slaves or freedmen, apart from that Tyrannus Tiberi of doubtful identification. The total absence of imperial slaves or freedmen in the context of one of the Empire's official institutions is hard to imagine.

Another group that I believe to be ruled out, despite the opinions of Herzog and Barlow,[25] is that of the professional bankers, the *argentarii* and *nummularii*. It is true that the slaves mentioned on the *tesserae* were assayers of coins, and we do not know what the name for them was (*num-*

---

[24] Herzog 1937: 1434–5; Cary 1923: 112–13. The legend is repeated by Barlow (1978: 106, 109, 111–15, and 117), and also, of course, by Petrucci (1991: 261–2).
[25] See, for example, Barlow 1978: 117–18, 167–8 and 172–4.

mularii? spectatores?), but they were not professional, independent assayers/money-changers, working in their little shops, for the general public. It is my belief that they were working within the framework of larger-scale business ventures and services than those of the counters of professional bankers. Even if Camodeca was right in his claim that the Sulpicii of Puteoli were professional bankers, such bankers' businesses on the whole remained relatively modest, focussing on local affairs rather than contacts in far-flung places. Besides, if professional banks had been identified on the *tesserae*, the name of the banker himself would have been inscribed, not that of the slave-assayer.

What of the family names of the masters? C. Nicolet noticed that on the 73 *tesserae* dating from before 44 BC, sixteen of the family names are also the family names of knights. But under the Empire the situation is different: only one family name, Maecenas, appears in both groups.[26] Some of the masters seem to be identifiable, but most are not. Eunus Fidiclani was almost certainly a slave of the senator Caius Fidiculanius Falcula, mentioned by Cicero, or of one of his relatives.[27] Athamas Maecenatis was the slave of a close relative of Maecenas,[28] and Flaccus Rabiri may have been a slave of Caius Rabirius Postumus.[29] Alfius may be confused with a known moneylender of that name.[30] But does the family name Caecilius warrant our identifying Atticus (in 52 BC, after the death of his uncle)? Or C. Octavius, the grandfather of Augustus (in 53 BC, after the death of Augustus' father)? I think it would be risky to do so. Furthermore, at least three of the slave owners mentioned on the *tesserae* are women: Tragonia, Rupilia, and Attia.[31] And three are *socii*, members of not just any company, but tax-collectors' companies (*societates publicanorum*).[32]

These observations lead to two conclusions. Firstly, that in this case prosopography is of little use to us. It does not make it possible to identify the group of financiers who owned the slaves on the *tesserae*. The second conclusion stems from the presence of women: in all likelihood, some of the slaves named here had been hired, so their master would not be the head of the business. In that case (and we do not know how

---

[26] Demougin 1988: 114. [27] *Tessera* 40, dated 62 BC. See also *tessera* 43 ([Pilar]gurus [Fidic]lani).
[28] *Tessera* 108, dated to AD 13. [29] *Tessera* 39. [30] *Tessera* 73; Horace, *Epod.* 2.67.
[31] *Tesserae* 99, 104, and 122.
[32] *Tesserae* 10, 15, and 102. If it were a matter of bankers or private financier associates, it would be the family name of the master or masters of the slave that would be indicated on the *tessera*, not the word *socii*. Two banker associates could be co-owners of a slave, but the company that they formed did not have the legal power to own slaves as a company (whatever the claims of Barlow 1978: 113).

frequently it occurred), the family name inscribed is that of their master (which was also part of the slave's name), and not that of the head of the business in question.

It is, at this stage, impossible to be certain. But two hypotheses appeal to me more than the rest, and of those two, I definitely prefer the second. Let me describe them.

The first is closer to Herzog's theories, but very much reduces the circle of the 'happy few'. According to this hypothesis, a number of important financiers were involved, who specialized in, for example, the transfer of funds, with or without the material coins being transported (particularly, but not exclusively, in Rome or within Italy), or they may have been very large-scale moneylenders and credit-intermediaries who, as such, all knew one another and belonged either to the elite or to the group of big businessmen. The texts do not attest any such cooperation between a few important financiers (who were not associates, and some of whom had interests in the tax-collectors' companies). But it may have existed, even if no text refers to it. In that case, the slaves would be treasurers, acting as cashiers, coin-assayers or money-changers, working within the framework of their respective masters' businesses, or else hired out by their masters to work in other individuals' businesses. As for the assayers who were free men, they would be employees of one or other of these large-scale financiers.

According to this hypothesis, the appearance of *tesserae* would be explained by the growing importance of financial business in Rome, and by the need to facilitate the circulation of coins without having to check them repeatedly. Their gradual disappearance in the course of the first century AD could be explained by the greater dispersion of financial businesses, which became far less concentrated in Rome, or by a progressive and general slowing down of financial affairs.

It is worth noting that the appearance and disappearance of *tesserae* are not necessarily as dramatically significant as we might like to make out, for both before and after the time of the *tesserae*, it is possible to imagine other forms of labelling that have not come down to us, or inscriptions painted on sacks. In fact, the amount of coins never was indicated on the *tesserae*: was it painted on the sack?[33]

The other possible conclusion, and the one that I prefer, is that the *tesserae* were all produced by the great companies of tax-collectors (the *societates publicanorum*) that were recognized legally.[34] The sacks were used

---

[33] Petrucci 1991: 256, note 15.
[34] On this privilege of the great tax-collectors' companies, see Nicolet 1979: 70–82.

in transactions between the companies, in transactions with the State, for transferring the companies' funds, particularly back to Rome, and for transporting the State funds for which the companies were responsible.

It would not be very surprising to find that the assayers included slaves belonging to companies, slaves belonging to individuals, some of whom had probably been hired (in particular, those belonging to women), and free men, too, for as V. Ivanov already noted, these tax-collectors' companies employed a very mixed workforce, and free men and slaves seem to have worked for them on the same professional level.[35] The expression *familiae publicanorum* was used to designate all those who worked for the companies, slaves and free men alike. Moreover, the graph of the numbers of knights' family names (far more numerous on the *tesserae* of the Republic than on later ones) would tally well with this hypothesis, for in the first century of the Empire there are far fewer references to knights with interests in the *publica*.[36]

According to this hypothesis, which I believe to be the best one, the masters of the slaves would have been either officials of the tax-collectors' companies, or people with interests in those companies, or else the owners of slaves whom they had hired out to one of the companies. The disappearance of the *tesserae* could be satisfactorily explained by the progressive fragmentation of the *societates publicanorum*, whose size, political importance, and even numbers waned sharply in the course of the first century AD, even if they did not necessarily disappear totally as early as this period.[37]

---

[35] Ivanov 1910: 74–86.   [36] Demougin 1988: 103–12.   [37] Demougin 1988.

CHAPTER 8

The interest rate

The documentation available on interest rates is relatively abundant, but very dispersed and tricky to interpret. The literary texts cite a few examples of loans, and also include general remarks on the current rates and the measures taken by the public authorities (generally to limit the interest; very occasionally to prohibit it). The rate of interest was, in fact, one of the aspects of financial life that most frequently exercised the public authorities. As we shall see, the legal texts, for their part, provide interesting information on the variation in interest rates.

Curiously enough, the tablets recovered from the villas of the Vesuvius region tell us nothing about this subject. It is the papyri that provide the most interesting information. But, at the same time, we should not forget the inscriptions relating to euergetistic foundations, for these sometimes indicate the rate of interest that should be charged for lending the money donated in order for this to produce an annual income.

Over recent years, very little research has been devoted to the subject of interest rates.[1] It is true that a century ago it gave rise to a major work that still commands respect, despite the discovery of new evidence.[2]

This chapter is divided into three sections. The first concerns the interventions made by the public authorities. The second comprises a few remarks on the practice of charging interest. The last is devoted to variations in the interest rate.

According to Tacitus, the Twelve Tables prohibited the lending of money at a rate higher than the *fenus unciarium*. This expression has been the subject of much discussion, and some historians, such as T. Frank and Barlow, for instance, have surmised, following Billeter, that it designated an annual rate of 8⅓ per cent (one twelfth of the capital) or of 10

---

[1] See, however, Barlow 1978.   [2] Billeter 1898.

per cent (if calculations are based on a year of 10 months). The conclusion drawn by H. Zehnacker, who for his part interprets this as a rate of 100 per cent per annum (one twelfth per month), seems to me preferable by far.[3] The years 350 and 340 BC were both marked by a serious debt crisis. In 357 BC, the limit fixed by the Twelve Tables was reimposed by law.[4] Ten years later, the rate was cut to the *fenus semiunciarium*, that is to say 50 per cent per year (half a twelfth per month). The payment of debts was staggered over three years, with four instalments (the first to be paid right at the start). Eventually, in 342 BC, interest-bearing loans were banned altogether by the famous *lex Genucia*.[5]

The consequences of that law are not known. In other periods, a legal abolition failed to eradicate the practice of lending money at interest, but did lead to the elaboration of ways of getting around the prohibition. Such evasions were flagrant in the Middle Ages. Under the Early Empire, Palestine provides another example where such procedures were rife.[6]

How long did the *lex Genucia* remain in force? We do not know. In principle, it probably never was abrogated. In 89 BC, when there was another serious debt crisis, the *praetor* A. Sempronius Asellio decided to apply an old law that had fallen into disuse, which prohibited interest-bearing loans altogether.[7] Was this the *lex Genucia*? Or had money-lending at interest been again prohibited in the meantime? It is known for certain that in the second century BC the law of 342 was no longer applied. Was it at about this time (between 200 and 170 BC) that a new law reformulated the prohibition? Both Billeter and Barlow believe so: Billeter thinks that this was the *lex Marcia*, while Barlow suggests the *lex Iunia de feneratione*.[8] However, the alternative thesis, namely that the old *lex Genucia* was the one invoked by Sempronius Asellio, cannot be ruled out. The works of Cato the censor, Plautus, and Terence make no mention of any legal ban on lending money at interest. Their silence would be more understandable if no new ban on interest had been introduced in their time.

The *lex Cornelia Pompeia* of 88 BC legalized interest-bearing loans and once more fixed a maximum *unciarium* rate, namely, at this date, 12 per cent per year (one ounce per pound for each month) by T. Frank's reck-

---

[3] Tac. *Ann.* 6.16. See Billeter 1898: 115–33 and 157–62; Frank 1933–40: vol. 1, 17 and 28–9; Barlow 1978: 75 and 122–3; De Martino 1980: 143–7; Zehnacker 1980.   [4] Liv. 7.16.1.

[5] Billeter 1898: 134–57; Barlow 1978: 56–8.   [6] Safrai 1994: 293–5.

[7] On the praetorship of A. Sempronius Asellio, see Appian, *B.C.* 1.134.232–9; Frank 1933–40 : vol. 1. 268–9; Bulst 1964: 331–2; Gabba 1967: 158–61; Badian 1969: 475–81.

[8] Billeter 1898: 144–53 and Barlow 1978: 59–60.

oning,[9] or 8⅓ per cent per year (one twelfth of the capital per year). In 51 BC, the Senate again limited the interest rate to 12 per cent per year, which proves that the maximum of 88 BC (whatever it was) was no longer being applied.[10] The maximum rate of 12 per cent per year reappears in the provincial edict issued by Cicero in Cilicia. From then on, in the Latin world, interest was calculated at so many hundredths per month. The rate of 12 per cent per year was thus called *centesimae usurae* (that is to say an interest of one hundredth, 1 per cent per month). This method of calculation was probably imitated from the Greek custom, for the Greeks calculated in drachmas per *mina* per month, and given that one hundred drachmas made up a *mina*, one drachma per month was the equivalent of 1 per cent per month.[11]

Was the limitation formulated by the Senate in 51 BC confirmed by Caesar and later by Augustus? We do not know. I, like Billeter, do not believe that Caesar's law *de modo credendi possidendique intra Italiam* set a limit on the interest rate.[12] However, he may have passed some other law, no trace of which has come down to us. Was the interest rate limited to 12 per cent per year under the Principate, in lasting fashion and through-out the imperial territory? Two things, at any rate, are certain: under the Principate, interest-bearing loans were never prohibited; and even if there is scarcely a mention of any limitation of the rate in the texts of that period, it was limited to 12 per cent in certain provinces, such as Egypt. But was that limitation applied generally? Very possibly, but we cannot be absolutely certain.

Thus, the Roman State tended to fix a maximum interest rate which, however, did not become a basic rate. It set an upper limit. Under the Principate, as well as in the last century of the Republic, we know of many cases in which the interest charged was well below that limit, and not only for the capital from new foundations.

Moreover, the Roman State was very sensitive to two other matters. One was the question of compound interest (the interest that was added to capital each year, or even each month, thereby bringing in yet more interest). Compound interest was frequently forbidden: the *senatusconsul-tum* of 51 BC authorized only loans that were *perpetuo fenore*, that is to say which produced simple interest. Compound interest was more likely to be permitted or tolerated for annual capitalization than for monthly cap-

---

[9] Frank 1933–40, vol. 1: 269–71.
[10] Cic. *ad Att.* 5.21.13; Billeter 1898: 169–75 and Barlow 1978: 172.
[11] Barlow 1978: 130, 134, and 171. [12] Billeter 1898: 175–7.

italization.[13] In Cilicia, while Cicero was governor, annual capitalization was allowed, but not monthly capitalization.

In times of crisis, the public authorities were particularly attentive to the matter of interest payments that were owed. They decided frequently to limit such payments to a sum equal to that of the capital loaned. This is what Lucullus did in Asia to relieve the cities that had fallen into debt. The same rule was regularly applied in Roman Egypt.[14]

As Tacitus remarked, usury and debt were inveterate evils in Rome and the Roman world, and they were never totally eradicated. Nevertheless, whenever the public authorities were firmly resolved to reduce them severely, they managed to do so, as the examples of Cato in Sardinia and Lucullus in Asia certainly show.[15] A. Gara stresses the fact that in Egypt Roman domination produced a fall in the interest rate and a more effective weapon against usury.[16] But the affair of the loan to Salamis in Cyprus shows how even a relatively honest governor, anxious not to oppress the natives, could be led to procrastinate and prevaricate so as not to displease his peers (one of whom, Brutus, was creditor to the people of Salamis).

J.-Y. Grenier emphasizes the fact that, in modern France, the rate of interest depends on the supply of and demand for money, but also that the supply of money, for its part, results in the first place from the manner in which savings are divided between hoarding and loans. Depending on whether a moneylender is concerned more with profit or with safeguarding his patrimony, he decides to lend or, on the contrary, to hoard. It depends upon how confident he feels. Over the decades, there have been noticeable phases characterized either by confidence or by a lack of it.[17] At the end of the Roman Republic and in the first two centuries of the Empire, it was certainly confidence that predominated, at least among members of the elite on whom we possess documentation. Whereas we find no examples of men unprepared to advance loans, there are several mentions of holders of capital unable to find borrowers.[18] Hoarding does not appear to have been a problem in those periods, and it is hardly mentioned. By the end of the third century and in the fourth century AD, the situation was quite different. Many Christian texts allude to hoarding, and it is con-

[13] Barlow 1978: 171 and notes 130–1.   [14] Plut. *Lucull.* 20.3; and Johnson 1936: 450–1.
[15] Liv. 32.27.3–4; and Plut. *Lucull.* 20 and 23.   [16] Gara 1988: 943–6.
[17] Grenier 1996: 188–91.   [18] See, for example, Petr. *Satir.* 53.4 and Pliny, *Epist.* 10.54 and 55.

demned much more frequently than at the beginning of the Empire. The centuries with which the present work is concerned probably constituted a prolonged period of confidence, when men were keen to lend their money.

The variations in interest rates that have been traced fluctuated between 4 and 12 per cent per year. It is extremely rare to come across an interest rate of less than 4 per cent,[19] and one of the authors of the *Historia Augusta* calls 4 per cent the *minimae usurae*.[20] Except in cases of manifest usury, the 12 per cent rate is hardly ever exceeded.[21] There were no terms in Latin that exactly translate 'usury' or 'usurious'. Nevertheless, Billeter was correct when he declared that any interest rate over 12 per cent would have seemed usurious to them, even when the interest rate was not legally limited.[22] That is borne out by the fact that one hardly ever comes across a loan at 15, 16, or 18 per cent interest per year. If the rate rose above 12 per cent, it soared straight to 24, 48, or even 60 per cent per year.[23]

When, after the battle of Actium, the treasury of the kings and queens of Egypt was taken to Rome and partly converted into money, the interest rate fell from 12 to 4 per cent,[24] that is to say it plummeted from its normal maximum to its lowest level.

Another question, posed by, for example, I. Shatzman and A. Gara, is the following: how are we to explain the fact that the interest rate was so often greater than the income from land (which apparently hardly ever exceeded 6 per cent)?[25] How could people continue to farm their land in those circumstances? Gara's explanation is that the social and ethical values of the ancient world dissuaded the people from seeking to raise interest from their possessions as a whole. Perhaps. But another point to take into account is the element of risk: advancing interest-bearing loans is always more risky than agriculture. When a rich man's aim is above all to safeguard his capital and derive a modest but sure income from it, land is always a better option than moneylending.

Finally, we must also bear in mind that in one and the same place a number of different rates of interest could be applied at the same time, even without counting the case of usurious loans. Given the poverty of

---

[19] In *Dig.* 33.1.21.4 (Scaev.), a rate of 3% per year is mentioned.
[20] Scr. Hist. Aug. *Anton. Pius* 2.8.
[21] One foundation seems to indicate the extraordinarily high rate of 15% (*CIL* v, 5134).
[22] Billeter 1898: 164–5.
[23] 24%: see Cic. 2 *Verr.* 3.165–70. 48%: Brutus' loan to Salamis in Cyprus. 60%: Hor. *Sat.* 1.2.14.
[24] Dio Cass. 51.21.5; Suet. *Aug.* 41.2.   [25] Shatzman 1975: 49, note 6; Gara 1988: 943–6.

our documentation, this makes it enormously complicated to try to work out how situations evolved in different sets of circumstances.

The rate of interest would vary, firstly, depending on the personality of the lender and that of the borrower. Two of Cicero's letters provide a good illustration of the difficulties that this could provoke. In 62–61 B C, Cicero was trying to borrow money, as he had bought a house on the Palatine. In December 62, he wrote that money at 6 per cent could easily be found and that, in any case, he was a *bonum nomen* in the eyes of moneylenders, because during his consulate, at the time of Catiline's conspiracy, he had pursued policies that favoured their interests.[26] Less than one month later, at the very beginning of January 61, he wrote that Q. Caecilius was not advancing loans at less than 12 per cent, even to those close to him.[27] Taking into account Cicero's personality and Q. Caecilius', Billeter's conclusion is that the interest rate had, in fact, probably not changed between December and January. The difference (the doubling of the rate) was due to the identities of the lender and the borrower.[28] I cannot go along with him all the way here; I think that the interest rate did increase in the last weeks of 62. All the same, the difference could certainly be explained in part by the prestige of Cicero and the greed of Caecilius.

Pliny the Younger explained to Trajan that, interest rates being equal, the Bithynians preferred to borrow from private funds rather than from public ones;[29] so, in order to invest their money, the public authorities were forced to lower their interest rate. Another point: the borrowing rate of money invested in foundations was normally very low, as it was important that the foundation's capital should be continuously invested. In practice, however, one comes across some foundations that charged 12 per cent. Was such a rate a consequence of imprudent investment on the part of the founder? Or did it correspond to regional peculiarities or to a particular set of circumstances?

The size of a loan and its duration were also factors to be taken into account when determining the interest rate.

Differences in interest rates also corresponded to the various preoccupations and strategies of the moneylenders. A strategy of provident management stood in contrast to one of self-enrichment and quick profits, but the latter was far more risky. A passage from Persius contrasts two investments, the first of which brought in a modest 5 per cent while

---

[26] Cic. *ad Fam.* 5.6.2.   [27] Cic. *ad Att.* 1.12.1.   [28] Billeter 1898: 163–5.
[29] Pliny, *Epist.* 10.54–5.

the second aimed for a greedy 11 per cent. A passage such as this shows that at the very same time and in the very same place, some interest rates could be twice as high as others without, however, reaching a usurious level.[30]

Finally, wherever intermediaries took a hand, there were, of course, two separate rates of interest, the one that the intermediary paid to the investor and the one that he himself received from the borrower. But we have no information on the difference between these two rates, either when the intermediary was a banker or when he was a credit intermediary such as Cluvius or Vestorius. We have virtually no documentation at all on the interest rates charged by bankers.

According to a remark in Suetonius, Augustus issued a censorious *nota* of blame to knights who first borrowed money at interest and then invested it, charging a higher interest rate.[31] How to interpret this passage is a delicate question. The simplest interpretation is that Augustus wanted to deter knights from engaging in the most specialized and most profitable financial operations. Of course, credit intermediaries were bound to lend money at a higher interest rate than that on the money that they had borrowed. The reproaches that Augustus aimed at those knights could not be extended either to bankers or to other financiers short of wiping out their financial activities as a whole.

Would the interest rate at a particular date vary from one place to another? Definitely yes, as a number of jurists' texts testify.[32] The cause of the variations is not always explained in these texts, and when it is, it is not always the same. Sometimes the text implicitly refers to a limitation imposed by a provincial edict.[33] In other cases, it seems that the circumstances are at least partly responsible, and that the variation depends on the relation between the supply of cash and the demand for it.[34] Gaius thus comments that in some places the interest is lower and the supply of money greater, while in other places the interest is higher and the supply more limited. Finally, this jurist sometimes refers to some custom of the particular locality, that is to say to a durable tradition that does not depend upon ephemeral circumstances.[35] So supply and

---

[30] Persius, *Sat.* 5.149–50.   [31] Suet. *Aug.* 39.

[32] *Dig.* 13.4.3 (Gaius); 17.1.10.3 (Ulpian); 22.1.1 pr. (Papin.); 22.1.37 (Ulpian); 26.7.7.10 (Ulpian); 27.4.3.1 (Ulpian); 30.39.1 (Ulpian); 33.1.21 pr. (Scaev.).

[33] *Dig.* 17.1.10.3 (Ulpian); 26.7.7.10 (Ulpian).

[34] *Dig.* 13.4.3 (Gaius); probably 26.7.7.10 (Ulpian) and 27.4.3.1 (Ulpian).

[35] *Dig.* 33.1.21 pr. (Scaev.); 22.1.1 pr. (Papin) (if, that is, *mos* designates a lasting custom; *consuetudo* is probably more revealing than *mos*, for the question that interests us here); 30.39.1 (Ulpian) (*mos regionis*).

demand were not the only factors at work; local and regional customs also needed to be taken into account.

In practice, it is hard to put figures on these variations since, in our meagre documentation, geographical variations are invariably intertwined with chronological ones. It is frequently said that, under the Principate, interest was lower in Italy and the western Mediterranean (4 to 6 per cent) than it was in the Greek part of the Empire (8 or 9 per cent) and, above all, in Egypt (12 per cent).[36] The Egyptian documentation is evidently the richest. As for the rest of the Empire, close investigation of the available evidence (including those cases that give figures relating to foundations), suggests that there is no clear difference between the East and the West. In North Africa, for example, four foundations foresaw interest rates of 5 or 6 per cent, but a fifth expected a rate of 12 per cent. We have to assume that geographical variations existed, but it is not easy to come up with precise figures.

And what of variations in time? In Italy, we are faced with two very different situations in succession. In the last century of the Republic, it is well known that there were a number of sudden variations. Under the Principate, in contrast, there is no indication of any significant variation, and the rates cited in the literary and legal texts and the inscriptions are low, frequently 5 or 6 per cent per year.[37]

Between 88 and 62 BC, the average rate must have fluctuated on several occasions. At the end of 62, in Rome, it was quite low (6 per cent), but seems to have risen over the last weeks of the year. In 54 BC, following a serious scandal involving electoral corruption, it doubled, rising from 4 to 8 per cent.[38] As can be seen, before the scandal it was very low. The *senatusconsultum* of 51 BC shows that it had risen greatly between 54 and 51. What with the civil war and the debt and liquidity crisis that marked it, we may be certain that it did not fall. Caesar himself writes that the interest rate invariably rises in times of war, because of the exceptional taxes that are required from everyone.[39] As noted already, in 31 BC, after the confiscation of the treasure of Egypt, the interest rate fell by two-thirds, from 12 to 4 per cent per year.

This relatively full documentation gives some idea of the rapidity of interest rate variations, at least in Rome and central Italy, where aristo-

---

[36] For example Billeter 1898: 103–9 and 181; Sartre 1991: 155 and 171.

[37] Colum. *De re rust.* 3.3.9; Persius, *Sat.* 5.149–50; Pliny, *Nat.Hist.* 14.56; *Dig.* 15.4.3 (Ulpian); *Dig.* 22.1.13 pr. (Scaev.); 22.1.17.6 (Paulus); 26.7.7.10 (Ulpian); 45.1.134.2 (Paulus); 46.3.102.3 (Scaev.); etc. See Billeter 1898: 179–220. This is not to mention the inscriptions of foundations, whose rate, logically, could not be very high.

[38] Cic. *ad Att.* 4.15.7 and 4.17.2–3; *ad Quint. Fr.*, 2.14.4. On this subject, see Billeter 1898: 163–5; Früchtl 1912: 130–3 and Shackleton Bailey 1965–8: volume 2, 213–4.   [39] Caes. *B.C.* 3.32.5.

cratic finance was then concentrated. It also shows that the variations do not have economic causes, as they do in modern Europe.[40] The dominant factors were political and military events (civil wars, the booty produced by wars), and the ups and downs of senatorial political life. In this period, variations in the interest rate stemmed not from economic developments, but from the vicissitudes of politics and aristocratic finance.

Under the Principate, the textual documentation for Rome and Italy presents a very different picture, that of an extremely stable situation with very low interest rates (5 to 6 per cent).

In the tablets of Murecine, the interest rate is not mentioned in those of *mutua cum stipulatione*; in fact, the subject does not arise at all. Yet the loans made by the Sulpicii were surely not interest-free. Should we conclude that separate tablets relating to interest have chanced not to come down to us? Camodeca thinks not. He believes that the interest was subtracted from the total of the capital at the point when the debtor received the money. But why should that have been the procedure? According to him, because the interest rates were extremely high, exceeding the legal maximum.[41] In contrast to the picture presented to us by the literary and legal texts, he suggests another, which is very different, according to which usurious interest rates were extremely common in first-century AD Italy.

However, in the case of the Sulpicii we cannot rule out the possibility that other tablets, as yet undiscovered, recorded all the information to do with interest rates. Given that fragments of the *Digest* cite simple contracts of *mutuum cum stipulatione* without mentioning interest, we should not suppose there to have been any illegality about the situation.[42] If such a procedure had constituted a way of concealing an usurious rate of interest, the jurist would not have failed to say so. Besides, it was legally normal that *mutuum* interest should be the subject of a special stipulation.[43]

Sometimes the interest was not mentioned because it was included in the sum to be repaid. P.W. Pestman has shown that in the papyri from Egypt, *atokos* and *aneu tokou* do not always signify that the loan was interest-free; the interest might be included in the sum due to be repaid.[44] But should one necessarily conclude that, if this was the case, the interest rate was usurious?

---

[40] Grenier 1996: 191–201.   [41] Camodeca 1992: 165–98.
[42] Camodeca 1992: 175–6 (on *Dig.* 12.1.40 (Paulus), and 45.1.126.2 (Paulus)).
[43] Michel 1962: 103–27.
[44] Pestman 1971; see also Foraboschi and Gara 1981: 337.

I am not convinced that the testimony of the (few) literary texts and, above all, that of the legal texts should be rejected solely in favour of an *ex silentio* argument (and in the absence of any other proof). To do so would be, in my view, far too distrustful of the textual tradition.

If Camodeca were right (and I do not believe he is), it would be impossible to avoid the following alternative: either the Sulpicii were even more greedy usurers than most, or else Roman financial life was far more primitive than the other available evidence would suggest. The drop in the interest rate was, in fact, connected with an intensification of financial life, an increase in the monetary stock available, and also in the number of monetary transactions. The current practice of usury, despite the laws (Camodeca is convinced that the rate of interest in Italy under the Empire was limited to 12 per cent), would thus be a consequence of the State's inability to institutionalize financial practices and to apply its decisions. It should be remembered that some of the money-lenders of Murecine were imperial slaves and freedmen! It would also reveal the predominance of an ethos of self-enrichment of the most brutal kind, at the expense of the smooth running of commerce and relative security for wholesalers. Should Camodeca's hypothesis on the interest rate ever come to be confirmed, it would indicate a high degree of archaism in Roman commercial and financial life.

CHAPTER 9

Rome's responses to financiers and financial crises

The relations of first the city, then the Empire, with financial life and the world of financiers pose various problems. This chapter will examine the attitude that the State, as such, as the ruling authority, adopted toward private business and the various categories of private businessmen. To give the other side of the picture, chapter 10, in contrast, will examine the operations by which the State itself became a private financier or a client of private financiers. It will thus be concerned with the financial operations of first the city of Rome, then the Empire, and also those of various cities within the Empire.

How did the city, then the Empire, behave as public authorities, in respect of private financial life? The best way to answer that question is to draw a clear distinction between 'normal' periods and periods of crisis. For in normal times, the attitude of the public authorities and the measures taken by them were not at all the same as in times of crisis. What constituted a crisis? The word, for which there was no equivalent in Latin, is often used and is the subject of much disagreement. Many writers consider it to be too sweeping, or over-charged with a variety of connotations, either Marxist (as in the 'crisis of the slave-based mode of production') or 'modernizing'. Some refer to 'the third-century crisis' as if to a long period of decline, degeneration, and many changes. Others reject the term absolutely, for it does suggest that every domain of social and economic life was simultaneously undergoing the same kind of disorders and that these related more or less directly to the political and military history.

I shall be using the word 'crisis' in a very neutral sense, aiming to imbue it with the minimum of theoretical and ideological content. What I mean by it is a point when public opinion and the public authorities were aware of dysfunctional elements that it seemed essential to remedy. Those elements affected, not Roman society and the Roman economy as a whole, but one particular aspect of the economy. I shall be using the word 'crisis' so as to avoid more ponderous terms such as 'dysfunctioning'.

I shall be concerned only with monetary and financial crises and shall not be referring to those that affected other aspects of the economy (such as agricultural crises, crises in food supplies and trade), unless, that is, they produced serious monetary or financial effects.

In the financial domain, the 'crises' experienced in the Roman period can be classed in three categories. First, there were the payment or liquidity crises and debt crises, which the present chapter will be considering. These malfunctions occurred in private transactions. Some began as debt crises (which, however, soon led to dire consequences for payments). Others were provoked by a blockage in payments (but soon turned into debt crises). Neither was directly caused by financial difficulties on the part of the public authorities, although it is believed that in some cases low spending by the State contributed to sparking them off or aggravating them.

Then there were major monetary crises, of which there were essentially two: one at the time of the Second Punic War, the other in the third century AD. These thoroughly upset the monetary system. The financial difficulties of the State were largely responsible for provoking them. The earlier crisis, at the time of the Second Punic War, will be analysed in chapter 10. The financial and banking effects of the later crisis have already been discussed, in chapter 3.

What happened when times were 'normal'? In the first place, a praetor's edict and edicts promulgated by provincial governors set out the rules of private law. These rules applied to all financial transactions. But they did not apply in identical fashion to all statuses: peregrines were not necessarily subject to the same rules as Roman citizens. Take the example of the debt crisis of 193 BC. As the Roman laws on interest-bearing loans did not apply to the Allies, debt-claims were placed in the names of the latter.[1] How should the details of this manoeuvre be interpreted? It is hard to say. Unlike Barlow, I do not think it can be explained by the practice of literal contracts. At any rate, it made it possible to get around the Roman rules, even where the debtor and the true creditor were both Roman citizens. It was then decided by a new law that the regulations

[1] Liv. 35.7 and 35.41.9–10; see Frank 1933–40: vol. 1, 206–8 and Barlow 1978: 58–67, 72–3, 78–80 and 83–6.

should also apply to persons of Latin status and to Allies. Clearly, measures affecting the interest rate were included in this law.

Secondly, the beginnings of a law governing the profession had been set in place; this applied solely to professional money-changers/bankers: it concerned the opening and holding of deposit accounts, the maintenance of professional registers, the production of these registers in courts of law, and the modes of compensation for debt-claims. It changed very little between the end of the Republic and the end of the Principate, and it appears to have been applied effectually. It was justified by the fact that money-changers/bankers constituted a profession. But at the same time it was specifically aimed at the banking function. Professional bankers constituted the only category of financiers that was subject to a specific set of regulations applied on a permanent basis.

In normal times, the public authorities intervened very little in the affairs of private financiers, except in that they saw to it that justice and the law were habitually observed. And, since no office for the registering of contracts existed, it may be that they had no way of knowing the details of all contracted debts. Whenever a census was taken, the citizens declared their debts and their credits, but we do not know whether the census documents recorded the details of each loan and the name of the other contractor. We know of only one occasion when the Roman Empire tried to obtain an overall view of one entire category of debts. This was in 192 BC, within the framework of the episode mentioned above. To that end, the city of Rome required the Allies to declare all the sums that they had lent to Roman citizens. Only then did the city realize how bad things really were, for the census registers had not provided the means to assess the situation.

But the debt and liquidity crises that afflicted Rome were by no means rare: for instance, they occurred in 193–192 BC, during the 80s BC, in 63 BC, in 49 BC and in AD 33. Furthermore, at those same dates and also at others, there were problems of usury in various regions and provinces. For example, in 198 BC, Cato the Elder had to deal with a debt crisis in Sardinia.[2] In 173 BC another debt crisis developed in Thessaly and Aetolia. Ap. Claudius Pulcher alleviated the debts and staggered the dates of repayment, arranging for this to be made in yearly instalments.[3] Even if, in ordinary times, the public authorities hardly considered intervening in financial life, except to set in place a few emergency measures

---

[2] Liv. 32.27.3–4; see Barlow 1978: 56–7 and 71.   [3] Liv. 42.5.7–10; see Barlow 1978: 65–6.

(not always applied), extraordinary times came round often enough, and then they did need to intervene. Sometimes the consequences of such crises were very indirect, as interest-bearing loans were linked with every aspect of social life. According to Appian, for example, many money-lenders who charged interest (*daneistai*) were opposed to Tiberius Gracchus in 133 B C, because their debt-claims were guaranteed by mort-gages on public estates which he was planning to recover from their occupants.[4]

I shall now analyse three of these debt and liquidity crises, and then make a few observations relating to them and also to State objectives.

The first is the crisis of 64–63 B C, an essential factor in Catiline's con-spiracy. It arose from the debts that were prevalent in a number of social circles (former soldiers of Sulla, who had become small-scale landown-ers; shopkeepers in Rome; etc.), but above all in sectors of the senatorial aristocracy. There were wealthy debtors who, without selling some of their possessions, could not repay their creditors. Some of them, Catiline, for example, could not bring themselves to part with any of their patrimony, for upon it their dignity and their rank were founded. As for the rest, as soon as they tried to sell, the price of land fell.[5] Catiline and his co-conspirators therefore demanded an abolition of debts, which the consul Cicero and a majority of senators refused to grant. The political and military defeat of the conspirators must have forced those debtors to sell some of their possessions.

Monetary circulation seemed to be frozen.[6] Cicero, sensitive to the sit-uation, banned the removal of precious metals from Italy and possibly even their transportation from one province to another.[7] Some creditors came to his aid by granting their debtors a *de facto* moratorium. One was Q. Considius, either a senator or a knight, who did not even demand the interest on his loans. He was the creditor of huge sums, 15,000,000 ses-terces in total (although it is not certain whether all this money belonged to him; he was probably acting as a credit intermediary). A *senatusconsul-tum* decided to thank him for his forbearance.[8]

A rather similar liquidity and debt crisis erupted fourteen years later, in 49 B C, when the civil war between Caesar and Pompey broke out. Because of this war, many creditors needed to recall their funds. But the debtors were not in a position to repay them immediately, as they were unable to sell their own properties (and clearly did not wish to). So

---

[4] Appian, *Bell. Civ.* 1.10.39; see Barlow 1978: 119–20. [5] Val. Max. 4.8.3.
[6] Nicolet 1971: 1221–5; Barlow 1978: 182–3; Yavetz 1963. [7] Cic. *in Vat.* 12 and *pro Flacco* 67.
[8] Val. Max. 4.8.3.

money became very hard to come by. It was what the Latins called an *inopia nummorum*, a deficiency of cash, or a *nummorum caritas*, an increase in the value of cash, resulting in a fall in the price of land.[9] The situation was the precise opposite of that of 63. In 49, it was a debt crisis that resulted in a liquidity crisis.

Caesar's response differed from Cicero's. He was anxious both to avoid an abolition of debts and, at the same time, to safeguard the honour of the debtors.[10] To this end, both the movable and the immovable possessions of the debtors were evaluated at their pre-war values, and some were then handed over as payment to their creditors.

The financial crisis that has been studied the most thoroughly is that of AD 33, under the reign of Tiberius. It has given rise to some extremely varied, even contradictory interpretations.[11] Julius Caesar had legislated on the minimum proportion of a patrimony that it was necessary to possess in land within Italy. By the same law (*de modo credendi possidendique intra Italiam*), he had tried to regulate debts and the lending of money, probably by fixing the maximum proportion of a patrimony that could be loaned.[12] Under Tiberius, one magistrate decided to apply this law of Caesar's, which had fallen into disuse – a fact that proves that a debt crisis had developed. Tacitus tells us that all the senators were more or less infringing the provisions of this law. The Emperor gave them eighteen months to set their affairs in order. Therefore the Senate passed a measure relating to the purchase of Italian land. It probably ruled that two-thirds of loaned sums should be invested in land in Italy, and was intended to avoid a sudden collapse in land prices, always a danger when such crises developed, for if land prices fell, debtors found themselves unable to repay the sums that they owed.

But, in any case, the result was disastrous. Even before this measure, Rome was faced with a shortage of liquid cash, which Tacitus attributes partly to the sale of the possessions of the condemned accomplices of Sejanus.[13] It is worth noting that Dio Cassius likewise blamed the abun-

---

[9] Cic. *ad Att.* 9.9.4; on the causes of the phenomenon, see Frederiksen 1966: 132.

[10] Caesar, *B.C.* 3.1.1–4. See Frederiksen 1966; Nicolet 1971: 1214–18; Pinna Parpaglia 1976; Piazza 1980: 91–6; Howgego 1992: 12. Frederiksen (1966: 138–40) thinks that the passage in the *De Officiis* devoted to debts was directed against certain aspects of Caesar's policies (*de Off.* 2. 22. 78 to 24. 85).

[11] See Rodewald 1976; Lo Cascio 1978a; 1978b; 1981; Andreau 1987a: 461–3; Demougin 1988: 117–23.

[12] The objective of Caesar's legislation was to remedy the *inopia nummorum* and reduce interest rates. But I believe that *de modo credendi* means that Caesar had fixed the maximum fraction of a patrimony that could be loaned.   [13] Tac. *Ann.* 6. 17. 1.

dance of goods confiscated and put up for sale for the collapse of land prices in 49 BC, a collapse that was still producing repercussions four years later. The sale of the confiscated goods cast many properties on to the market, and the result of this was the transfer of a large proportion of the monetary stock to the strongboxes of the State. But that was not the sole cause of this fall in prices. The deficit of liquid cash and the payment crisis were contributory factors.

In AD 33, the lack of cash continued to become increasingly serious. To remedy the situation, through the intermediary of *ad hoc* financial offices directed by senators, the Emperor himself offered interest-free loans amounting to an overall sum of 100,000,000 sesterces from his personal fortune for the duration of three years. The borrowers were required to offer security in the form of real estate or buildings. In this way they were not forced to divest themselves of their patrimony in order to pay off their debts. *Fides*, that is to say confidence, returned, and the situation was retrieved.

The first question to ask is, what could the State do to remedy a debt crisis? In my view, there were five possible ways of tackling the problem, all of which were employed at one time or another. They corresponded to five different political options:

(1) purely and simply to refuse to do anything about the debts and to repress any uprisings that this provoked (which was Cicero's policy in 63 BC);

(2) to introduce various measures designed to facilitate the repayment of debts, without wiping out either capital or interest: for example, a non-retroactive cut in the interest rate and a staggering of the deadlines for repayment;[14]

(3) to make public funds available in the guise of gifts, interest-free loans, or low-interest loans;

(4) to hand over to creditors certain possessions of their debtors or to organize public patrimony sales (the former measure being the more favourable to debtors);

(5) to abolish, either totally or partially, either the interest or the capital of the debts (in Rome a total abolition of debts was never implemented, but interest was sometimes reduced, or debts partially abolished).[15]

In times of financial crisis, the professional bankers were never the

---

[14] Liv. 7. 27. 3–4 (348–347 BC).

[15] Crawford (1971: 1229–31) also lists five means by which the State might remedy the shortage of cash, and so increase the monetary stock in circulation. Unsurprisingly, they only partly overlap with the means that I have indicated here.

State's preferred interlocutors. They were subject to measures with general effects, in the same way as anybody else. Despite the specialized nature of their profession, their activities in the field of loans and payments were in no way distinguished from those of other people. That is one indication, among others, of their social and financial limitations, and it confirms how much more extensive the monetary affairs of senators and knights were than those of the *argentarii*. Not until the third century AD do we find any (unfortunately indirect and fleeting) references to exceptional measures applicable solely to the banking businesses. We know of two inscriptions (one from the Gate of the *Argentarii*, which dates from AD 203 or 204, the other offered by *argentarii* to the son of Emperor Decius)[16] that testify to the existence of such measures, which related to commerce and food supplies for Rome.

The general financial measures introduced in times of crisis were applied only temporarily. At the time of the AD 32–3 crisis, Tiberius himself revived one of Caesar's laws, which had never been abrogated but had long ago fallen into disuse since, as Tacitus remarks, private interests tend to come before public well-being.[17] And the measures affecting the purchase of land taken by the Senate in AD 33 were soon abandoned, simply as a result of laxity.

On the other hand, these episodes reveal an economy in which real estate was considered enormously important, and attitudes were strongly influenced by the concept of the patrimony. In central Italy at least, the market for land was relatively active and was very much under the influence of the imperial elite, the senators and the knights. It was often hard for them to decide whether it would be more profitable to invest their money in land or in loans.

Did the lack of liquidity in some periods result from fewer coins being minted? There is disagreement on this in the case of the crisis of AD 33. T. Frank maintained that, before 33, Tiberius had issued relatively few coins and had not been spending a great deal. Rodewald stresses the weakness of the evidence presented by Frank and the considerable size of the batches of coins minted in the course of the 20s AD.[18] But his conclusions are debatable. The Roman State used the channel of public expenses to bring coins into circulation, but not all the coins that it spent were newly minted. It is quite true that, as an Emperor, Tiberius was not a lavish spender. The vitality of monetary transactions as a whole, as well

---

[16] *CIL* VI, 1035 and 1101. See Andreau 1987a: 122–8.   [17] Tac. *Ann.* 6.16,.1 and 6.17.14.
[18] Frank 1935 and Rodewald 1976.

as the monetary stock available, needs to be taken into account. But the contraction of monetary stock in AD 33 must certainly have accentuated the deficiency of liquid cash.

Finally, it is worth noting that these crises of liquidity and debt did not occur following a devaluation, nor did they directly provoke any change in the structure of coinage. To resolve a debt crisis, the public authorities certainly had no reason to exclude monetary manipulation as a matter of principle. During the extremely complex crisis at the beginning of the first century BC (91 onward), the *as* was revalued and became semi-uncial. Some scholars have interpreted this change as a measure that favoured debtors. If they are right (which is by no means certain), this would constitute an exceptional case.[19] As a general rule, to remedy these crises, the public authorities, rather than engage in monetary manipulation, brought more coins into circulation either temporarily (as in the case of the loans advanced by Tiberius) or definitively (when larger batches of coins were minted, when the State spent more, or cancelled taxes in arrears.)

Among numismatists and historians of antiquity, the most hotly debated question concerns the objectives of the State and the extent to which its magistrates were conscious of the monetary problem. The debate is always posed in the same terms, whether the subject in question is the minting of coins, changes in the structure of coinage, or the measures taken to eliminate financial crises.

Two opposed positions are invariably taken up. The first, which was widely adopted in the 1970s and 1980s, is that of, for example, M.H. Crawford and C. Rodewald.[20] It gives absolute priority to the fiscal and budgetary preoccupations of the State. Everything the State did was done in the interest of the public finances or, at a pinch, with social considerations in view. If Tiberius lent 100,000,000 sesterces, it was because social peace and the stability of the aristocracy were at stake.

According to the second position, the State was, on the contrary, seeking to promote an economic policy through its monetary policy. This position has been defended in caricatural fashion by M.E.K. Thornton.[21] In her article 'Nero's New Deal' (the title of which is a clear indication of its orientation!), she tries to show that Nero, by reducing

---

[19] On this crisis of the early 80s BC, see Badian 1969; Barlow 1980; Bulst 1964; Crawford 1985: 173–93; Lo Cascio 1979.   [20] Crawford 1970; 1985; Rodewald 1976.
[21] Thornton 1971; 1975.

the weight of gold coins and both the weight and the value of the silver denarius, in AD 64, had the needs of economic life at heart. According to her, after this devaluation, Nero minted far fewer coins and engaged upon an ambitious programme of public expenditure in order to remedy the economic stagnation.

Others, too, but with far more circumspection and historical perspective, think that the major objective of the Roman State's actions was to increase trade and agricultural prosperity. That is the view of, for example, Lo Cascio.[22]

I, for my part, draw a third, intermediate conclusion. It is close to the views defended in recent years by C. Howgego.[23] Rome certainly needed to spend in order to introduce new money (unlike Howgego, I very much doubt whether under the Republic and the Principate private individuals had the right to have coins freely minted by the authorized workshops).[24] However, its issues of new coins did not represent a response solely to fiscal, budgetary, and social preoccupations. On the contrary, not all its expenses were met with new coins. On the other hand, the Romans were conscious not of an overall economic system that functioned autonomously, but of a system limited to the overall monetary cash-flow, without reference to production and commerce as an economic whole.

After defeating Antony and Cleopatra at Actium in 31 BC, Octavian carried off the treasure of the kings and queens of Egypt to Rome. In a most illuminating sentence, Suetonius describes the consequences of the arrival of this treasure for Roman financial life: 'When the treasure of the kings of Egypt had been brought to Rome, Octavian provided such an abundance of money that, the interest rate having fallen, the value of land increased considerably.'[25]

Some commentators on this text doubt whether the ancients were conscious of the possible economic consequences of an increase in the quantity of money in circulation. They even doubt whether there *were* any economic consequences.[26] Others, Lo Cascio for example, believe, on the contrary, that there may indeed have been economic consequences, and think that the ancients were aware of them.[27] The former group doubts that prices as a whole rose (and it is true that Suetonius mentions only a fall in the interest rate and a rise in the price of land). Lo Cascio, however, tends to the view that other prices did rise along

---

[22] Lo Cascio 1978a; 1978b; 1981.   [23] Howgego 1990; 1992; 1994.   [24] Howgego 1990: 19–20.
[25] Suet. *Aug* 41.1–2.   [26] Crawford 1970: 46; 1974: 2, 633.   [27] Lo Cascio 1981: 82.

with the price of land, and that Suetonius was conscious of the situation and even of its economic consequences.

My own conclusion establishes a clear distinction between, on the one hand, an awareness of an economic system (including the combination of production, the distribution of material goods, and services) and, on the other, an awareness of a financial system limited to the overall monetary cash-flow. It differs both from that of Lo Cascio (who tends to overlook that distinction) and from that of Rodewald (who takes into consideration only the fiscal and budgetary domain). In my opinion, the Romans were conscious of a system of financial relations that functioned in an autonomous fashion, mechanically, and knew that it was important to get it going again when it broke down. But they did not theorize this idea; they did not turn it into the subject of a financial science, which would have produced theoretical treatises. And the financial policy of the public authorities was far more in evidence when the system broke down. When times were 'normal', they tended not to intervene.

This idea of an autonomous financial system, limited to the overall monetary cash flow, is detectable in the way in which Livy writes of the situation in Rome in 207 B.C.[28] The victory at the Metaurus river repaired the situation in Rome. The Romans once more dared to conclude transactions, buying and selling, lending money and settling their debts. It is remarkable that Livy refers solely to the monetary transactions of the Romans, not even mentioning their willingness to work hard or the results of their efforts.

This awareness of a financial system is also manifest from the way in which the Latin authors wrote about financial crises. The crisis of 49 B C, for example, had a political cause (the civil war). But once it had erupted, it was presented as part of a mechanical chain of causes and effects: payments were no longer made, money was hard to come by, the interest rate rose, the price of land and buildings fell.

The passage of Suetonius cited above is also in line with this way of thinking. It shows that Suetonius was conscious of some of the effects that could be produced by an increase in the quantity of money in circulation.[29] But his point of view is financial rather than economic. As Suetonius sees it, what really matters is not the possible effects of a rise in prices on production and trade. It is the ways in which money can be invested and the profits that one can thereby make.

[28] Liv. 27.51.10 (*vendendo, emendo, mutuum dando argentum creditumque solvendo*). I am grateful to Xavier Colin (who is preparing a thesis on loans and social relations) for having drawn my attention to this text of Livy.   [29] Guey 1966: 472–4.

According to this financial point of view, the three most important elements were the following:

(1) the abundance or scarcity of the coins available in practice, which itself depended upon the quantity of coins issued by the State;

(2) the rate of interest, which rose when cash was scarce and fell when it was abundant;

(3) the price of land, which was inversely proportional to the interest rate. Land prices were not affected purely and simply by the state of agricultural life. They varied in accordance with the autonomous functioning of the financial system, since land represented a means of investment. Suetonius' text is not at all concerned with agricultural production.

Over and above the budgetary interests of the State and its social preoccupations, that text implies a (non-theorized) awareness of the autonomous functioning of monetary exchanges as a whole. Everything else being equal, the more cash that was available, the better the financial system worked. *Fides*, confidence, existed so long as money was circulating normally, and it encouraged the autonomous interplay between payments and credits.

That *fides* is sometimes qualified by *publica*, but in such cases *publicus* is not to be applied to the State. It refers to the community as a whole. Livy recounts how, in 343 BC, to remedy the endebted state of the *plebs*, the State reduced the interest rate by half and spread repayments over three years. But despite the fact that, even then, part of the *plebs* remained deep in debt, the Senate did not decide to abolish their debts, because it valued *fides publica* more highly than the satisfaction of private interests. This passage, in which the adjective *publicus* does not apply to the State, reveals an abstract concept of financial life, since the Senate's action is taken notwithstanding the social difficulties (*privatae difficultates*).[30]

Other texts confirm that the word *fides* is, so to speak, emptied of its original moral meaning, and is instead used to refer to the functioning of an abstract system. One case in point is the famous passage in Cicero's *De imperio Cn. Pompei*, in which Cicero speaks of the financial consequences of Mithridates' ventures in Asia. 'We know that there was a collapse of credit at Rome owing to the suspension of payment', he declares.[31] And a little further on he speaks of this *ratio*, the financial accounting practised in the forum, which was inseparably linked to the gains and losses made by Italians in Asia. The use of the word *ratio* and

---

[30] Liv. 7.27.4.   [31] Cic. *de imp. Cn. Pompei* 7.17–19. On this speech by Cicero, see Torelli 1982.

of the verbs *implicare* and *versari* indicates that the whole collection of financial deals made in Rome is being compared to a single account of deposits in a bank. Such a deposit account was also called *fides*.

This text of Cicero's is of a social nature. It alludes to a number of groups that had suffered from Mithridates' activities. It is also economic, for it stresses the fertility of Asia and the wide variety of its crops. But the only passage in which it approaches to an abstract level of thought, independent of all social considerations, concerns neither the collection of taxes, nor production and commerce. It concerns monetary exchanges. No Latin text ever speaks in this fashion about the production of material goods and their circulation.

When those monetary exchanges failed to take place in a normal way, the situation had to be remedied by injecting new sums into the circulation. That is exactly what Tiberius did in AD 33. But that is not to imply that the Roman authorities were even vaguely conscious of the 'monetary needs' of the economy.

CHAPTER 10

The financial activities of the city of Rome and of the Empire

Did the city of Rome, and subsequently the Empire, lend money? And if so, to whom? And what of the cities of the Empire? What can be said of their activities involving credit?

This chapter, like the last, will touch upon the financial policies of the public authorities, but it will concentrate in particular on their own financial operations. It will consider the operations by which the State and the cities turned themselves into financiers, or became the clients of private financiers. But it will not be concerned with public finances nor with the State's income, expenses, or taxes.

The first section will be devoted to the Second Punic War, an unavoidable period for anyone seeking to understand the financial operations of Rome and their limitations. I shall then have some remarks to make about some of the financial interventions of Rome and the cities. Finally, I shall tackle the two principal points: public credit and public borrowing.

For any study of the budgetary and financial difficulties of the city and how these related to the development of the monetary situation, the Second Punic War is very instructive. My conclusions will be based on the works of the principal numismatists working on this period, M. Crawford, P. Marchetti, R. Thomsen, and H. Zehnacker.[1]

Around the mid-third century BC, the monetary standard was the one-pound *as*, that is to say a coin that weighed one Roman pound (about 324 g), minted in bronze. At this date, the denarius did not yet exist. But silver coins had also already been minted, in particular the Romano-Campanian didrachms, the most ancient of which probably date back to the end of the fourth century. By the time the Second Punic

---

[1] Crawford 1974; and 1985: 52–74; Marchetti 1978; Thomsen 1978; Zehnacker 1974; 1979; see also Burnett 1987.

War came to an end, in 201 BC, the monetary system had been completely transformed.

According to P. Marchetti, the bronze monetary standard which had been a semilibral *as*, at the outbreak of war in 218, was by then no more than an uncial *as*, that is to say the equivalent of one twelfth of a pound (about 27 g). According to Crawford, the *as* still weighed a pound in 218 and was only reduced to half a pound the following year. According to him, the uncial *as* dates only from after the war. Whichever of those two chronologies one favours, the *as* lost five-sixths of its weight between the beginning and the end of the war. That loss in weight took place in a rapid series of stages. Marchetti dates the triental standard, i.e. the equivalent of one-third of a pound, to the year 217. In 216 the quadrantal standard was introduced, in late 215 or early 214 the sextantal standard (2 ounces, or one sixth of a pound, about 54 g), and finally, in 211 BC, the uncial standard.

Before the war, silver coins, quadrigati, had been minted. Within the first few years of the war, these underwent a loss of both weight and value. To replace them, Rome issued two series of silver coins, probably in early 214 BC: the denarius, worth 10 *asses*, which weighed about 4.50 g and its smaller denominations, the quinarius and the sesterce; and then the victoriatus, worth 8 *asses*, which weighed three-quarters as much as the denarius. Finally, gold coins were minted, worth 60, 40, and 20 *asses*.

That reconstruction of the changes is faithful in its contents to what Pliny the Elder declares in a famous passage: 'The weight of a standard pound of bronze was . . . reduced during the First Punic War, when the state could not meet its expenditure and it was enacted that the *as* should be struck weighing two ounces. This effected a saving of five-sixths and the city debt was liquidated . . . In the dictatorship of Quintus Fabius Maximus [that is to say in 217 BC], *asses* of one ounce weight were coined . . .; by this measure the State made a clear gain of one half.'[2] However, Pliny's chronology is much higher than that favoured by virtually all numismatists of the present day. Whereas Pliny the Elder dated the creation of the denarius to about 269 BC, nowadays it is dated to 214 BC.[3]

It is worth noting, nevertheless, that Pliny establishes a direct link between these monetary devaluations and the Punic War, which necessitated such high expenditure that, without those measures, the city would have been unable to cope.

---

[2] Pliny, *Nat. Hist.* 33.44.   [3] Crawford dates it to 211.

Livy has plenty to say about the difficulties of the public exchequer in this period. But it is hard to put any figures on them. Using what are known as 'hypothetico-deductive' methods,[4] Marchetti has nevertheless attempted to do so. On the basis of the number of soldiers called up by Rome, he has estimated the outlay for the equipment and food supplies of the army and the fleets, and also for wages; he has calculated the total income provided by taxes, to which he has added the booty, the value of which is frequently known. He concludes that there was a definite deficit. The figures that he suggests (62,000,000 sesterces of income, 65,000,000 of expenses) are disputable (the deficit was probably over 3,000,000 sesterces). However, the reality of the deficit is in no doubt.

In this situation, what measures did the city take? In 216 BC, Rome asked Hieron of Syracuse for money and wheat.[5] In 215, it obtained credit from its suppliers, in particular the tax-collectors (*publicani*). They agreed to make the city a free loan (*commodare*) for supplies for the army in Spain, using the money they had won from adjudications in their favour. Contracts were drawn up with them; Livy observes that the Republic was thus administered by means of private money (*privata pecunia res publica administrata est*). The tax-collectors also provided for the upkeep of public buildings, agreeing to defer payment for their services until the end of the war.[6]

In 214 BC, equipment for the fleet was provided as a compulsory public service, assigned directly to the wealthier of the tax-payers, in particular senators.[7] In the same year, it was decided to defer payment for public works. The money that belonged to widows and orphans was deposited in the public Treasury, and Livy explains that they were obliged to appeal to the quaestor (that is to say the ordinary financial magistrate) in order to pay for the expenses to which they were already committed.[8]

In 205 BC, Rome appealed for voluntary contributions from both cities and individuals.[9] In that same year, large portions of public land (*ager publicus*) were sold.[10]

The city thus appealed either for advances from the tax-collectors, or for contributions, voluntary or otherwise, from its citizens – undertaking to reimburse some of those sums at a later date. This was what Crawford has called 'credit financing'. Rome resorted to this on a number of occasions between 216 BC and the end of the war. In 210, it tried to recruit

---

[4] See chap. 11 (pp. 127–8).   [5] Liv. 23.21.5–6.
[6] Liv. 23.48-49 and 24.18.10; Nicolet 1963: 422–4 and 426.   [7] Liv. 24.11.7–9.
[8] Nicolet 1963: 426–31; Maselli 1986: 15–16.   [9] Liv. 28.45.13–21.   [10] Liv. 28.46.4–6.

oarsmen, but there was not enough money in the public exchequer to pay them. One of the consuls begged the senators to set an example by handing over to the State all their gold, silver, and bronze coins. The senators brought along their precious metals and their coins with such enthusiasm that the knights and the *plebs* were keen to follow suit. At the end of the Second Punic War, those sums were reimbursed in three stages, the last portion being repaid in the form of real estate, not in money.[11]

Clearly, money manipulations must be related directly to these budgetary difficulties. As Pliny observed, the State went all out to raise money wherever possible. But there was also a crisis of private liquidity. In 216 BC, it was *per inopiam argenti*, because of a lack of liquidity, that a commission of three magistrates was set up to act as public bankers (*triumviri mensarii*).

Not much is known of this commission of public bankers (all three of whom were senators). In 214 BC, they were responsible for paying the owners of eight thousand slaves who had volunteered and been enrolled in 216, and subsequently manumitted. In that instance, the commission acted as accountants. In 210 it received the deposits of all the gold, silver, and bronze offered to the city by the senators, the knights, and the *plebs*. But there is no indication that they managed the State income, even partially. This was a period during which the city's credits and, above all, debts were quite exceptional. Serving as financial intermediaries between the public exchequer and the citizens, this triumvirate played the role of accountant to all these credits and debts, and also in the reception and payment of money.[12] Nicolet has rightly pointed out that the institution of this commission reflected an influence from the Hellenistic world.[13]

One further remark: at this point the monetary system was in the throes of a spectacular breakdown; the city was facing serious budgetary difficulties (which had sparked off the breakdown), and a crisis of private liquidity (which was in part a consequence of it). Such a conjunction of all three factors – budgetary, monetary, and financial – had seldom occurred in Rome. It did not recur until the third century AD. In the meantime, debt and liquidity crises did develop at times when the public finances were not in such bad shape and when the structure of coinage was reasonably or even very stable. Even in the first century BC, despite

[11] Liv. 29.16.3 and 31.13.5–8. [12] Andreau 1987a: 233–7. [13] Nicolet 1963.

the political and administrative disorganization, the monetary system was not as unstable as appearances might lead one to believe.[14]

Public banks similar to the banking commission of 216 BC also existed in certain Greek cities, but mostly on a permanent basis (rather than a temporary one, as in Rome). The most ancient of these Greek public banks known to us date from the fourth century BC and one continues to come across them down to the first century BC, in cities that were by then part of the Roman Empire, such as Temnos.[15] Under the Principate, no more is heard of them. These *demosiai trapezai* were generally directed by magistrates. They were responsible for some of the operations connected with the city's exchequer, and received a proportion of its income. They accepted deposits from the city, and in its name organized loans and guaranteed payments. They had no clientele of private depositors.[16]

According to Livy, a commission of five public bankers of this type (*quinqueviri mensarii*), composed of senators, had already existed in Rome in 352 BC, when there was a debt crisis. These *mensarii* were responsible for distributing sums advanced by the city to enable creditors to be reimbursed. In some cases, they proceeded to evaluate the possessions of debtors, whose property then passed to their creditors in lieu of the sums owed. So they, too, according to Livy, at least, thus acted as temporary treasury officials, in the service of the city.[17]

The royal banks of Ptolemaic Egypt, which in the Roman period were known as public banks (*demosiai trapezai*), were a sub-variety of those public banks. They played an important fiscal role.[18]

Elsewhere in the Roman Empire, in the second and third centuries AD, there were contracted private banks, which engaged in money-changing for the public, and some (but apparently not all) of which held a monopoly. We know of a number in Egypt,[19] and also in several cities in the Greek part of the Empire: Pergamum, Mylasa, and probably Sparta.[20] Virtually nothing is known about the advantages and constraints that accompanied the privileges that they enjoyed. Such contracted banks, used by both private and professional bankers, never existed in Rome itself.

To facilitate the task of organizing the public exchequer (until such

---

[14] Burnett 1987.   [15] Cic. *pro Flacco* 44; see Bogaert 1968: 243–4.   [16] Bogaert 1968: 403–8.
[17] Liv. 7.16.1 and 7.19.5; 7.21.5–7. See Andreau 1987a: 230–3 and Storchi Marino 1993.
[18] Bogaert 1994: 1–24, 47–57, and 133–152; Gara 1979; 1988.   [19] Bogaert 1994: 8–10 and 77–93.
[20] Bogaert 1968: 401–3.

time as the Treasury was opened, which happened only from time to time), some Greek cities deposited public funds either in private banks or with individuals who were particularly trusted (but who were not bankers). This Greek tradition, which never existed in Rome, continued in the Roman period in Greek-speaking regions. We know of one example in Taormina in the first century AD, and another in Delphi, at the beginning of the reign of Constantine.[21]

We have very little information about the transportation of public funds. The city of Rome, and subsequently the Empire, must certainly have tried to keep such transportation to the minimum, but material transfers were inevitable, since provinces where no troops were stationed brought in, through taxes, more money than the State spent on the spot.[22] At the end of the Republic and the beginning of the Empire, it was the large tax-collectors' companies that organized these transports on behalf of Rome. We are told this by the *Verrines*, which also indicate that the sums that the State left deposited with tax-collectors were left with them as a favour, and must have constituted a source of profit for them.[23] Such deposits also enabled the State, thanks to the mediation of the tax-collectors, to transfer funds without having to organize any material transportation (*permutationes*).[24] As we have seen (chapter 7), it is possible that the *tesserae nummulariae* may have related to the transportation of coins.

We do not know how the public authorities managed when the companies of tax-collectors gradually lost their importance and eventually disappeared. We can only suppose that they organized these transports themselves, or with the aid of the army. So far as I know, no documentation is available on the subject.

In the Republican period, in normal times Rome did not lend money to its citizens, nor did the tax-collectors lend money in the name of the city. The city certainly granted payment facilities, for example to the tax-collectors and, as we have seen, it would keep non-remunerated deposits in their strongboxes. But those were not, strictly speaking, loans.

Nor can tax arrears, where they existed, be counted as loans. Shatzman claims that in the Republican period private individuals could borrow from the Treasury. But there is nothing to prove that the texts

---

[21] Bogaert 1968: 215 and note 440, 220–1.   [22] Gara 1986: 106–7.   [23] Cic. 2 *Verr.* 3.165–70.
[24] Cic. *ad Att.* 11.1.2; 11.2.3; 11.13.4; see p. 20, in chap. 2, and also Andreau 1978: 51–5; Barlow 1978: 168–71. On the activities of the tax-collectors as moneylenders and as 'State bankers', see Badian 1972: 76–81.

that he cites relate to loans. They are more likely to relate to arrears (of taxes, for example).[25]

In exceptional situations, when there were debt and liquidity crises, Rome did sometimes lend money, but the loans would be interest-free or virtually interest-free. As we have seen, according to Livy, in 352 B C, in order to resolve the debt problem, it advanced money to creditors.[26] In 216 B C it lent money against securities, but without interest, to individuals wishing to ransom prisoners.[27]

It also sometimes happened that Rome would advance interest-free loans both to other cities that were subject to it and to independent foreign ones. The loans consisted of money, or sometimes of wheat. Between 101–99 B C, for example, Rome lent wheat to the cities of Sicily, which had been ravaged by the slave war.[28]

Under the Empire, all the above activities continued but were extended. Rome often took measures to provide aid when crises of liquidity or debt arose, or to help the poor. For example, it would advance interest-free or low-interest loans. It is worth remembering that Maecenas, in the famous speech that Dio Cassius attributes to him, recommended such loans.[29] Under the reign of Augustus, whenever there was a superabundance of funds in the Treasury, the Emperor advanced free loans to those who were capable of offering pledges worth twice as much.[30] Alexander Severus advanced free loans to the poor so that they could buy land.[31]

Also worth noting are the cancellations of tax arrears, which really amounted to cancellations of debts – in other words gifts. Hadrian and Marcus Aurelius, for example, both authorized such cancellations.[32]

But during the Principate, two or three innovations were greatly to increase the volume of public loans. The first concerned the imperial patrimony. Like any member of the elite, but probably more so than any

---

[25] Shatzman 1975: 81. He cites: Appian, *Bell. Civ.* 3.17 and 20; Ascon. 73; Plut. *Cato Minor* 6.4 and 17.2; and Suet. *Aug.* 32.12. In the life of Cato the Younger, State debts are mentioned. Those could also be debts in arrears (for example, payments due to tax-collectors). The only text favourable to Shatzman's thesis is Appian's, in which, however, it is a matter of the civil wars, and Antony and Octavian were not 'private individuals'. Such an exceptional situation provides no basis for his argument.

[26] Whether or not they are authentic, these episodes of the fifth and fourth centuries B C reveal what Livy and his contemporaries considered to be probable. That is why they are of interest within the framework of the present book.   [27] Liv. 22.60.4.   [28] Cic. *de Lege agr.* 2.30.83.

[29] Cass. Dio, 52.28; see Gabba 1962: 41–58.   [30] Suet. *Aug.* 41.2.

[31] Scr. Hist. Aug. *Al. Sev..* 21.2. as well as 26.2 and 40.2. See also Gabba 1962: 58–61. I am not concerned here with the credibility of the *Historia Augusta*. My comment above on the episodes of the fifth and fourth centuries B C (see note 26) also applies to the *Historia Augusta*.

[32] Scr. Hist. Aug. *Hadr.* 7; Cass. Dio, 72.32: see Gabba 1962: 64–6.

other (in view of the growing volume of his possessions), the Emperor lent money, albeit through the intermediary of slaves and freedmen. The Murecine tablets mention several imperial slaves and freedmen who were lending money either to the Sulpicii or to traders operating in Puteoli.[33] The Sulpicii borrowed a sizeable sum, 94,000 sesterces, from an imperial slave, Phosphorus Elpidianus.

It is well known that the strict separation that existed at the beginning of the Empire between the personal patrimony of the Emperor and State possessions was later much relaxed. Nevertheless, for a long time loans of money advanced by the Emperor or by those responsible for managing his assets must have been considered as private loans, not as State loans. According to the *Historia Augusta*, that still applied in the Antonine and Severan periods. The loans made by Antoninus Pius are not presented in the same way as those made by Alexander Severus: the latter stemmed from the *fenus publicum*; the loans advanced by Antoninus, in contrast, were private (*patrimonio suo*).[34] Nevertheless, in practice, those private loans advanced by the Emperor or his entourage in effect represented an intervention by the State into financial activities.

The second major imperial innovation in the field of public loans were the *alimenta*. These loans, organized by Nerva and Trajan, have given rise to an extensive bibliography, particularly since the mortgage tablets of Veleia and the city of Ligures Baebiani have yielded interesting information relating to real estate at the beginning of the second century AD.[35] These sums were lent permanently to landowners of a number of Italian cities, in return for an annual payment of 5 per cent interest. It is hard to see why they should have accepted such loans, even if the interest rate was low. However, they appear to have done so voluntarily. What is certain is that the *alimenta* were intended, thanks to the interest derived from them, to assist in the upkeep and education of the little girls and, more particularly, little boys of Italy. Opinions differ as to whether the Emperor was also aiming to provide a kind of oxygen boost for agriculture.

The Empire probably controlled large financial resources. The problem lay in managing them as well as possible, that is to say in investing them wisely. The *alimenta* provided one solution to this problem of management. Organized at first by prefects, then by procurators, they

---

[33] See chap. 6, pp. 71–9; Camodeca 1992; 1994a.
[34] Scr. Hist. Aug. *Anton. Pius* 2.8 and *Al. Sev.* 21.2.
[35] See Veyne 1957–58; Garnsey 1968; Duncan-Jones 1974: 132–8 and 288–319; Lo Cascio 1978c; 1980; Woolf 1990.

guaranteed a certain continuity. The expense that they incurred was not too heavy a burden for landowners who paid no land tax. In fact, indirectly, it was a means of getting them to pay just that. It also stimulated the circulation of money in Italy.

Finally, there may have been a third innovation under the Empire. In a letter to Trajan, Pliny the Younger refers to public funds (*pecuniae publicae*) that he, as governor, was having difficulty in investing in Bithynia.[36] Some scholars consider these to have been funds belonging to the cities. Others, myself included, think, rather, that they were funds belonging to the province.[37] If the latter opinion is correct, it would prove that the Roman State, as such, was at this time lending money in return for interest, in the same way as any individual member of the elite, which was something that it had never done under the Republic. Unfortunately, we cannot be sure from Pliny's letter.

And what of the cities? The evidence available indicates that as early as the Republican period some were lending money, and probably at interest. But was this current practice in Italy? And were the sums involved very large? I doubt it, but it is hard to be more specific. It does appear that in 44 BC Cicero owed money to his home town of Arpinum.[38] In the Greek world, certain sanctuaries loaned money at interest, so, given that such a sanctuary belonged to its city, it was in fact the city that was advancing the loans.[39] Under the Empire, lending money at interest was frequently practised by cities in both halves of the Empire. Many cities received foundation money, the capital of which needed to be invested in order to produce interest.[40] Those foundations were frequently managed separately from the rest of the city's revenues, and such management was called *kalendarium*.[41] Some cities possessed a number of different *kalendaria* and a special magistrate, the *curator*, was put in charge of them. Epigraphical evidence testifies to this in a number of localities, which proves that it was a common enough institution. We know, for example, that there was a *curator Kalendarii pecuniae Valentini* in Pesaro,[42] a *curator muneris pecuniae Aquillianae* in Grumentum,[43] a *curator muneris Catiniani* in Venosa,[44] and *curatores kalendarii* in Nola and Suessa,[45] etc. But for how long did these foundations function? One wonders, particularly where the interest rate was high. And who were the borrowers?

---

[36] Pliny, *Epist.* 10.54.
[37] See Magie 1950: 591; Garzetti 1960: 363; Gabba 1962: 63–4; Howgego 1992: 14, note 124.
[38] Cic. *ad Att.* 15.15.1; 15.17.1; 15.20.4.   [39] Bogaert 1968: 288–94.
[40] On Italy, see Andreau 1977.   [41] Manacorda 1977.   [42] *CIL* xi, 6369.
[43] *CIL* x, 226.   [44] *CIL* ix, 447.   [45] *CIL* ix, 1160 and x, 4873.

Did such loans have some social function in the cities? Did they help to limit the burden of usury? All these questions remain impossible to answer.

Rome was not accustomed to borrow money; and the Empire remained faithful to that tradition. Cases of public borrowing are extremely rare.

Under the Republic, Rome would frequently buy in wheat from outside, however, and sometimes received it as a gift, from Hieron of Syracuse, for example, or from Massinissa.[46] Occasionally, but rarely, it would borrow it or buy it on credit. Thus in the 220s BC, Hieron supplied wheat for the Roman army, for which he was paid once the wars against the Celts were over.[47]

As for money itself, throughout its history down to the mid-third century AD, Rome borrowed only in two quite exceptional periods (and even then did so indirectly): during the Second Punic War, and during the civil wars of the first century BC. In the course of the Second Punic War, Rome borrowed money several times, but that was a matter of 'credit financing' rather than borrowing in the strict sense of the term. This has been mentioned above. In 210 BC, when the senators, knights, and *plebs* offered their precious metals and their coins to the city, this was regarded as a voluntary gift. Only in 204 BC was it decided to reimburse those contributions, which Livy thenceforth called *mutuae pecuniae*, instead of *conlatae*.[48]

During the civil wars, Brutus and Scipio, in order to finance the anti-Caesar forces, borrowed funds from the cities of Asia, by virtue of a *senatusconsultum* and in the name of the Roman public authorities.[49] This borrowing should be distinguished from that negotiated by the political and military leaders, who were certainly acting within the framework of their State responsibilities but on an altogether personal basis and without the backing of the Senate.[50] But civil war situations such as these were in any case altogether exceptional: there were two centres of public power in Rome, and the borrowing contracted by one faction was designed to be used to overcome the other. We do not know how the borrowing was arranged, but it was clearly engaged in only under duress.

On the other hand, at the beginning of AD 70, 'whether the treasury

---

[46] Garnsey 1988: 168–72 and 182–91.   [47] Garnsey 1988: 184.

[48] Liv. 31.13.2; 31.35; 31.36.3–6; see Nicolet 1963: 431–2.

[49] Cic. *ad Fam.* 12.28; *ad Brut.* 2.4; Cic. *Philipp.* 10.26; Caes. *Bell. Civ.* 3.31.2 and 3.32.6. I am grateful to X. Colin for the information he provided on this subject, as well as on the *mutuum*.

[50] On these enforced loans, see Cass. Dio. 42, 50–51, and Frank 1933–40: vol. 1, 336–7 and 342.

was really poor or it was deemed advisable that it should appear so'
(*verane pauperie aut uti videretur*), the Senate, according to Tacitus, 'voted to
accept a loan of sixty million sesterces from private individuals' (*a priva-
tis mutuum acciperetur*).[51] However, soon the need to do so no longer
seemed pressing, and the loan was never contracted. It is an astonishing
text, despite the fact that this was just after the civil war of AD 68–9. For
never before had the Senate explicitly decided to organize a public borrowing. Even during the Second Punic War the measures taken were far
more indirect. However, even if the decision was taken in principle, in
the event this important innovation was never applied.

It is worth noting that in such exceptional circumstances Rome always
turned (or tried to turn) to its citizens as a whole, or to a good many of
them. Never did it appeal to some foreign sovereign when needing to
borrow money. Nor did it ever appeal to specialist financiers (except
when, in 215 and 214 BC, it used 'credit financing' to set up the public tax
farms assigned to its tax-collectors).[52] That behaviour persisted under
the Empire. Likewise, the Emperor never borrowed money for public
needs. The case of Licinus, under Augustus, constituted no exception,
for that was a completely private deal between this Emperor and one of
his dependants.[53] Moreover, when the Republican city did turn to its
members, it did so only on a temporary basis, in the context of particularly critical circumstances. The debt was subsequently paid off without
delay.

Public debt existed neither in Greece nor in Rome. As Hamilton commented, 'that was one of the rare phenomena that was never rooted in
Graeco-Roman Antiquity'.[54]

In western Europe, however, it was a phenomenon that appeared as
early as the thirteenth or fourteenth century. It took two forms. One was
public borrowing (in France the first large loan obtained was probably
that of 1295, for Guyenne's campaign against England; the most
'modern' country at this time was Italy). As the royal financiers were
eventually unable to repay the loans, those credits that could be
demanded back at a predetermined date were 'consolidated', that is to
say thenceforth they continued as debt-claims, and on the grounds that
they were debt-claims, their owners had the right to cede them. The
other form taken by the public debt was that of 'constituted' dividends

---

[51] Tac. *Hist.* 4.47.1.   [52] Liv. 23.48.9.
[53] Macr. *Sat.* 2.4.24; see Meyers 1964: 67; Bénabou 1967. It was not rare for a master to borrow
money from one of his slaves or freedmen; see Dumont 1987: 110–12.
[54] Hamilton 1947: 118.

guaranteed by immovable property. The royal exchequer or the town that issued these received a large sum from the owner of the property first, in return for which it paid him a yearly rent or dividend. In both cases it was the public authorities (the king or the towns) that did the borrowing. In the sixteenth century, such dividends became a means of credit of the greatest magnitude.[55]

In Rome, the State would never appeal to major private financiers (as the European monarchies of the modern period frequently did), nor was there any system of dividends or public debt. The *alimenta* did represent constituted dividends of a kind, but the way that they functioned was the precise reverse of medieval and modern dividends. In the case of the *alimenta*, it was the State, not private individuals, that advanced the capital in the first place, and the private individuals then owed the State yearly sums for which their land provided the security. The State underwrote a constituted dividend, and it was the State that received perpetual annuities.

The absence of any public debt, which was a macroscopic phenomenon of the late Middle Ages and the modern period, is, of course, significant. It is certainly true to say that in those times money was borrowed in anticipation of other resources, and then more and more was borrowed to cover the charges of the debt run up from previous borrowing; also, the consolidation of the debt was regarded by contemporaries as a swindle, a partial bankruptcy.[56] But how is it that the ancient cities never resorted to such ploys? Was it because they possessed a large patrimony of both real estate and property in the form of buildings, and because, in the case of Rome, its conquests multiplied the value of its patrimony and made it possible to levy vast amounts in taxes? I shall not attempt a quantitative comparison between the resources of Rome and those of the kings or cities of the modern period. Some scholars, such as B. Laum, have sought the explanation in the relationships that bound citizens to their city in antiquity: the nature of the ancient city ruled out the possibility of concluding with it any freely agreed contract between equal partners.[57]

At any rate, the absence of public borrowing in antiquity, whatever the explanation for it, produced effects of major importance on the economy and society as a whole. J.F. Drinkwater believes that that absence greatly limited the social possibilities of the *feneratores*. According to him, it thwarted the development of powerful financial circles inde-

[55] On this, see Boyer-Xambeu 1986: 87–91; Braudel 1979: vol. 2, 462–8; Schnapper 1957: 41–64; Vilar 1974: 178–82.   [56] Boyer-Xambeu 1986: 86 and 90.   [57] Laum 1924.

pendent of the landowning elite, circles interested above all in money matters.[58] Economically, the absence of a public debt explains how it was that financial businesses and the credit system never developed as they did in Modern Europe. By the last centuries of the Middle Ages, there already existed establishments designed to control the management of loans and to ensure the payments of interest, and it would be hard to overestimate the importance of those establishments, known as 'Monti' in Italy. Furthermore, markets such as those of Genoa, and later Amsterdam, which were – to use Braudelian terminology – the centres of the European 'World Economy', owed much of their activity to transactions involving loans and public dividends.[59]

The Greek world did practise public borrowing rather more often than Rome did. It took three different forms, to which L. Migeotte has devoted an excellent study in a recent book.[60] All three forms originated in the classical period (we know of several cases of public borrowing in the fifth century B C), and they persisted until the end of the Hellenistic period and even under the Principate. They were loans from temples and from foreign sovereigns; loans from the members of the city, by subscription; and loans from private individuals.[61]

The raising of loans from private individuals was a feature of, in particular, the second and first centuries B C. The provinces, and above all the Greek world, at this time enjoyed a privilege that by no means contributed to their prosperity: they had to turn to private individuals, for the most part Italians, who would advance them large loans. These individuals either would be domiciled in the province in question (and were called *negotiatores* by the Latin writers), or else they lived in Italy but had interests in one or several provinces. Some were knights or even senators, others were not. In Tenos, it was L. Aufidius Bassus, who had been a trapezite, and his son, who may also have been one, who advanced such loans; in Caria, it was the procurators of Marcus Cluvius; in Athens, twenty or thirty years earlier, it was Atticus; etc. The loans advanced by these figures, which were sometimes euergetistic but more often usurious, shows that the cities in question were facing serious difficulties, particularly in paying the taxes demanded by Rome. The gravity of this situation became all too manifest at the point when Lucullus became governor of the province of Asia.[62] The kings of the modern period also had their financial difficulties. But they managed to

[58] Drinkwater 1977–8; 1981; Pleket 1983: 206, note 49.
[59] Braudel 1979: vol. 2, 462–71 and vol. 3, *passim*.   [60] Migeotte 1984.
[61] Migeotte 1984: 363–77.   [62] Plut. *Lucull.* 20 and 23.

institutionalize their bankruptcies, so to speak, and to integrate them into a financial interplay that became ever more intense and diversified. That did not happen in the Greek provinces of the Late Republic.

From the period of Augustus on, it is certain that Rome did its best to limit borrowing on the part of the cities, in both the East and the West. Consider the edict of P. Fabius Persicus, which dates from the mid-first century AD. The magistrates of Ephesus were permitted to borrow money in the name of the city only if repayment could be made out of the revenues of the same year. If they mortgaged the income of the subsequent year, their own possessions had to be submitted as security.[63] In the West, it is worth mentioning the *lex Irnitana*, according to which borrowing by cities was allowed, but could not exceed 50,000 sesterces per year (except, it seems, where the authorization of the governor of the province was obtained).[64] Several passages that appear in the *Digest* also mention cases in which the responsibility for repayment devolved upon not the city as a whole but only the magistrates or the order of the decurions.[65] Under the Principate, Rome looked with favour upon euergetistic gifts to the cities (provided they actually materialized and were not just empty promises), but it did its utmost to discourage public borrowing. Redistribution was preferable to dependence upon credit.

An inscription in Nîmes provides the example of a member of the elite, Quintus Avilius Hyacinthus, who frequently came to the aid of the city's Treasury by supplying the loans requested by the magistrates.[66] This inscription shows that we should not necessarily draw a hard and fast contrast between the Eastern and the Western cities. Throughout the Empire, the cities could borrow money, but Rome did all it could to limit that borrowing to the minimum, and it never allowed long-lasting or consolidated debts. At an early period, Greek customs, which have been studied by Migeotte, were different from Roman practice. Later, however, the customs of the Greeks were kept under strict control by their Roman governors.

There was a real difference between Republican Rome and the Greek cities. But, as Migeotte has pointed out, in the Greek tradition, public borrowing was neither frequent nor, financially, all that important. When one compares the whole of antiquity to the last centuries of the Middle Ages or to the modern period, the difference between the Greek cities and Rome seems strictly relative, no more than a matter of degree.

---

[63] Magie 1950: 545–6 and 1403–4; Bogaert 1968: 247–8; Migeotte 1984: 290–1.
[64] Gonzalez 1986: 194 and 226.   [65] *Dig.* 3.4.7.1 (Ulpian); 3.4.8 (Javolenus); 12.1.27 (Ulpian).
[66] *AE* 1982: 681; see Christol 1992.

Where public debt is concerned, the difference between antiquity, on the one hand, and medieval and modern Europe, on the other, is much greater.

There was really no 'public debt problem' either in Greece or in Rome.[67] In one period only, things could have gone the other way: in the second and first centuries BC, in peregrine cities, particularly in the Greek world. However, the restoration of order under Caesar, first, and then Augustus, definitively confirmed the traditions of the ancient cities.

---

[67] Howgego (1992: 13, note 111) writes, 'Cities in the Roman world could borrow, and did so.' Yes, but clearly the limitations of that conclusion should be recognized.

The problem of quantities and quantitative developments

This book is essentially devoted to financial life in the Roman world between the end of the fourth century BC and the end of the third century AD. It barely touches upon the more ancient periods of Roman history, for which documentation on this subject is virtually non-existent. Nor does it touch upon late antiquity. I have chosen, so far, to present a non-chronological, static picture of the six centuries upon which the book focuses.

In the present chapter I shall be considering whether it is possible to discern developments within that long period of six centuries. It is a difficult task, given the limited nature of the documentary evidence.

We are prone, in the late twentieth century at least, to express developments in the field of finance in terms of quantities, so in this chapter I shall also tackle the problem raised by the study of quantities.

After World War I, many efforts were made to collect and study all the quantitative evidence that could be gleaned from the ancient texts and inscriptions concerning – for instance – prices and interest rates (not that the data amounted to much, and anyway some historians considered what there was to be unreliable). One of the major scholars who embarked upon that course was T. Frank.[1] Later, he was followed by R. Duncan-Jones, in his first book, and by S. Mrozek, both of whom researched categories of data that had not yet been satisfactorily marshalled.[2]

Conscious of the limitations of such a way of proceeding, other historians, myself included, sought additional ways of studying the ancient economy, striving to show that, even where the economy was concerned, the major cleavages were qualitative rather than quantitative.[3] In the 1960s and 1970s, not many historians of antiquity devoted themselves to problems of quantification. In Britain and the United States, the

---

[1] Frank 1933–40.   [2] Duncan-Jones 1974; Mrozek 1975.
[3] For example, Andreau 1974b and Parise 1978.

growing authority of Finley initially tended to dismiss quantification,[4] although subsequently his disciples have played a major role in the new wave of quantitative history.

That new wave began to spread in the early 1980s, and it enjoyed real success, particularly in Britain and the United States, although there is now a strong reaction against it.[5] In default of new quantitative data elaborated by the ancients themselves, it proved necessary to discover new ways of establishing quantities. Two kinds of methods have been used, chiefly elaborated by British historians, who describe the first as 'inductive' and the second as 'deductive'.

The inductive method consists of enumerating the available documents, in particular archaeological materials (but coins, inscriptions, etc. are also enumerated). It presupposes thinking about ways of counting, about the statistical treatment of enumerations, and about their historical significance. It has made a valuable contribution to the history of various forms of production and commerce.[6] The 'deductive' method consists in elaborating hypothetical quantities not provided by the documentation, reasoning on the basis of other quantities and probability, either by analogy or by comparison. It was introduced by Finley and has been widely used by his disciples, in particular K. Hopkins. This is not, however, the place to give a critical assessment of the use of such methods.[7]

Roman banking and financial life have so far not been the subjects of quantification, which is hardly surprising, given the state of the documentary evidence. However, K. Hopkins and H. U. von Freyberg have recently produced 'quantitative studies' of economic and social inspiration which tackle the financial and fiscal equilibrium and touch upon the history of private finances.

The rest of this chapter is composed of three sections. In the first, I set out the broad lines of the forms of research indicated above and explain how they relate to the subject of the present work. In the second, turning once again to our documentation on banking and financial life, I consider how this should be treated in order to form some idea of quantities and to describe developments. Finally, the last section constitutes a conclusion on those developments.

Neither Hopkins nor von Freyberg helps us directly to acquire a better understanding of the chronological evolution of financial affairs

---

[4] See Finley 1985: 27–46.   [5] For example, Cohen 1992: 26–40.
[6] See Peacock and Williams 1986; Giardina and Schiavone 1981; Giardina 1986; Tchernia 1986a.
[7] See Andreau 1995c.

between the fourth century BC and the third century AD (this is not intended as a criticism, though), for Hopkins and von Freyberg deal only with the Principate, and they treat it in a static fashion. However, their reflection upon quantities may help us to think about their chronological evolution. Furthermore, central to their thinking is the significance of geographical differences (differences both between Italy and the provinces and between one province and another).

The research work of von Freyberg is closely connected to that of Hopkins, for Hopkins's 'Taxes and Trade Model'[8] provides the starting point for Freyberg's comments and complementary material.[9] Both believe that from the beginning of the Empire on, the commercial balance between Italy and the provinces shifted considerably, to the advantage of the latter and the disadvantage of Italy. It is a point that has provoked disagreement: some scholars have questioned the representative nature of the products most familiar to us from archaeology (for example, ceramic tableware). However, the most recent research does, on the whole, seem to confirm the point.[10] How should this be explained?

According to M. Rostovtzeff, this development was caused by the respective qualities of the entrepreneurs and workers in the various regions, and those qualities were connected with the social balance there. He believes that the provincials, thanks to their managerial flair and the quality and profitability of their products, had managed to conquer the markets. This supply-side explanation is no longer considered convincing and has been replaced by economic explanations based upon demand: centres of production moved because the centres of consumption were moving (the latter, at least, is uncontestably true), and the nature of what was produced changed to suit the preferences of the consumers (this, however, is impossible to verify).

Hopkins, arguing at the level of macro-economics, links the development of commercialization with taxation. He distinguishes three types of regions: the provinces without troops, which paid taxes directly without themselves receiving much in return from the imperial Treasury; the provinces where troops were stationed, which paid taxes but received those military credits from the Empire; and Italy, which paid no taxes but, more than any other region, benefited from civilian State expenditure.

It was the provinces without soldiers that took to selling more and

---

[8] Hopkins 1980.   [9] Von Freyberg 1989. On this book, see Andreau 1992b; 1994b.
[10] See Andreau 1991.

more, to Italy's cost. They sought thereby to compensate for the flow of valuable items, both monetary and non-monetary, that they were losing and Italy was gaining. That may have been the reason, or one of the reasons, why, in the first century AD, Gallo-Roman pottery and that of proconsular Africa replaced Arretine ware at western Mediterranean sites.

Von Freyberg tackles the same question of the commercial imbalance between Italy and the provinces under the Principate. But his explanation differs from that of Hopkins. It is based on what would be called in modern terms the theory of the movement of capital and the balance of payments.

He thinks that, whatever the degree of archaism or modernity of the ancient economy, significant transfers of buying power from one region to another (whether or not accompanied by material transfers of cash) inevitably produced consequences, just as they still do today. Either they triggered a second, equally large counter-flow, or else a balance was restored in other ways, which differed according to whether or not the two regions belonged to the same State and whether or not they used the same currency. If they did use the same currency, the imbalance in payments produced a rise in prices in the region into which capital was flowing and a fall in prices in the other region. This was the situation of the Roman world under the Principate.[11]

Prices rose in the region into which money was flowing, in this case Italy. They fell in the regions from which that money was flowing, that is to say the provinces, or some of them. The price discrepancies encouraged the Italians to purchase provincial merchandise. Of course, this depended upon the cost of transport, and the situation would have been quite different had the Roman Empire not been situated around the coasts of the Mediterranean. The result was an inversion of the commercial relations between Italy and the provinces, a phenomenon that gathered pace over the first and second centuries AD.

By his reasoning, the last stage concerns the effects of this development on the wealth produced by Italy and the provinces as a whole. The region receiving the inflow of capital eventually grew poorer instead of richer, since it returned that capital to the provinces when it bought their merchandise, without itself producing any new wealth. Furthermore, von Freyberg believes that euergetism and the taste for economically useless buildings accentuated that poverty, since that capital which did

[11] Von Freyberg 1989: 140–56.

remain in Italy by no means always resulted in furthering production.

Hopkins does not, so far as I know, refer to banking and private financial life. But von Freyberg is interested in monetization[12] and makes a number of general remarks about banking and money.[13] He is most directly concerned with the private transfers of funds between the provinces and Italy but, quite rightly, declines to put figures on them because the data available are insufficient.[14]

Von Freyberg believes that those transfers, which probably amounted to less than the State budget, were also favourable to Italy. They became so more and more as the senatorial and equestrian elite increased the proportion of its patrimonies located in the provinces. Its revenues were spent at least partly in Italy, since Rome, with its prestige and diversity of merchandise that poured into it, still represented an important centre of consumption. In short, von Freyberg concludes that throughout much of the Principate period, the transfers of private capital resulted in transfers of buying power to Italy.[15]

Within the framework of a deductive approach, there is no reason why one should not evaluate the overall volume of debts or of bank deposits. But so far this has not been attempted, and it is true that the documentary evidence is particularly poor on financial matters, far poorer than in the domain of production and commerce.

A number of other approaches are possible. The first is a study of all the elements of political and social history that throw light on the development and volume of business, such as the role of money in political life, the general impression of wealth or poverty or debt and liquidity crises. It is an approach that has often been adopted for the end of the Republic, thanks to the rich documentation provided by authors such as Cicero, Sallust, Plutarch, Dio Cassius, and others.

On the individual members of the elite, prosopography has produced good results, and could produce more if used to tackle new questions. But whatever the category studied (the *feneratores*, the tax-collectors, the *negotiatores*, etc.), the same difficulty always arises: the documentation is far more abundant for the last century of the Republic than for other periods. As for bankers, I have attempted a quantitative study of their funerary inscriptions, with a view to fixing their geographical distribution and forming some idea of how their numbers evolved chronologically.[16] According to De Ligt, the results that I obtained should be

---

[12] Von Freyberg 1989: 74–7.   [13] Von Freyberg 1989: 93–6.   [14] Von Freyberg 1989: 134–8.
[15] However, this is not the place to discuss all the hypotheses of Hopkins and von Freyberg; see Andreau 1992b; 1994b.   [16] Andreau 1987a: 257–329.

regarded with caution, as their credibility depends upon the evolution of epigraphical customs.[17] It is quite true that the name of a man's profession is not indicated in all cases, and the proportion of inscriptions available to study varies from one level of wealth to another and also from one region to another, but without any clear pattern. Nevertheless, I do not disown the conclusions that I reached, in particular those relating to the city of Rome and to Italy.

The third approach is valid only for well-defined and well-delimited professions, such as professional financiers, but not elite financiers. Here, it is a matter of establishing a qualitative history of the professions, taken collectively, from which to deduce developmental tendencies.

Now let me draw a few conclusions relating to chronological and geographical differences. From the end of the third century BC to the time of Caesar and the second triumvirate, financial transactions in general and the money deals of the elite in particular continued to expand. We do not know how much or how fast, and it is even hard to prove that this happened. But there can be hardly any doubt that it did.[18]

It is true that moneylenders had already long existed, and deposit bankers had appeared upon the scene between 318 and 310 BC. In addition, the Second Punic War had certainly provided an opportunity, both for the city and for private individuals, to assimilate a number of Hellenistic procedures and techniques. But it was after this that business picked up, particularly for the elite. This progression went hand in hand with a growing differentiation between financial operations and increasing specialization among financiers.[19]

Maritime loans, which Rome took over from the Hellenistic world, are first attested at the time of Cato the Elder, but we do not know precisely when they were introduced into Rome. The *permutatio* that made it possible to transfer money without shifting material funds must originally have involved an operation of foreign exchange, or so its name would suggest. Whether it was conducted by a company of tax-collectors or by private individuals, its origins probably go back to the first half of the second century BC. In the course of the second and first centuries BC, private law underwent a number of profound changes, which resulted in part from the development of financial affairs and which, in return, must have exerted a considerable influence on financial life. But those changes had their limits: no endorsable cheques ever existed, nor did negotiable bills.

---

[17] De Ligt 1991: 493–4 and 496.
[18] Hopkins 1980; Crawford 1985: 173–93; Howgego 1992: 2–16.   [19] Barlow 1978: 232–4.

Plautus' plays present specialized moneylenders, but no credit inter-mediaries. In contrast, at the time of Cicero the latter clearly existed.

Most historians agree that in Italy this development was accompanied by new ways of thinking, and that money deals became more and more accepted by the elite. The Roman sources themselves say so. In truth, members of the elite had long been lending money at interest, as every-one apparently knew. On the other hand, such lending never had a very good reputation, even at the end of the Republic or under the Principate. But it is true that towards the end of the fourth century BC, lending money for interest had been prohibited by the *lex Genucia*. Was it banned again in 191 BC?[20] Even if it was, which is unlikely, the ban did not last for long. Subsequently, lending money at interest was never pro-hibited again, and the practice was mentioned perfectly openly.

The progress of private financial affairs correlated with a number of other major developments. Of these it is worth mentioning the diversification of the agriculture of the *villae*, which became increasingly oriented towards the sale of their produce; the growth of the city of Rome; the increasing security of transport, which facilitated these devel-opments; and the progressive diffusion of new life-styles in the western provinces.

The ever-widening dispersion of their patrimonies obliged the elite to provide themselves with more liquid money and to organize money transfers. In their desperation to maintain their rank, senators and knights sought to increase their patrimonies, or at least to manage what they possessed as profitably as possible. To this end, they launched them-selves into as many ventures as possible, both private and political.[21]

Many factors were at work here: the large incomes, legal or otherwise, that senators derived from their political life; the profits that came their way from private business pursued in the provinces; the size of the profits made by companies of tax-collectors (*societates publicanorum*). Aristocratic finance was much more closely linked with politics and public adjudica-tions than with private commerce. But the way in which it was funded depended directly upon the commercialization of agricultural products and, during this period, this expanded in tandem with the expansion of commerce.

The history of the banking professions between the third and the first centuries BC confirms the progress made by financial businesses.[22] The regular participation of bankers in sales by auction, and the appearance

[20] Barlow 1978: 55–67.   [21] See Jaczynowska 1962 and Shatzman 1975.
[22] Andreau 1984; 1987a: 61–167.

of *coactores argentarii* and *nummularii* can be understood only in connection with a widening diffusion of monetary transactions and credit, both within the framework of economic life and outside it. For while sales by auction are attested in particular ports, in certain wholesale and retail markets and in the *nundinae* of central Italy, auctions also played a major role in the sales of portions of the patrimonies of members of the elite (slaves, buildings and movable chattels, land, etc.) and also in the sales of securities put up for loans. Their diffusion was linked to the progress of monetization and moneylending. The qualitative history of the financing and banking professions thus does provide clear indications of tendencies relating to the volume and diffusion of financial business.

In the western provinces, the Roman presence, although character-ized by exploitation of the native inhabitants in the second and first cen-turies BC, was at the same time accompanied by the undeniable progress of financial businesses. The *Pro Fonteio* of Cicero is a fine document that testifies to this.

As for the eastern provinces, they went through three periods that were so different that it is hard to see how the transitions were made from one to another. The first was the Hellenistic period, in the strict sense of the expression, before the Roman conquest. The second was the period of exploitation, after the conquest, a phase dominated by the presence of *negotiatores* which more or less ended at the same time as the Republic did. The third was the period of a new provincial equilibrium, within the Empire, beginning by and large with the reign of Augustus. The second period was probably catastrophic with regard to the prosperity of the native populations. But how did the volume of transactions develop from one to the next of these periods? It is very hard to say.

Let me make two or three more observations. The first is that from Cicero's time, the overall progress of financial affairs was, curiously enough, accompanied by a relative loss of status and wealth for the pro-fessionals. In the second century BC and the early years of the first century, we know of bankers in Italy and in the conquered territories – Delos, for example – whose financial and social standing was very high. But later the situation changed. As monetization and financial transac-tions spread, they increasingly involved middle-range circles. At the same time, banking professions became more modest. In the Athenian classical period, Pasion possessed one of the largest fortunes in the city. That was not the case with the Italian bankers of the period of Augustus. This development worked increasingly against the emergence of a bour-geoisie, since the financiers situated above the professional bankers were already connected with the world of landowners with patrimonies. One of the features of this development was that the growing financial activity propelled the ancient economy into greater dependence upon the landowning oligarchy.

Secondly, let me point out that, if one works back along the chains of causes, one arrives at the conquest of an Empire and at the political and military unification that resulted from it. Without the conquest, things would not conceivably have worked out the way that they did. Whereas the financial life of the medieval and modern periods developed on the margins of States and between one State and another, that of the Roman Empire grew within the sphere of Roman domination. The existence of the Empire multiplied financial transactions but, at the same time, by providing facilities that stemmed from the political unification, it hampered the elaboration of new financial techniques. In this respect, the brilliant achievements of the last two centuries of the Republic and the early years of the Empire eventually, in the domain that interests us here, led to the seeds of a decline that later – much later, it must be said – did indeed materialize.

What can be said of the diffusion of financial businesses in the various provinces under the Principate? In Hopkins's 'Taxes and Trade Model', the provinces in the first group (those that paid taxes and received no troops) seem to have been destined for a particularly active financial life, since they became the active centres of commercial transactions. Outlying provinces, however, were also obliged to pay taxes, and the military camps there were centres of consumption and monetization; but wholesale commerce and the more elaborate kind of financial businesses should, logically, have been less developed there.

What does the documentation tell us? Very little, unfortunately, as, under the Principate, the literary texts do not provide information on all the provinces. Inscriptions relating to professional bankers are too few in number in the provinces, and in some provinces are not to be found at all (probably on account of variable epigraphical customs). In any case, the models of Hopkins and von Freyberg take into consideration only the relations between the provinces and Italy; they comment on neither the relations between the various provinces nor the transactions that took place within the different provinces. And the activity of professional bankers appears to have been, above all, local and regional.

The last point I would like to make concerns the history of Italy. Here, it is easier to reach some conclusions. However one explains the financial decline of central and southern Italy, there seems no doubt that it occurred. In the second and first centuries B C, the financial life of Italy (particularly central Italy) had profited, as had its commercial life, from an exceptional coincidence of favourable factors: the presence of members of the elite, who appropriated a large proportion of the benefits that stemmed from the conquest, growing steadily richer; the emigration of many Italian *negotiatores*; massive sales of, for instance, wine; and the growing importance of Rome, which was unquestionably the major financial centre.

In the course of the first two centuries AD, those factors became dissociated, and various signs indicate that Italy was sinking into financial decline, and Rome in particular, even if it still was the foremost town in the Empire. Of course, each of those signs was no more than relative, but their coincidence is telling.

The number of bankers known from inscriptions decreases sharply. Not one is attested after the first century AD outside Rome and the major ports (Ostia, Portus, and Aquileia). That does not necessarily mean that there were none anywhere, but there appears to be no doubt that their numbers shrank and that they were now mainly to be found only in Rome and in its ports.[23]

From the second century onward, in Italy, much less credit was provided in auction sales by the *argentarii* and the *coactores argentarii*, and it disappeared altogether during the second half of the third century AD. That credit provided at auction sales had been important for three reasons: it had affected the commerce on which the supplies of Rome depended; its existence had favoured transactions involving elements of the elite members' patrimonies; and it had stimulated moneylending, for it helped to make it possible to auction the security put up for such loans. In the second and third centuries AD, the contacts of the *argentarii* and the *coactores argentarii* still attested in Italy seem to have been mostly with wholesale markets (for example, the *forum boarium* in Rome). The other two functions of auction sales must necessarily have undergone a definite decline at this date throughout Italy, and even in Rome.[24]

There are other signs which are as telling, such as the disappearance or decline of the *Janus medius*, the disappearance of the *negotiatores*, and also of the great companies of tax-collectors. At the end of the Republic and the beginning of the Empire, the *Janus medius* in Rome had attracted financiers who were higher fliers than the professional bankers and who, in particular, acted as intermediaries between creditors seeking to lend

---

[23] Andreau 1987a: 257–329.   [24] Andreau 1986.

money and potential borrowers.[25] After the period of the Julio-Claudians, we hear no more of these intermediaries, and it does not seem possible to ascribe that disappearance purely to the vagaries of the available textual documentation.

In the last century of the Republic, members of the Italian elite groups, the senators, knights, and others, would invest their money through the mediation of certain *negotiatores*, Italian businessmen established in the provinces or even in regions outside the Empire. In the course of the first century AD, these *negotiatores* likewise disappear. From then on, the word *negotiator* no longer designated such businessmen, but was used instead of wholesalers.

Finally, the great companies of tax-collectors, which used to play an important financial role, began to disappear. Even if the decline of these companies was in truth more gradual and less continuous than it used to be believed, there can be no doubt that they became increasingly rare between the time of Augustus and the second century AD.

Moneylending at interest certainly continued to flourish and was practised by many elite members. A portion of their patrimonies was made up of debt-claims. Maritime loans also continued to be advanced. In the course of the Principate, money-changers and bankers are quite frequently attested in the Greek part of the Empire. However, it is impossible not to recognize the decline or even disappearance of social institutions and circles which, at the end of the Republic and under Augustus and the Julio-Claudians, had imparted great vitality to the financial life of Italy.

The most affected by decline were not the commercial transactions of the markets and ports of Rome, but the major financial business that concerned Italy itself and the relations between Italy and the provinces, and that cannot be reduced simply to the counterpart of commercial operations. For that reason, this kind of business may be considered as extra-economic; it stemmed at least in part from the elite members' customary ostentatious consumption, which, however, did create a specific financial space. To be sure, toward the end of the Republic, some credit intermediaries were lending money to traders (for example, Cluvius and Vestorius). However, their activities and those of their fellow-*feneratores* by no means simply constituted an extension of commercial operations.

Eventually, all these financial phenomena linked with the aristocracy disappear from view, probably for two reasons. The first was the manner

---

[25] Andreau 1987a: 707–9; 1987b.

in which the aristocracy of the Empire evolved, becoming more and more linked with the provinces and less so with Italy. The second was that, increasingly, inevitable financial operations (such as the transportation of money from the provinces to Italy) were organized within the framework of commercial business or through close relations with the world of commerce. The dichotomy between commercial life and aristocratic finance, which is detectable in certain works of Cicero, such as his *Verrines*, in particular, faded away later, at least in Italy. That development may be partly accounted for by the explanatory schema suggested by von Freyberg. The decline was very gradual; there was no single cause for it, and not all of its multiple causes were economic. Far from it! However, the aspect to which Hopkins, followed by von Freyberg, has drawn attention does help to explain it.

Although wealth flowed into Italy, either in the form of cash later spent elsewhere in return for merchandise, or else in the form of merchandise, Rome, which had become the destination for the products of the entire Roman world, was no longer as important financially as it had been, because the financial flow became increasingly a one-way affair: the money went mostly in one direction, the merchandise in the other. Even the decline of the professional moneylenders in Italy, and their increasing links with commercial centres may, at least in part, be explained by the imbalance of those exchanges and the structure of the financial flow.

Of course, the major financial business conducted by the elite, sometimes with contacts in the commercial circles, but still independent of them and autonomous, to some extent shifted to other places. It was never again concentrated in a single place as it had been at the end of the Republic; and it certainly thereby lost some of the brilliance that had resulted from that concentration.

CHAPTER 12

Financial life in Roman society and economy

To what extent did the people of ancient Greece and Rome seek individual profit at the expense of social solidarity and the traditions of reciprocity and non-profit-seeking exchange? And what economic role (in production and commerce) was played by financial life?

Those are two totally distinct questions, yet they are often linked in discussions on the ancient economy. They were, for example, treated together by P. Millett (1991) in relation to Athens in the classical period. That is why I shall be addressing both questions in the present chapter.

First, let me make a few observations on Millett's method and results. He divides financial loans and operations into three groups:

(a) free operations, founded on personal and social relations, with no thought of profit ('non-professional lending: loans without interest');

(b) loans and transactions effected for some remuneration, but conducted only occasionally, by anyone, with no financial specialization ('non-professional lending: loans bearing interest');

(c) 'professional money-lending.' In my view, this third category is really twofold. It includes, on the one hand, operations conducted by specialist financiers who, in some cases, were profit-seeking and competent businessmen but did not practise any urban profession, strictly speaking, for instance, elite members who loaned part of their fortune at interest, for the sake of the income or to increase their patrimony; on the other hand, professional men, money-changers/bankers (trapezites and, in Rome, *argentarii*), traders, and wholesalers who also conducted financial business.

In his book on fourth-century Athens, Millett discusses all four categories of loans, but particularly emphasizes the first. He believes that the practice of advancing free loans was very common in Athens and fitted into the framework of relations of kinship, neighbourliness, and civic solidarity. So, first and foremost, he contrasts free loans with those that 'professionals' advanced with an eye to profit (whether those 'professionals' were professional bankers or elite financiers; his use of the word 'professionals' simply denotes that they specialized in this activity).

I broadly approve of his classification (although I should prefer a classification into four groups, for Millett minimizes the importance of non-banker specialist lenders and underestimates the specificity of banks). And I believe, like him and Bogaert,[1] that loans provided by professional bankers ('bank loans', in the third category) were quantitatively less important than the rest. That is why I have always insisted upon the distinction between professional bankers and elite financiers. However, I have paid far less attention than Millett to relations of free lending and to the connections between social links and loans. There were, of course, free loans. But for three reasons I have never made them one of my central preoccupations.

My first reason is connected with the particular questions that I have posed. Millett's point of departure is the notion of profit, of remunerated loans and credit with economic purposes. Following in the footsteps of M. I. Finley, he tries to show that those three ideas did not play a significant role in antiquity. I, for my part, have been drawn toward questions relating to the organization of the economy and, above all, of work. In my studies of economic history, I have operated to some extent as a sociologist of work. That is how I encountered the debate on the ancient economy known as the 'primitivist/modernist controversy'.[2]

I have studied not loans as a whole, but only remunerated loans, distinguishing between the role of the professional bankers (to whom I have applied the term 'professional' in a different sense from that used by Millett) and that of members of the elite.

Conscious of the specificity of ancient societies, I have sought that specificity particularly in the difference between, on the one hand, the elite (senators, knights, and at least certain elements in the municipal aristocracy) and, on the other, the professional men (a difference that tends to be ignored or denied by the 'modernists'). To pinpoint that difference, I introduced the concept of a 'work status' or 'the conditions of the activity'. I refer the reader to my remarks in chapter 1.[3]

Despite their anthropological interest, some of the oppositions upon which Millett builds his argument do nothing to clarify the problems posed by the ancient economy. Take, for example, the opposition between what is economic and what is not. Peasants who help one another at harvest time are not operating outside the economy. And con-

---

[1] Bogaert 1968: 373–4 and Millett 1991: 15.   [2] Millett 1991: 9–15.   [3] See above, pp. 3–4.

sumption, too, is part of the economy. Or consider the opposition between remunerated loans and free loans. It sometimes happens that the interest is not indicated because it has already been included in the sum to be repaid. P. W. Pestman has shown that in the papyri of Egypt, *atokos* and *aneu tokou* do not necessarily signify that the loan was free; the interest may have been included in the sum due to be repaid.[4]

Furthermore, the absence of financial remuneration does not necessarily mean that there was no remuneration at all. We know that in Roman Egypt, in poor and working-class communities, many loans were remunerated, not by interest, but by work or services.[5] Reciprocity, social practices that foster *philia* or *amicitia*, and that cannot be avoided, are not always disinterested. Nor do they inevitably fall outside the economy. In the Roman senatorial elite of the Late Republic, many loans were accompanied by great declarations of *amicitia* and stemmed from reciprocity. Yet in many cases they were remunerated and were even prompted by a definite desire for profit. Such kinds of practices existed in all pre-industrial societies, including western Europe in the seventeenth and eighteenth centuries. They do not betoken an extreme archaism.[6]

And here is one more reason: the Roman world was different from the world of classical Athens, and the documentation available for the two also differs. In Athens, thanks to the Attic orators, in particular, we hear much more about the traders, the artisans, and the small-scale landowners than we do in Rome. The Roman documentation mostly relates to the elite. When studying the social solidarities that led an Athenian to advance free loans, Millett describes them as a series of concentric circles: the family and kinship, the neighbourhood, the city.[7] Such a progression, working outward from the centre, where solidarity was strongest, toward the extreme periphery, where reciprocity was 'negative', cannot really be made to apply to the Roman elite.

Like the Athenians, the Romans had a tradition of helping and rendering services to all those close to them, such as kin, neighbours, and friends. At the end of the Republic and under the Principate, for example, they were still in the habit of depositing money or valuable objects in the houses of individuals who were not to invest these deposits and eventually returned them intact. These were known as regular deposits, also accepted by bankers, and were not remunerated.[8] They

---

[4] Pestman 1971; see also Foraboschi and Gara 1981: 337.   [5] Johnson 1936: 452–4.
[6] Grenier 1996: 87–91.   [7] Millett 1991: 109–59.
[8] Michel 1962: 56–73; Andreau 1987a: 529–30; Kaser 1971–5: vol. I, 534–6.

would also contract free loans, which in principle raised no interest, *mutuum*. However, the *mutuum* evolved. It became legally possible to require interest not included in the contract which, in itself, remained free. Down to the time of Justinian, the stipulation of interest on the *mutuum* was not legally regarded as a contradiction of the interest-free nature of the contract itself.[9]

From Cicero's period on, the use of the words *mutuari, mutuus,* or *mutuum* in literary texts did not imply that the loan was interest-free. Certain passages in Plautus, for instance, seem to imply this.[10] But when they reappear, the words frequently turn out to designate loans at interest.[11] The vocabulary connected with *mutuum* is, certainly, more often to be found in a context of friendship and trust than in one of speculation or usury. But it is not possible to rely on that when attempting to understand the history of interest-free loans in Rome.

Interest-free loans did continue to exist in Roman Italy.[12] But they were probably less common than in classical Athens. For the Romans were traditionally very meticulous where money and contracts were involved. Under the Republic, the acts of generosity recorded in certain literary texts confirm, *a contrario*, the customary firmness of their behaviour, even towards those close to them.

The most spectacular case is that of the dowries of the sisters of the adoptive father of Scipio Aemilianus.[13] Aemilia Tertia, the wife of Africanus, had paid her two sons-in-law (Ti. Sempronius Gracchus and P. Cornelius Scipio Nasica) half of her daughters' dowries, which in each case amounted to fifty talents. In 163/162 BC she died. Scipio Aemilianus was anxious to pay off the debt. Legally, he could do this in three instalments, the first of which was supposed to be paid within ten months. He instructed his banker to pay all that was owed as soon as the first instalment fell due. When the husbands of his aunts visited the banker, they were amazed to receive twenty-five talents each, thought that there had been some mistake, and were then embarrassed to find that Aemilianus knew perfectly well what he was doing and was acting out of generosity toward them.

---

[9] On the *mutuum*, see Michel 1962: 103–27 and Kaser 1976: 271–82.

[10] Particularly Plautus, *Asin.* 248; see Barlow 1978: 55–6.

[11] For example, in Apul. *Metam.* 1.22.2, where *mutuor* concerns the activities of a pawnbroker, Milo of Hypata, who, of course, insisted upon interest!

[12] On the place of reciprocity and redistribution in the circulation of money, see Howgego 1994 and Shatzman 1975: 82.

[13] Pol. 31.27. Note that Greek writers (here Polybius and Plutarch) used Greek monetary units, i.e. talents and drachmas, to stand for sums paid in Italy in denarii or sesterces.

A century later, customs had probably relaxed somewhat, and Cicero expressed surprise that Atticus' uncle, Quintus Caecilius, gave those closest to him no advantage at all when it came to interest rates.[14] This shows that it was customary to charge even close relatives interest. Plutarch relates that Cato of Utica, having inherited one hundred talents from a cousin, changed it into money and loaned it all, without charging interest, to those of his friends who were in need. He had decided to act in accordance with his morals, rather than according to common practice.[15]

Neither interest-free loans nor gifts of money were expected. They did not constitute social customs that an individual felt bound to observe. And in Roman law, gratuitous generosity was a concept that, on its own, was irrelevant. It had meaning only in contrast to the burdensome nature of interest.[16]

However, there can be no doubt of the generosity of certain high-placed Romans. Their actions were completely individual, the result of a personal choice; for Millett's theory of concentric circles (family and kin, neighbourhood, city) is not applicable to the Roman elite. Each *paterfamilias* was surrounded by an individual network of *propinqui*, that is to say, more or less close relatives, friends, neighbours, and connections. From amongst them, he would select the beneficiaries of his generosity on various grounds, some of which would stem from his philosophical ethos or his aristocratic scale of values.[17] Even the behaviour of the most grasping financiers was not invariably prompted by the profit motive.

Consider the example of Atticus, who was certainly not one of the greediest financiers. He may have advanced interest-free loans to the city of Athens.[18] According to Cornelius Nepos, he also lent money interest-free to Fulvia, Antony's wife, out of gratitude and despite his friendship with Cicero.[19] But his interest-free loans to the city of Athens and to Fulvia did not prevent Atticus, on other occasions, from insisting on the interest due to him and manifesting undeniable intransigence. Consider his behaviour relating to his debt-claim on the city of Sicyon.[20] And,

---

[14] Cic. *ad Att.* 1.21.1.
[15] Plut. *Cato Min.* 6.7; on financial relations between kin, see Andreau 1990.
[16] Michel 1962: 318–22.   [17] Andreau 1990.
[18] Corn. Nep. *Atticus* 2.4 (the manuscripts use the words *numquam* and *unquam*, which indicate that he never demanded interest when he advanced loans to this city; but some editors have emended this to *iniquam*).   [19] Corn. Nep. *Att.* 9.2–7.
[20] Cic. *ad Att.* 1.13.1; 1.19.9; 1.20.4; 2.1.10; 2.13.2; 2.21.6. In 58 BC, works of art, particularly paintings, located in Sicyon, were transferred to Rome and delivered to the creditors of that city (Pliny, *Nat. Hist.* 35.127). See Maselli 1986: 62–3; Verboven 1993b; Labate and Narducci 1981.

during the civil wars, he was very much in two minds about whether to allow his brother-in-law Quintus Cicero, then in debt to him, a deferment of payment. He made a number of large gifts – Brutus received 400,000 sesterces from him[21] – yet in 45 BC he refused to help out Quintus' son.[22]

In my opinion, G. Maselli should not be sarcastic on the score of Atticus' cupidity.[23] For he was not a *fenerator* on the model of his uncle Q. Caecilius, and his example shows how a scrupulous concern for his patrimony and great financial caution could go hand in hand with moral obligations. But this was an aristocratic society in which room for traditions of interest-free loans and reciprocity was limited. More often than not a gift would result from a personal choice, and not be prompted by social custom. The giving of gifts was a manifestation of the power of a *paterfamilias*.

There were, however, three contexts that tended to encourage indulgence or one-way generosity. The first was that of one's clientele.[24] The second was that of euergetism, for example towards a particular city. By taking it under his protection, the elite member would demonstrate his lack of self-interest (particularly if the city was faced with financial difficulties). The advancement of interest-free loans as well as the giving of gifts could constitute acts of euergetism.

The third context was that of the political life of Rome, which, at the end of the Republic, as we know, occasioned some major financial operations. It has often been observed, rightly, that senators would have no compunction about being successively (or even simultaneously) both debtors and creditors of their peers. Caesar's debts, which (we are told) amounted to as much as 25,000,000 sesterces in 61 BC, are particularly notorious.[25] The need at certain points in a political career to incur huge expenses, electoral corruption, the desire to win support by providing financial help for potential allies, and the considerable inequality of fortunes within senatorial circles all helped to foster the urge to engage in massive financial transactions.

I shall not dwell upon these practices, which were very much modified under the Early Empire, but which did not disappear completely, as they have been studied often.[26] Political life gave rise to loans that appeared

---

[21] Corn. Nep. *Att.* 8.6.

[22] See Maselli 1986: 62–6 and 99–201; Labate and Narducci 1981; Verboven 1993a.

[23] Maselli 1986: 64.   [24] Saller 1982: 120–2.   [25] Shatzman 1975: 346–56.

[26] Deloume 1889; Früchtl 1912; Shatzman 1975; etc. See also D.R. Shackleton Bailey's commentaries on the letters of Cicero, which are always accurate and very illuminating (Shackleton Bailey 1965–8; 1977).

to be interest-free yet were by no means disinterested. They were loans
for political profit. The lender would be a politician who reckoned that
his gesture would advance his political career. The interest from the loan
would be low or non-existent, precisely because the desired advantage
was not of a financial nature. But there certainly would be an advantage
(or at least the hope of it). So in operations such as these (in which both
Crassus and Caesar were much involved), generosity is hardly the word
to use.[27]

These loans 'for political gain' should not be confused with other
political loans, which were not disinterested either and which, moreover,
were not interest-free: these were 'loans with political objectives'. The
borrower would be a politician in need of money to promote his political career, to organize an electoral campaign, etc. He would be planning
to use the borrowed money for political ends. In such a case there was
no reason for the lender to waive his own financial profits (in other
words, the payment of interest).

One of the strangest things about this private financial life was that
an unbridled desire to make profits tended to go hand in hand with a
somewhat theatrical sense of the liberal gesture. A characteristic
example is provided by the Cloatii (who were neither senators nor
knights). Numerius and Marcus Cloatius, who were established in the
port of Gytheion in the first century BC, advanced the city three loans
at usurious rates (48 per cent compound interest in the case of the third
loan, at a time when a rate of less that 12 per cent simple interest, with
extended time for repayment, was considered normal in Rome).
Subsequently, however, they accepted a remission of at least part of the
first debt of the people of Gytheion, contented themselves with partial
repayment of the second, and for the third limited their claims (to 24 per
cent simple interest, with remission of the interest already due). The city
thanked them for this generosity – with all the greater fervour, given that
they had managed to persuade the Roman authorities that Gytheion
should be exempted from a levy of troops and the requisitioning of
wheat and cloth.[28]

Now let us consider the economic role of financial activity. Some historians have denied that it was of any economic importance. Others have
exaggerated its modernity. My own position is intermediate, above all

---

[27] Shatzman 1975: 78, 346–56 and 375–8. Verboven 1993a contains some excellent observations on
   the interaction of economic and financial life with the social and political traditions of the city.
[28] *IG* v, 1.1146. See Bogaert 1968: 100–1; Le Roy 1978; Andreau 1985a: 180.

because this was a pre-industrial economy and one which, in my opinion, despite its achievements, had come nowhere near to reaching the state of imbalance that preceded the Industrial Revolution. Many historians of the Industrial Revolution stress the fact that the development came about within the framework of 'a structure of changing structures'. A previously stable economy had changed into a situation of instability in which any kind of impulsion was liable to swing it over into a different system.[29] Rome never came to experience such instability, partly because it constituted an Empire. It experienced political and social upheavals, but never any such dynamics of structural change.

On this important point, the conclusions of A. di Porto, A. Petrucci, A. Carandini, and D. Manacorda – despite appearances – all concur with those of M. I. Finley. Nor are they wrong. For they all aim to show that, by the second century B C (or perhaps even as early as the late fourth or third century), Rome had acquired all the economic, social, legal, and psychological structures upon which it continued to depend until well into the Principate. All of them thus stress the extraordinary, extremely long-term stability, which of course helps to account for the brilliant achievements of Roman civilization.

However, those merits of the Roman economy, which also constituted limitations, did not prevent financial life from being interwoven to some extent with the functioning of the economy. Quite apart from advancing credit, the bankers and financiers provided many services for economic agents. The assayers/money-changers, who had appeared in Greece by the late sixth century B C, greatly facilitated foreign exchange and liquidity. It was certainly not by chance that money-changers were so often to be found in ports and in markets, nor that, in Pergamum, in the reign of Hadrian, tensions arose between them and the traders.[30] It is true that, as Plato tells us,[31] traders and shipowners themselves checked and changed foreign money, and that touchstones have been found in the wrecks of ships.[32] All the same, the existence of money-changers/bankers was very useful to commerce, as were bank deposits. The latter made it possible to keep money in a town where one did not live but to which one went regularly on business. The services regarding payments that money-changers/bankers provided were useful too, because they made payments more flexible. For clients on the move (traders and pedlars, and also certain members of the elite, usually the

---

[29] Verley 1985: 175–6; see also Crouzet 1966.
[30] See the inscription *OGI* 484 + II, 552; Bogaert 1968: 231–4 and 401–3; Gara 1976: 115–24.
[31] Plato, *Polit.* 289c; see Bogaert 1968: 329 note 143.   [32] Hesnard 1988: 92.

more important ones), the fact that, in the Roman world, bankers and professional deposit-keepers were specialists in local transactions was not always a drawback, quite the reverse.[33]

The services that the professional bankers provided influenced the process of monetization. De Ligt complains that I do not prove the importance of the *argentarii*;[34] but does he not appreciate the importance of monetization and short-term commercial credit?

The gauge of monetization was the relation between goods that were the object of monetary transactions and those that were not; this was an indication of the extent to which money had penetrated the transactions of daily life.[35] In the case of antiquity, it is impossible to quantify this. The more or less substantial presence of coins of very low values is an indicator of the level of monetization.[36] At the end of the Republic and under the Principate, the level of monetization seems to have been higher in Italy than in most of the provinces. It is also in Italy that the greatest numbers of professional money-changers/bankers and money-receivers (*coactores*) are attested, and their history runs parallel to that of the evolution of money.[37] Their existence was both a cause and an effect of the rising level of monetization.[38]

Now let us consider loans and credit, and whether one should speak of loans for production and commerce, or whether all loans were, in effect, consumption loans. Did Roman financiers direct most of their efforts towards economic life in order to create an effective instrument for investments? Did any financial establishments specialize in the promotion of productive loans?[39] The answers to both questions must definitely be no. Did the ancient Greeks and Romans distinguish clearly between loans for production and loans for consumption? Did they divide loans into two categories, those destined to be economic, and the rest? Again, the answer must be no.

However, to move on from there to declare that the Roman bankers and financiers intervened neither in economic life in general, nor in commerce in particular, would be to take a huge step, one that should not be taken.

---

[33] Already in the Ptolemaic period, merchants and wholesalers made up part of the clientele of bankers (Bogaert 1994: 66–7).   [34] De Ligt 1991: 495–6.

[35] Crawford 1970; Goldsmith 1987: 7 and 41; Howgego 1992: 16–29.

[36] Howgego (1992: 18–19) nevertheless expresses a number of reservations on this point.

[37] Burnett 1989.   [38] Andreau 1994b: 197–9.

[39] The definition of 'productive' varies greatly in the bibliography. In the present book what I mean by the word is everything that contributes not only to production, but also to the transportation and distribution of goods.

In his condemnation of debts, Plutarch made an exception in the case of those who borrowed money in order to survive, because they had nothing to eat and drink. But then he writes in exactly the same terms of those who borrow in order to buy land or productive slaves and those who do so because of their taste for luxury or for euergetism.[40] In another passage, he writes of borrowing money in order to buy wheat fields, vineyards, and olive groves.[41] Such texts, which confuse the various possible functions of loans, reveal both that the Greeks and Romans had no concept of productive loans, and also that such productive loans nevertheless did exist. Certain fragments in the *Digest* refer to cases where loans were contracted with the objective of buying some land, repairing a ship, feeding sailors, or purchasing merchandise.[42] Millett and Cohen both cite a remark of Demosthenes on the role of loans in commerce.[43] A similar remark is to be found in the letters of Seneca to Lucilius. It refers to a man who wants to launch himself into business, maritime commerce, or public tax-farming, needs to borrow money, and turns to an intermediary in order to find credit.[44]

Roman financiers (whether professional or not) did not limit themselves to loans for consumption, which is not to suggest that most loans were productive. What proportion of loans were linked with production or commerce? We have no idea. Probably only a minority. On that point, I agree with Cohen's conclusions on classical Greece. As for Millett, at one point he declares that there were no productive loans in antiquity since, according to him, they are not known in any pre-industrial societies; yet at another point he compares classical Greece to situations in modern India, where 30 to 40 per cent of all loans are productive.[45] I do not believe that the Graeco-Roman world was a 'developing country', as India now is (or an under-developed one). But while I reject the first of his conclusions, I do accept Millett's second conclusion (namely, that only a minority of loans were productive, although they remain impossible to quantify).

Loans were advanced by all categories of financiers.[46] And all were capable of advancing the productive variety and thereby influencing economic life; but they did not all operate in the same fashion, nor on the same scale. Let us just say that short-term commercial credit was

---

[40] Plut. *Moralia* 830E.   [41] Plut. *Moralia* 523 F.
[42] *Dig.* 12.1.4 pr. (Ulpian); *Dig.* 14.1.1.8-11 (Ulpian); *Dig.* 14.1.7 (Africanus).
[43] Dem. 34.51. See Millett 1991: 188 and Cohen 1992: 151.   [44] Sen. *ad Lucil.* 119.1.
[45] Millett 1983: 43; 1991: 71–2.
[46] Howgego (1992: 14) lists all the categories of people and institutions that advanced loans.

made available by several categories, particularly by bankers and merchant-financiers. Longer-term credit, probably less common, lay more
in the province of elite *feneratores* and 'entrepreneurs'.[47]

At sales by auction, the *argentarii* and the *coactores argentarii* would pay
the sellers the sums due to them immediately, or almost immediately, as
soon as the sale was over, and they would advance the borrowers short-
term loans for a few months only (never for more than a year, in the
examples available to us). Such auctions would frequently be held in
commercial places: ports, or wholesale or retail markets. In Rome, for
example, they would take place at the *Portus vinarius superior* (on the bank
of the Tiber, upstream from the centre of Rome), in the *Forum vinarium*
(a wholesale market specializing in wines), in the *Forum boarium*, the
Macellum Liviae, and the *Macellum Magnum*. We know of a *praeco vinorum*
in Ostia, who organized auctions of wine. Outside Rome, money-
receivers and money-changers/bankers were to be found in towns where
fairs were held, such as Cremona, or where there were periodic markets,
nundinae.

In southern Latium and in Campania, all the towns in which money-
changers and bankers are known at the beginning of the Empire have
one point in common. They all appear on the *indices nundinarii*, the lists
of towns in which periodic markets used to take place. In Pompeii, sales
by auction were held on the days of *nundinae*. Right at the end of the
Republic and in the age of Augustus, money-changers/bankers and
auction credit were thus available in markets that were already holding
their own auctions.[48] As well as serving as rural markets for the peasants
and smallholders of the neighbourhood, the *nundinae* fulfilled two other
functions, as is clearly shown by the tablets of Jucundus.

They constituted a place for patrimonial transactions where landowners, even large-scale ones, could sell and buy land, houses, livestock, and
slaves, and where they could sell at least some of the produce from their
estates. In Cato's *De Agricultura*, there are references to auctions of agricultural goods. Two and a half centuries later, a letter from Pliny the
Younger provides another example.[49] Pliny was auctioning the produce
of his vineyards, and the buyers were *negotiatores*. The letter shows,
however, that in this case, no banker was lending money to the buyers at
the auction.

The *nundinae* were also markets that traders frequented, so they played
a significant role in the commercialization of agricultural (and even

---

[47] Andreau 1985c; 1987a.   [48] Andreau 1976; 1984.   [49] Pliny, *Epist.* 8.2.

manufactured) products, which were then transported to Rome. These traders attended the *nundinae* in order to auction whatever they themselves had imported or had had imported from overseas. In the mid-first century A D, a certain Ptolemy of Alexandria sold a consignment of linen at the *nundinae* of Pompeii.[50] J. Frayn rightly points out that bankers such as Jucundus contributed, albeit modestly, to the financing of the wool trade.[51]

Situations clearly varied enormously depending upon whether the seller, the buyer, or both were consumers, retailers, or wholesalers. For traders who were buyers, the short-term commercial credit that the bankers provided made it possible to purchase goods without paying out the necessary sums immediately. Sometimes they were even able to resell the merchandise before paying for it. A pseudo-Acronian scholium to Horace, intended to explain the meaning of the words *coactor* and *argentarius*, provides a good example of such a case. It refers to olives sold by *foranei* (wholesalers established in or close to the forum?). The buyers at the auction are *circumforanei*, travelling traders, who would resell them, as retailers, in the surrounding neighbourhoods. The banker (*argentarius*) pays the sellers on the spot. Through a *coactor* (a money-receiver), he is later reimbursed by the buyers, the travelling traders, to whom he has advanced credit and who have probably been able to resell the purchased products before paying for them.[52]

The *argentarii* and *coactores argentarii* sometimes likewise played a part in auctions devoted to the wares of craftsmen or the products of mining. Here, too, the buyers were sometimes traders. Thus, in Rome, the *coactor argentarius* Aulus Argentarius Antiochus, who plied his trade *inter aerarios*, very probably did so at auctions of objects manufactured by those bronze-workers.[53] The bronze plaques discovered at Aljustrel, in the Iberian peninsula, refer to auctions in which *argentarii* and *coactores argentarii* played a part. The *lex metalli Vipascensis* shows that mine shafts were sold at the auction, as were slaves, mules, and horses, that is to say, men and beasts for working in the mines.[54] In Vipasca, the short-term credit provided by the *argentarius* was thus a short-term credit advanced to men who exploited mines. Sometimes it happened that what was sold by auction was some agricultural product, and that the seller was either a landowner or a man farming the land of others.

But the professional bankers were not alone in providing short-term

---

[50] *CIL* IV, 3340, tabl. 100; see Andreau 1974a: 218, 284, and 289.   [51] Frayn 1984: 156.
[52] Ps. Acr. *ad Hor. Sat.* 1.6.85–6; see Andreau 1987a: 586 and 717–20.   [53] *CIL* VI, 9186.
[54] *CIL* II, 5181; see Domergue 1983.

credit. The tablets of Murecine show that an imperial slave (formerly the slave of an imperial freedman), Hesychus, although not a banker, advanced this kind of credit on either a short- or a medium-term basis. Similarly, a fragment of Paulus included in the *Digest* concerns a slave who, while being employed by his master to lend money for interest, also advanced commercial credit on his own initiative, paying barley-merchants for their merchandise in place of the buyers.[55] Maritime loans also constituted a form of short-term commercial credit, but of a very particular kind. These were probably advanced mainly by elite *feneratores*, by 'entrepreneurs', or by merchant-financiers.

The known examples of middle- or long-term productive loans[56] are extremely rare (they are particularly rare among the actual documents of day-to-day legal business that have come down to us). Many people find this surprising, but are probably wrong to do so, for the following two reasons.

The first is that, even in eighteenth-century England, such long-term loans were neither as common nor as massive as has long been believed. P. Verley sums up the most recent results of research on initial capital and self-financing, and on fixed capital and circulating capital, as follows: 'Little need for initial capital, rapid growth subsequently made possible by a massive reinvestment of profits, internal financing predominating over external financing, less need for fixed capital than for circulating capital'.[57] It would really not be surprising if those comments applied, *a fortiori*, to Roman antiquity! Self-financing was not unknown in Rome either.

Furthermore, there existed in Rome institutions that made middle- or long-term financing possible without any need to resort to loans. The chief among such institutions was a *societas*, the sleeping partnership, in which one of the associates provided the capital for another who was responsible for all the work and the management. This was very well suited to members of the elite particularly keen to increase their patrimonies. It gave them the chance to make a profit from commercial, industrial, or even financial businesses, without themselves having to adopt the life of 'entrepreneurs.' The medieval *commenda* resembled this type of contract, and J. Le Goff has commented on it as follows: 'The contractors were regarded as associates to the extent that they shared the risks and the profits, but in other respects the relations between them

---

[55] *Dig.* 14.5.8 (Paulus). [56] In the sense in which I use the word 'productive': see n. 39 above.
[57] Verley 1985: 48–52. See also Crouzet 1972; Feinstein and Pollard 1988; Wrigley 1988; Verley 1991.

were those that existed between a lender and a borrower'.[58] Thus, it would be mistaken to assume that a senator who had concluded a contract of this kind was a trader or an industrialist.

Nevertheless, traces do exist of productive middle- or long-term loans. Some were advanced by patrons to their freedmen. A fragment included in the *Digest*, attributed to Q. Cervidius Scaevola, relates to just such a case of commercial credit loaned for a period of several years. A *negotiator marmorum*, providing security in the form of marble blocks, borrowed money from a creditor whose identity is not given. The loaned money served to pay the sellers of the marble. The wholesaler had meanwhile leased some warehouses belonging to the Emperor.[59] This, too, was a loan that helped to finance circulating capital.

In recent years, the question of the financing of eastern commerce has again been raised, particularly that of trade between the Red Sea and India. Who provided the large sums necessary for setting up such trade? M. Crawford and L. Casson, for example, have insisted that it could have been members of the Roman imperial elite, and Crawford even mentions the imperial family as a possibility.[60] But I myself am simply indicating a few ways in which commerce may have been financed. I do not possess any new information on the identity of those who invested in eastern commerce. Like Casson and G.W. Bowerstock, I rule out, at any rate, the idea that the Emperor in person may have financed eastern trade to promote some commercial policy applied throughout the eastern regions.[61] So far as I can see, there is no convincing evidence that such a policy existed. However, that does not exclude the possibility that highly important figures, possibly even those very close to the Emperor, may have pursued private interests in this sector.

Roman banking and business certainly did not constitute a tool deliberately designed to further economic investment. All the same, they should not be totally denied an economic role.

This chapter relating to the traditions of reciprocity and non-profit-seeking exhange, and to the economic role of financial life constitutes a suitable conclusion to this study of banking and business.

Pre-industrial historical societies were familiar with writing and with

---

[58] Le Goff 1956: 20.   [59] *Dig.* 20.4.21.1 (Scaev. *lib. XXVII digg.*).
[60] Crawford 1980 and Casson 1989.
[61] Casson 1989: 32–9 and Bowersock 1988. On the relations between the Roman public authorities and trade, see Andreau 1995a. On eastern trade, see Drexhage 1988; Sartre 1991; Millar 1993; Tchernia 1995.

money; they were so firmly divided socially that they may be called class societies. They were also merchant (but not bourgeois or capitalist) societies.

The Greek cities constituted one such example, the Roman Empire another. One comes across disinterestedness and reciprocity in both, but also profit, cupidity, and avarice. Both societies made use of consumer loans, but also of a minority of productive loans; they engaged in many political operations, related to warfare and conquest, but engaged in activity that may properly be called economic. The types of behaviour that stemmed from cupidity or avarice were by no means invariably economic, however; far from it. Many were linked with social and cultural traditions. One example is provided by dowries, which gave rise to many complicated strategies, although they were not, strictly speaking, an 'economic' matter. The same goes for inheritances – a patrimony was not solely an 'economic' phenomenon.

However contradictory these patterns of behaviour and practices seem to us, they continued alongside one another and interacted (just as some of them even continue and interact in our own 'modern' societies).

If one tries to eliminate some of them to simplify one's historical view of antiquity, one will inevitably fail to understand it, or one's understanding of it will be flawed. For it was not characterized purely and simply by archaism, but by a complex combination of archaic elements and elements that were more 'modern'.

It would be relatively pointless to assess its archaism (or its modernity) on, for example, a scale ranging from 0 to 10. What is important is to understand how these so very disparate elements interacted, and to compare pre-industrial economies with one another.

For the non-agricultural economic sectors, what I would propose would be, for example, to compare them from the point of view of the two major social groups that are involved: on the one hand, the aristocracy, whose members possessed a real-estate patrimony; on the other, the men with urban professions, the artisans, the traders, and the bankers. In between those two major groups are the circles of big businessmen, the 'entrepreneurs', who did not belong either to the landowning aristocracy or to the world of professions, but who would nevertheless have occupied a substantial place. The consistency and success of these circles situated on the margins of the aristocratic elite vary enormously from one society to another.

In Rome, their position was truly marginal. They never formed a homogeneous group and never constituted a real bourgeoisie; they were just a few isolated and heterogeneous figures. Is that one of the important features that differentiates the ancient economy from the economies of the modern period? It is, but not the only one. There are plenty of other aspects to compare. Where financial life is concerned, some are studied in this book. Others have escaped me or, rightly or wrongly, seemed to me irrelevant. But a comparative approach is certainly indispensable.

Bibliographical essay

The themes touched upon in this book have given rise to partly separate bibliographies, for the diverse aspects of Roman financial life are not usually treated all together (for the Republican period, Barlow 1978 is the only useful study that treats all aspects).

The first of those bibliographies relates to the big business deals of the senatorial elite, particularly at the end of the Republic. A number of works have been specifically devoted to them, some recent (Rauh 1986a, 1989, and Verboven 1993a, which are extremely stimulating), some of much earlier date but still useful (Früchtl 1912). But they are also frequently mentioned in prosopographical works on the senators, the knights, their patrimonies, and their entourages (the various articles in Pauly & Wissowa's *Realencyclopädie*, Nicolet 1974, Shatzman 1975, who is very useful because he provides information on all the Republican senators known to us). They are also studied in relation to political life and the debt crises (Yavetz 1963, Amsden 1986, Frederiksen 1966), or monetary and economic developments (Yavetz 1970, Lo Cascio 1979 and 1981, Barlow 1980, Crawford 1985, Duncan-Jones 1974 and 1990, Verboven 1994, see also Greene 1986: 45–66). Much information is to be found in commentaries on the works of Cicero, particularly in Shackleton Bailey 1965–8 and 1977, both of which are very valuable editions, with commentaries, of his correspondence.

Over the past twenty years, the economic role of the senators and knights outside agriculture has been a subject of much debate. While Finley 1973 considered it to be minimal, D'Arms & Kopff 1980 and D'Arms 1981 have insisted on its importance. Within the financial domain, this question is studied in detail in Andreau 1985c.

On the tax-collectors (*publicani*), the most interesting work remains Badian 1972; see also Nicolet 1966 and 1979. Hill 1952, who has attracted far too much attention, is at all costs to be avoided. On the Italian *nego-*

tiatores who went off to do business in the provinces, the standard works of reference are Hatzfeld 1919 and Wilson 1966.

A study of the financial interests of members of the elite involves their values and strategies and so engages one in a history of modes of thought, or cultural anthropology. In this domain, Labate & Narducci 1981 is extremely perceptive and measured. The article should be complemented by a number of other works by Narducci (Narducci 1983, for example) and by Veyne 1991: 131–62.

Aristocratic attitudes cannot be understood without reference to the aristocracy's clienteles, kin, families, and friends. On clienteles, see, for example, Wallace-Hadrill 1989, David 1992, and Deniaux 1993.

There is now an abundant bibliography on the family and kinship. I recommend Andreau & Bruhns 1990, Bradley 1991, Corbier 1990 and 1991, Dixon 1992, Dondin Payre 1993, Rawson 1986 and 1991, Rawson & Weaver 1997. On the financial and economic implications of friendship, see Rauh 1986b.

Finley 1973 contains few references to professional banking, but the work nevertheless underlined the rigidities that hampered the development of financial life and the fact that, in the ancient world, loans were not 'productive'. (Actually, the meaning of 'productive' varies from one author to another, and it is preferable to define it when one uses it. In the present work, what I mean by productive is whatever relates to the production, transportation, or distribution of goods.) Over the past dozen or so years, professional banking has been the subject of a whole series of works, strongly marked by the discussions surrounding Finley's *oeuvre*. Rather as with Millett 1991 and Cohen 1992, who disagree about Athenian banking, Bürge 1987, who is 'minimalist' or 'primitivist', disagrees with Petrucci 1991, who is 'modernist'. As for myself, I accept some of the conclusions of Finley and his disciples, while on other points I find myself more in agreement with the 'modernists'. It is time to progress beyond this debate, which means understanding it first (Andreau 1974a, 1982, 1984, 1985c, 1987a, etc.). On professional banking in Graeco-Roman Egypt, the articles of R. Bogaert are to be recommended. They are collected together in Bogaert 1994. The author, like myself, is not altogether on the side of either the 'primitivists' or the 'modernists'. Rathbone 1991 gives a clear account of the uses of banking in a rural community in third-century AD Egypt and of how it was used by the managers of a large estate. The information on professional banking provided by the Heroninos archive seems to me to tally with the picture presented in the present work.

Some categories of documents have been studied separately, for example the nummulary *tesserae*, on which, unfortunately, the extremely disputable works of Herzog (1919 and 1937) cannot be avoided; likewise tablets. On those of L. Caecilius Jucundus, see Andreau 1974a and Jongman 1988. On those of Murecine, see Wolf & Crook 1989, Camodeca 1992, and, more recently, Gröschler 1996.

The tablets of Herculaneum were published at the time of their discovery by V. Arangio Ruiz & G. Pugliese Carratelli (1946–61). However, G. Camodeca realized that, despite its positive qualities, that publication could be improved and, besides, was not complete. He therefore decided to republish the entire collection. He has, to date, written three articles on them: Camodeca 1993a, 1993b, and 1994b.

The epigraphy of the *instrumentum* (that is to say, the epigraphical study of the marks, painted inscriptions, and graffiti on instruments and objects used in daily life: pottery, amphorae, lamps, metal objects, etc.) is clearly not directly related to financial life. It can be useful, nevertheless, from a prosopographical point of view, for example. For a synthesis, see Harris 1993.

There are many studies on maritime loans. Recent titles of fine works in which the earlier bibliography may be found include Biscardi 1974; de Ste. Croix 1974, Vélissaropoulos 1980, Casson 1980, 1986 and 1990; De Salvo 1992: 336–43, Tchernia 1995. Articles devoted to other financial and accounting techniques are much more rare. On the interest rate, no recent work bears comparison with Billeter 1898. But Frank 1933–40 and Barlow 1978 contain much interesting information. As for accounting, apart from Andreau 1987a, see Mickwitz 1937, de Ste. Croix 1956, and Rathbone 1991.

Over the past decades, the role of slaves and freedmen in commerce, manufacture, and financial life has increasingly been seen as one of the defining characteristics of Roman society, and one of the points at which economic logic becomes closely intermingled with the most deeply rooted social structures and cultural traditions. Di Porto 1984 is a very stimulating essay and is certainly reliable from the legal point of view. However, the conclusions of the old book by Juglar (1894) definitely remain more convincing. See also Bradley 1984 and Kirschenbaum 1987.

The relations between banking and private business, taxation, and the financial and monetary policy of the State are central to the two studies upon which I have commented at length in chapter 11 of this book, Hopkins 1980 and von Freyberg 1989. But see also Gabba 1962 and

1988, Nicolet 1988 (which contains a chapter of fundamental importance entitled 'The economic thought of the Romans'), and Andreau, Briant & Descat 1995.

Were the city of Rome and subsequently the Empire exclusively preoccupied with taxation? Or did they, as I believe, appreciate the financial need to maintain a sufficient supply of coins? Behind the measures that they took, is it possible to detect a veritable economic policy in embryo? These are questions touched upon in chapter 9, the notes of which provide the necessary bibliography.

Bibliography

AMPOLO, C. (1974) 'Servius rex primus signavit aes', PP 29: 382–8

AMSDEN, D. M. (1986) 'Debt and politics in the age of Cicero'. Diss. Rutgers University

ANDREAU, J. (1974a) Les Affaires de Monsieur Jucundus. Rome

(1974b) Review of Duncan-Jones 1974, REA 76: 444–9

(1976) 'Pompéi: enchères, foires et marchés', BSAF: 104–27

(1977) 'Fondations privées et rapports sociaux en Italie romaine (Ier-IIIe siècles ap. J.-C.)', Ktèma 2: 157–209

(1978) 'Financiers de l'aristocratie à la fin de la République', in Frézouls, E., ed., Le dernier siècle de la République romaine et l'époque augustéenne, 47–62 Strasbourg.

(1980) 'Echanges antiques et modernes (du présent faisons table rase?)', Les Temps Modernes, 35: 412–28

(1982) 'Brèves remarques sur les banques et le crédit au Ier siècle av. J.-C.', AIIN 28: 99–123

(1983a) 'A propos de la vie financière à Pouzzoles: Cluvius et Vestorius', in Cébeillac-Gervasoni, M., ed., Les 'Bourgeoisies' municipales italiennes aux IIe et Ier siècles av. J.-C., 9–20. Paris and Naples

(1983b) 'La lettre 7*, document sur les métiers bancaires', in Les lettres de Saint-Augustin découvertes par Johannes Divjak (Actes du Colloque des 20–21 septembre 1982), 165–76. Paris

(1984) 'Histoire des métiers bancaires et évolution économique', Opus 3: 99–114

(1985a) 'Les financiers romains entre la ville et la campagne', in Leveau, ed., 177–96

(1985b) 'Enrichissement et hiérarchies sociales: l'exemple des manieurs d'argent', Index 13: 529–40

(1985c) 'Modernité économique et statut des manieurs d'argent', MEFRA 97: 373–410

(1986) 'Declino e morte dei mestieri bancari nel Mediterraneo occidentale (III-IV d.C.)', in Giardina, A., ed., Società romana e Impero tardoantico. I. Istituzioni, ceti, economie, 601–15 and 814–18. Rome and Bari

(1987a) La vie financière dans le monde romain, Les métiers de manieurs d'argent (IVe siècle av. J.-C.-IIIe siècle ap. J.-C.). Rome

(1987b) 'L'espace de la vie financière à Rome', in *L'Urbs, Espace urbain et histoire (Ier siècle av. J.-C.-IIIe siècle ap. J.-C.)*, 157–74. Rome

(1990) 'Activités financières et liens de parenté en Italie romaine', in Andreau and Bruhns, eds., 501–26

(1991) 'Mercato e mercati', in Schiavone, A. ed., *Storia di Roma*, vol. 2, 367–85. Turin

(1992a) 'Mobilité sociale et activités commerciales et financières', in Frézouls, E., ed., *La mobilité sociale dans le monde romain*, 21–32. Strasbourg

(1992b) Review of von Freyberg 1989, *Gnomon* 64: 418–22

(1994a) 'Affaires financières à Pouzzoles au Ier siècle ap. J.-C.: les tablettes de Murecine', *REL* 72: 39–55

(1994b) 'L'Italie impériale et les provinces, déséquilibre des échanges et flux monétaires, in *L'Italie d'Auguste à Dioclétien*, 175–203. Rome

(1994c) 'Pompéi et le ravitaillement en blé et autres produits de l'agriculture (Ier siècle ap. J.-C.)', in *Le ravitaillement en blé de Rome et des centres urbains des débuts de la République jusqu'au Haut Empire*, 129–36. Rome and Naples

(1995a) 'La cité romaine dans ses rapports à l'échange et au monde de l'échange', in Andreau, Briant and Descat, eds., 83–98

(1995b) 'Italy, Europe and the Mediterranean: relations in banking and business during the last centuries BC', in Swaddling, J., Walker S., and Roberts, P., eds., *Italy in Europe: Economic Relations, 700 BC–AD 50*, 305–12. London (British Museum, Occasional Paper 97)

(1995c) 'Vingt ans après *L'économie antique* de M. I. Finley', Présentation du dossier 'L'économie antique', *Annales, Histoire, Sciences Sociales* 50: 947–60

ANDREAU, J., BRIANT, P., AND DESCAT, R., eds. (1995) *Les Echanges dans l'Antiquité: le rôle de l'Etat*. Saint-Bertrand-de-Comminges

ANDREAU, J. AND BRUHNS, H., eds. (1990) *Parenté et stratégies familiales dans l'Antiquité romaine*: Rome

ANDREAU, J. AND ETIENNE, R. (1984) 'Vingt ans de recherches sur l'archaïsme et la modernité des sociétés antiques', *REA* 86: 55–83

ANKUM, H. (1978) 'Tabula Pompeiana 13: ein Seefrachtvertrag oder ein Seedarlehen?', *Iura* 29: 156–73

ANKUM, H. (1988) 'Minima de tabula pompeiana 13', *CH* 33: 271–89

ARANGIO RUIZ, V. (1948) 'Les tablettes d'Herculanum', *RIDA* 1: 9–25

(1974) Studi epigrafici e papirologici. Naples

ARANGIO RUIZ, V. AND PUGLIESE CARRATELLI, G. (1946–61) 'Tabulae Herculanenses', I, IV, V and VI, *PP*, 1, (1946): 373–85; 9, (1954): 54–74; 10, (1955): 448–77; 16, (1961): 66–73

AUBERT, J.-J. (1993) 'Workshop Managers', in Harris, ed., 171–81

(1994) *Business Managers in Ancient Rome, A Social and Economic Study of Institores 200 BC–AD 250*. Leiden

BADIAN, E. (1969) 'Quaestiones variae', *Historia* 18: 447–91

(1972; second edition 1983) *Publicans and Sinners, Private Enterprise in the Service of the Roman Republic*. Oxford

BAGNALL, R. S. AND BOGAERT, R. (1975) 'Orders for payment from a banker's archive', *Ancient Society* 6: rev. ed. 79–108 (Bogaert, R. (1994) 219–52)

BARLOW, C. T. (1978) 'Bankers, moneylenders and interest rates in the Roman Republic'. Diss. University of North Carolina, Chapel Hill

(1980) 'The Roman government and the Roman economy, 92–80 BC', *AJPh* 101: 202–19

BENABOU, M. (1967) 'Une escroquerie de Licinus aux dépens des Gaulois', *REA* 69: 221–7

BILLETER, G. (1898) *Geschichte des Zinsfusses im griechisch-römischen Altertum bis auf Justinian*. Leipzig

BISCARDI, A. (1974) *Actio pecuniae traiecticiae, Contributo alla dottrina delle clausole penali*. Turin (First edition in *Studi Senesi* 40 (1947) 567ff)

(1984) 'Minima de iure civili', in *Sodalitas, Scritti A. Guarino*, vol. 4, 1525–36. Naples

BODEI, G. (1978) 'Pecunia fanatica, L'incidenza economica dei templi laziali', in *Studi su Preneste*, 3–46. Perugia (= *RSI* 89 (1977) 33–76)

BOGAERT, R. (1966) *Les origines antiques de la banque de dépôt*. Leiden

(1968) *Banques et banquiers dans les cités grecques*. Leiden

(1976) 'L'Essai des monnaies dans l'Antiquité', *RBN* 122: 5–34

(1985) 'Le rôle économique et financier des banques dans le monde grec', *Cahiers de Clio* 84: 77–94

(1994) *Trapezitica Aegyptiaca, Recueil de recherches sur la banque en Egypte gréco-romaine*: Florence

BOULVERT, G. (1973) 'Nouvelles "Tabulae Pompeianae": note sur un affranchi de Tibère et son esclave', *RD* 51: 54–61

BOVE, L. (1971) 'A proposito di nuove "tabulae pompeianae"', *Labeo* 17: 131–56

(1973), 'Tabulae Pompeianae 19–22', *Labeo* 19: 7–25 (= *RAAN* 1972: 167–86)

(1975) 'Rapporti tra "dominus auctionis," "coactor" ed "emptor" in Tab. Pomp. 27', *Labeo* 21: 322–31

(1979) *Documenti processuali dalle Tabulae Pompeianae di Murecine*. Naples

(1984a) 'Tabellae Eupliae, Testationes ex codice accepti et expensi', in *Sodalitas, Scritti A. Guarino*, vol. 4, 1861–67. Naples

(1984b) 'Le Tabulae ceratae', in *Atti del XVII° Congresso internazionale di Papirologia*, 1189–200. Naples

(1984c) 'Prêts d'argent et sûretés dans les "tabulae Pompeianae" de Murécine', *RD* 62: 537–52

(1984d) *Documenti di operazioni finanziarie dall'archivio dei Sulpici, Tabulae Pompeianae di Murecine*. Naples

BOWERSOCK, G. W. (1988) Review of Sidebotham, S. E. (1986), *CR* 38: 101–4

BOYER-XAMBEU, M.-TH, DELEPLACE, G. AND GILLARD, L. (1986) *Monnaie privée et pouvoir des princes*. Paris

BRADLEY, K. R. (1984) *Slaves and Masters in the Roman Empire. A Study in Social Control*. Brussels, (Collection Latomus 185)

(1991) *Discovering the Roman Family*. Oxford

BRAUDEL, F. (1979) *Civilisation matérielle, économie et capitalisme, XVe–XVIIIe siècle*, 3 vols. Paris

BRUNT, P. (1965) 'The Equites in the late Republic', in *Second International*

Conference of Economic History (Aix-en-Provence, 1962), vol. 1, 117–37. Paris and The Hague (Reprinted in Seager 1969)

BULST, C. M. (1964) 'Cinnanum tempus', *Historia* 13: 307–37

BÜRGE, A. (1987) 'Fiktion und Wirklichkeit: Soziale und rechtliche Strukturen des römischen Bankwesens', *ZRG, Roman. Abteilung* 104: 465–558
(1988) Review of Di Porto 1984, *ZRG, Roman. Abteilung* 105: 856–65
(1995) 'Zum Edikt De edendo', *ZRG, Roman. Abteilung* 112: 1–50

BURNETT, A. M. (1987) *Coinage in the Roman World*. London
(1989) Review of Andreau 1987a, *CR* 39: 323–4

BUTI, I. (1976) *Studi sulla capacità patrimoniale dei 'servi'*. Naples

CAMODECA, G. (1982–9) 'Per una riedizione dell'archivio puteolano dei Sulpici', *Puteoli*, 6 (1982): 3–53; 7–8 (1983–4): 3–69; 9–10 (1985–6): 3–40; 12–13 (1988–9): 3–63
(1992) *L'Archivio puteolano dei Sulpicii*, 1. Naples
(1993a) 'Per una riedizione delle *Tabulae Herculanenses*, 1', *Cronache ercolanesi* 23: 109–19
(1993b) 'Per una riedizione delle *Tabulae Herculanenses*, 11', *Ostraka*, vol 2.2, 197–209
(1994a) '*Puteoli* porto annonario e il commercio del grano in età imperiale', in *Le ravitaillement en blé de Rome et des centres urbains des débuts de la République jusqu'au Haut Empire*, 103–28 Rome and Naples
(1994b) 'Riedizione del trittico ercolanese TH 77 + 78 + 80 + 53 + 92 del 26 gennaio 69', *Cronache ercolanesi* 24: 137–46

CARLSEN, J. (1992) 'Dispensatores in Roman North Africa', in Mastino, A. ed., *L'Africa romana*, vol. 9. 1, 97–104

CARY, M. (1923) 'Tesserae gladiatoriae sive nummulariae', *JRS* 13: 110–13

CASSON, L. (1980) 'The role of the State in Rome's grain trade', in D'Arms and Kopff, eds., 21–33
(1986) 'New light on maritime loans: P. Vindob. G 19 792 (= S.B. VI, 9 571)', in Bagnall, R. and Harris W. V. eds., *Studies in Roman Law in Memory of A. Arthur Schiller*, 11–17. Leiden
(1989) *The Periplus Maris Erythraei*. Princeton
(1990) 'New light on maritime loans: P. Vindob. G 40 822', *ZPE* 84: 195–206

CEBEILLAC-GERVASONI, M., ed. (1983) *Les "bourgeoisies" municipales italiennes aux IIe et Ier siècles av. J.-C.* Paris and Naples

CHIUSI, T. J. (1991) 'Landwirtschaftliche Tätigkeit und actio institoria', *ZRG, Roman. Abteilung* 108: 155–86

CHRISTOL, M. (1992) 'Les ambitions d'un affranchi à Nîmes sous le Haut Empire: l'argent et la famille', *Cahiers du Centre Gustave Glotz* 3: 241–58

COARELLI, F. (1985) *Il Foro Romano*, II, *Periodo repubblicano e augusteo*. Rome

COELLO, J.M. (1989) 'Officium dispensatoris', *Gerion* 7: 107–19

COHEN, E. E. (1992) *Athenian Economy and Society. A Banking Perspective*. Princeton

CORBIER, M. (1990) 'Les comportements familiaux de l'aristocratie romaine (IIe siècle av. J.-C.-IIIe siècle ap. J.-C.)' in Andreau and Bruhns, eds., 225–49
(1991)'Divorce and adoption as Roman familial strategies', in Rawson, ed., 47–78

CRAWFORD, M. H. (1970) 'Money and exchange in the Roman world', *JRS* 60: 40–8

(1971) 'Le problème des liquidités dans l'Antiquité classique', *Annales (ESC)* 26: 1228–33

(1974) *Roman Republican Coinage*. 2 vols. Cambridge

(1976) 'The early Roman economy (753–280)', in *L'Italie préromaine et la Rome républicaine. Mélanges offerts à J. Heurgon*, I, 197–207. Rome

(1980) 'Economia imperiale e commercio estero', in *Tecnologia, economia e società nel mondo romano*, Atti del Convegno di Como (27–29 settembre 1979), 207–17. Como

(1985) *Coinage and Money under the Roman Republic, Italy and the Mediterranean Economy*. London

CROUZET, F. (1966) 'Angleterre et France au XVIIIe siècle. Essai d'analyse comparée de deux croissances économiques', *Annales (ESC)* 21: 254–91 (revised in Crouzet, F., (1985) *De la Supériorité de l'Angleterre sur la France*, 22–49. Paris

(1972) *Capital Formation in the Industrial Revolution*. London

D'ARMS, J. H. (1981) *Commerce and Social Standing in Ancient Rome*. Cambridge MA

D'ARMS, J. H. AND KOPFF, E. C., eds. (1980), *The Seaborne Commerce of Ancient Rome: Studies in Archaeology and History*. (=*MAAR* 36) Rome

DAVID, J.-M. (1992) *Le patronat judiciaire au dernier siècle de la République romaine*. Rome

DEGRASSI, A. (1957–63) *Inscriptiones Latinae Liberae Rei Publicae*. 2 vols. Florence

(1969) 'Epigraphica IV', *MAL*, series 8, 14: 111–41

DE LIGT, L. (1991), Review of Andreau, J. (1987a), *Mnemosyne* 44: 490–97

DELOUME, A. (1889) *Les manieurs d'argent à Rome*. Paris

DE MARTINO, F. (1980) *Storia economica di Roma antica*, 2 vols. Florence

DEMOUGIN, S. (1988) *L'ordre équestre sous les Julio-claudiens*. Rome

(1992) *Prosopographie des chevaliers romains Julio-claudiens*. Rome

DENIAUX, E. (1993) *Clientèles et pouvoir à l'époque de Cicéron*. Rome

DE SALVO, L. (1992) *Economia privata e pubblici servizi nell'Impero romano. I. Corpora naviculariorum*. Messina

DI PORTO, A. (1984) *Impresa collettiva e schiavo 'manager' in Roma antica (II sec. a. C.-II sec. d. C.)*. Milan

DIXON, S. (1992) *The Roman Family*. Baltimore and London

DOMERGUE, C. (1983) *La mine antique d'Aljustrel (Portugal) et les tables de bronze de Vipasca*. Talence (Publications du Centre Pierre Paris 9)

(1994) 'Production et commerce des métaux dans le monde romain: l'exemple des métaux hispaniques d'après l'épigraphie des lingots', in *Epigrafia*, 61–91

DONDIN PAYRE, M. (1993) *Exercice du pouvoir et continuité gentilice. Les Acilii Glabriones*. Rome

DREXHAGE, R. (1988) *Untersuchungen zum römischen Osthandel*. Bonn

DRINKWATER, J. F. (1977–78) 'Die Secundinier von Igel und die Woll- und Textil-industrie in Gallia Belgica: Fragen und Hypothesen', *TZ* 40–1: 107–25

(1981) 'Money-rents and food-renders in Gallic funerary reliefs', in King A. and Hennig, M. eds., *The Roman West in the IIIrd century*, London (BAR Int. series) 109, 215–33

DUMONT, J.-CHR. (1987) *Servus, Rome et l'esclavage sous la République*. Rome

DUNCAN-JONES, R. (1974; second edition 1982) *The Economy of the Roman Empire, Quantitative Studies*. Cambridge

(1989) 'Mobility and immobility of coin in the Roman Empire', *AIIN* 36: 121–37

(1990) *Structure and Scale of the Roman Economy*. Cambridge

EJGES, S. (1930) *Das Geld im Talmud*. Diss. Giessen

ELIA, O. (1960) 'La domus marittima delle tabulae ceratae nel suburbio di Pompei', *RAAN* 35: 29–33

(1961) 'Il portico dei triclini nel pagus maritimus di Pompei', *BA* 46: 200–11

Epigrafia (1994), *Epigrafia della produzione e della distribuzione*.Rome

ETIENNE, R. (1990) *Ténos II, Ténos et les Cyclades du milieu du IVe siècle av. J.-C. au milieu du IIIe siècle ap. J.-C.* Athens

FEINSTEIN, C. H. AND POLLARD, S. (1988) *Studies in Capital Formation in the United Kingdom, 1750–1820*. Oxford

FERRONNIERE, J. AND DE CHILLAZ, E. (1976) *Les opérations de banque*. 5th ed. Paris

FINLEY, M. I. (1973; second edition 1985) *The Ancient Economy*. London and Berkeley

(1975) *The Use and Abuse of History*. London

(1979) ed., *The Bücher-Meyer Controversy*. New York

(1985) *Ancient History: Evidence and Models*. London and New York

FORABOSCHI, D. & GARA, A. (1981) 'Sulla differenza tra tassi di interesse in natura e in moneta nell'Egitto greco-romano', in *Proceedings of the XVIth International Congress of Papyrology*, 335–43. Chico

(1982) 'L'economia dei crediti in natura (Egitto)', *Athenaeum* 60: 69–83

FRANK, T., ed. (1933–40) *An Economic Survey of Ancient Rome*. 5 vols. Baltimore

(1935) 'The financial crisis of 33 AD', *AJPh* 56: 336–51

FRAYN, J. (1984) *Sheep-rearing and the Wool Trade in Italy during the Roman Period*. Liverpool

FREDERIKSEN, M. W. (1966) 'Caesar, Cicero and the problem of debts', *JRS* 56: 128–41

VON FREYBERG, H. U. (1989) *Kapitalverkehr und Handel im römischen Kaiserreich (27 v. Chr.-235 n. Chr.)*. Freiburg

FRIER, B. W. (1980) *Landlords and Tenants in Imperial Rome*. Princeton

FRÜCHTL, A. (1912) *Die Geldgeschäfte bei Cicero*. Erlangen

GABBA, E. (1962) 'Progetti di riforme economiche e fiscali in uno storico dell'età dei Severi', in *Studi in onore di Amintore Fanfani*, vol. 1, 41–68. Milan (rev. in Gabba, E. (1988) 189–212

(1967) *Appiani Bellorum Civilium Liber Primus*. Florence, (second edition; first edition 1958)

(1988) *Del buon uso della ricchezza. Saggi di storia economica e sociale del mondo antico*. Milan

GARA, A. (1976) *Prosdiagraphomena e circolazione monetaria*. Milan
 (1979) 'Fiscalité et circulation monétaire dans l'Egypte romaine', in Van
 Effenterre, H., ed., *Points de vue sur la fiscalité antique*, 43–55. Paris
 (1986) 'Il mondo greco-orientale', in Crawford, M.H., ed., *L'Impero romano e le
 strutture economiche e sociali delle province*, 87–108. Como
 (1988) 'Aspetti di economia monetaria dell'Egitto romano', in *ANRW*, ii, vol.
 10.i, 912–51. Berlin and New York
GARNSEY, P. (1968) 'Trajan's Alimenta: some problems', *Historia* 17: 367–81
 (1983) 'Grain for Rome', in Garnsey, P., Hopkins K., & Whittaker, C. R., eds.,
 Trade in the Ancient Economy, 118–30. London
 (1988) *Famine and Food Supply in the Graeco-Roman World. Responses to Risk and
 Crisis*. Cambridge
GARZETTI, A. (1960) *L'Impero da Tiberio agli Antonini*. Bologna, ET 1972
GIARDINA, A., ed. (1986) *Società romana e Impero tardoantico*. Rome and Bari
GIARDINA, A. AND GUREVIC, A. J. (1994) *Il mercante dall'Antichità al Medioevo*.
 Rome and Bari
GIARDINA, A. AND SCHIAVONE, A., eds. (1981) *Società romana e produzione schi-
 avistica. Merci, mercati e scambi nel Mediterraneo*. Rome and Bari
GIORDANO, C. (1966) 'Su alcune tavolette cerate dell'Agro Murecine', *RAAN*
 41: 107–21
 (1970) 'Nuove tavolette cerate pompeiane', *RAAN* 45: 211–31
 (1971) 'Nuove tavolette cerate pompeiane', *RAAN* 46: 183–97
 (1972) 'Quarto contributo alle tavolette cerate pompeiane', *RAAN* 47: 311–18
GOLDSMITH, R. W. (1987) *Premodern Financial Systems, A Comparative Historical
 Study*. Cambridge
GONZALEZ, J. (1986) 'The Lex Irnitana: a new copy of the Flavian municipal
 law', *JRS* 76: 147–243
GRANT, M. (1956) 'The pattern of official coinage in the early Principate', in
 Carson, R. A. G. and Sutherland, C. H. V., eds., *Essays in Roman Coinage
 presented to Harold Mattingly*, 96–112. Oxford
GREENE, K. (1986) *The Archaeology of the Roman Economy*. London
GRENIER, J.-Y. (1996), *L'économie d'Ancien Régime, Un monde de l'échange et de l'in-
 certitude*. Paris
GRÖSCHLER, P. (1996) *Die Tabellae-urkunden aus den pompejanischen und herculanen-
 sischen Urkundenfunden*. Berlin
GUEY, J. (1966) 'De *L'Or des Daces* (1924) au livre de Sture Bolin (1958)', in
 Mélanges Jérôme Carcopino, 445–75. Paris
GUMMERUS, H. (1915) 'Die römische Industrie. Das Goldschmied- und
 Juweliergewerbe', *Klio*, 14: 129–89; 15: 256–302
HAMEL, J. (1966) *Banques et opérations de banques. I. Les comptes en banque* (Vasseur
 M., and Marin, X. eds.) Paris
HAMILTON, EARL J. (1947) 'Origin and growth in Western Europe', *American
 Economic Review* 2 (May): 118
HARRIS, W.V., ed. (1993) *The Inscribed Economy. Production and Distribution in the
 Roman Empire in the Light of Instrumentum Domesticum*. (*JRA* Suppl. Ser.) Ann
 Arbor

HATZFELD, J. (1919) *Les trafiquants italiens dans l'Orient hellénique*. Paris

HERZOG, R. (1919) *Aus der Geschichte des Bankwesens im Altertum, Tesserae nummulariae*. Giessen

(1937) 'Nummulärii', in P.W., *RE*, 17. 2: 1415–56

HESNARD, A. (1988) *L'épave romaine 'Grand Ribaud D' (Hyères, Var)*. (*Archaeonautica*, VIII), Paris

HILL, H. (1952) *The Roman Middle-class in the Republican Period*. Oxford

HOPKINS, K. (1980) 'Taxes and trade in the Roman Empire', *JRS* 70: 101–25

HOWGEGO, C. (1990) 'Why did ancient states strike coins?', *NC* 150: 1–26

(1992) 'The supply and use of money in the Roman world, 200 BC to AD 300', *JRS* 82: 1–31

(1994) 'Coin circulation and the integration of the Roman economy', *JRA* 7: 5–21

IVANOV, V. (1910) *De societatibus vectigalium publicorum populi Romani*. St Petersburg (Photographic reprint (1971) Rome)

JACZYNOWSKA, M. (1962) 'The economic differentiation of the Roman nobility at the end of the Republic', *Historia* 11: 486–99

JOHNSON, A. C. (1936) *Roman Egypt*, in Frank, T. (1933–40), vol. 2

JONGMAN, W. (1988; second edition 1991) *The Economy and Society of Pompeii*. Amsterdam

JUGLAR, L. (1894) *Du rôle des esclaves et des affranchis dans le commerce*. Paris. See also Juglar, L., *Quomodo per servos libertosque negotiarentur Romani*. (Latin tr., adapted (1902) Paris)

KASER, M. (1966) *Das römische Zivilprozessrecht*. Munich

(1971–5) *Das römische Privatrecht*. 2nd edn, 2 vols. Munich

(1976) *Ausgewählte Schriften*. 2 vols. Camerino

KIRSCHENBAUM, A. (1987) *Sons, Slaves and Freedmen in Roman Commerce*. Jerusalem

KUNISZ, A. (1978) 'Quelques remarques sur la réforme monétaire de Néron', in *Les Dévaluations à Rome*, vol. 1, 89–97. Rome

LABATE, M. AND NARDUCCI, E. (1981) 'Mobilità dei modelli etici e relativismo dei valori: il 'personaggio' di Attico', in Giardina A., and Schiavone, A., eds., *Società romana e produzione schiavistica*, vol. 3, *Modelli etici, diritto e transformazioni sociali*, 127–82. Bari and Rome

LAMBERT, E. (1906) 'Les changeurs et la monnaie en Palestine du 1er au IIIe siècles de l'ère vulgaire d'après les textes talmudiques', *REJ* 51: 217–44 and 52: 24–42

LAUM, B. (1924) 'Anleihen', in P. W. *RE*, suppl. 4, 23–31

LE GOFF, J. (1956) *Marchands et banquiers du Moyen Âge*. Paris

LENEL, O. (1881) 'Beiträge zur Kunde des Edicts und der Editcommentare', *ZRG* 2: 14–83

LE ROY, C. (1978) 'Richesse et exploitation en Laconie au 1er siècle av. J.-C.', *Ktèma*, 3: 261–6

LEVEAU, P., ed. (1985), *L'origine des richesses dépensées dans la ville antique*, (Actes du Colloque des 11 et 12 mai 1984) Aix-en-Provence

LIEBENAM, W. (1903) 'Dispensator', in P.W., *RE* 5: 1189–98

LIOU, B. AND TCHERNIA, A. (1994) 'L'interprétation des inscriptions sur les amphores Dressel 20', in *Epigrafia*, 133–56

LO CASCIO, E. (1978a) 'Moneta e politica monetaria nel principato: a proposito di due lavori recenti', *AIIN*, 25, 241–61

(1978b) Reviewed by Rodewald 1976, *JRS* 68: 201–2

(1978c) 'Gli *alimenta*, l'agricoltura italica e l'approvvigionamento di Roma', *RAL*, Sc. mor., stor. e filol., series 8, vol. 33: 311–51

(1979) 'Carbone, Druso e Gratidiano: la gestione della *res nummaria* a Roma tra la *Lex Papiria* e la *Lex Cornelia*', *Athenaeum*, 57: 215–38

(1980) 'Gli *alimenta* e la "politica economica" di Pertinace', *RFIC* 108: 264–88

(1981) 'State and coinage in the late Republic and early Empire', *JRS* 71: 76–86

MACQUERON, J. (1979) 'Un commerçant en difficulté au temps de Caligula', in *Mél. Alfred Jauffret*, 497–508. Aix-en-Provence

MAGIE, D. (1950) *Roman Rule in Asia Minor to the End of the Third Century after Christ*, 2 vols. Princeton

MANACORDA, D. (1977) 'Il *kalendarium Vegetianum* e le anfore della Betica', *MEFRA*, 89: 313–32

(1989) 'Le anfore dell'Italia repubblicana: aspetti economici e sociali', in *Amphores romaines et histoire économique, Dix ans de recherches*. 443–67. Rome

MANCINETTI, G. (1982) 'Filostrato di Ascalona, banchiere in Delo', *Opuscula Instituti Romani Finlandiae* 2: 79–89

MARCHETTI, P. (1978) *Histoire économique et monétaire de la seconde guerre punique*. Brussels

MASELLI, G. (1986) *Argentaria*. Bari

MEYERS, W. (1964) 'L'administration de la province romaine de Belgique', Diss. Bruges

MICHEL, J. (1962) *La gratuité en droit romain*. Brussels

MICKWITZ, G. (1937) 'Economic rationalism in Graeco-Roman agriculture', *The English Historical Review* 52: 577–89

MIGEOTTE, L. (1984) *L'emprunt public dans les cités grecques*. Quebec and Paris

MILLAR, F. (1977; second edition 1992) *The Emperor in the Roman World*. London

(1993) *The Roman Near East, 31 BC–AD 337*. Cambridge MA

MILLETT, P. (1983) 'Maritime loans and the structure of credit in fourth-century Athens', in Garnsey, P., Hopkins, K., and Whittaker, C. R., eds., *Trade in the Ancient Economy*, 36–52. London

(1991) *Lending and Borrowing in Ancient Athens*. Cambridge

MROZEK, S. (1975) *Prix et rémunération dans l'Occident romain (31 avant notre ère–250 de notre ère)*. Gdansk (Societas Scientiarum Gedanensis 55)

NARDUCCI, E. (1983) *Cicerone, La Vecchiezza*, with introd. by E. Narducci. Milan

NICOLET, C. (1963) 'A Rome pendant la seconde guerre punique: techniques financières et manipulations monétaires', *Annales (ESC)* 18: 417–36

(1966) *L'Ordre équestre à l'époque républicaine (312–43 av. J.-C.)*, I, *Définitions juridiques et structures sociales*. Paris

(1971) 'Les variations des prix et la "théorie quantitative de la monnaie" à Rome, de Cicéron à Pline l'Ancien', *Annales (ESC)* 26: 1202–27

(1974) *L'ordre équestre à l'époque républicaine (312–43 av. J.-C.)*. II. *Prosopographie des chevaliers romains.* Paris

(1979) 'Deux remarques sur l'organisation des sociétés de publicains à la fin de la République romaine', in Van Effenterre, H., ed., *Points de vue sur la fiscalité antique*, 69–95. Paris

(1988) *Rendre à César. Economie et politique dans la Rome antique.* Paris

PAGANO, M. (1983) 'L'edificio dell'Agro Murecine a Pompei', *RAAN* 58: 325–61

PARISE, N. (1978) 'Bilancio metodologico', in *Les Dévaluations à Rome*, vol. I, 319–23. Rome

PEACOCK, D. P. S. AND WILLIAMS, D. F. (1986) *Amphorae and the Roman Economy. An Introductory Guide.* London

PEDRONI, L. (1995) 'Censo, moneta e *Rivoluzione della plebe*', *MEFRA* 107: 197–223

PESTMAN, P. W. (1971) 'Loans bearing no interest', *Journal of Juristic Papyrology* 16–17: 7–29

PETRUCCI, A. (1991) *Mensam exercere. Studi sull'impresa finanziaria romana (II sec. a. C.-metà del III sec. d. C.).* Naples

PIAZZA, M.P. (1980) 'Osservazioni sul problema dei debiti nell'ultimo secolo della Repubblica', in *Atti del II° Seminario Romanistico Gardesano*, vol. 2, 39–107. Milan

PINNA PARPAGLIA, P. (1976) 'La lex Iulia de pecuniis mutuis e l'opposizione di Celio', *Labeo* 22: 30–72

PLATNER, S. B. AND ASHBY, T. (1929) *A Topographical Dictionary of Ancient Rome.* Oxford

PLEKET, H. W. (1983) 'Urban elites and business in the Greek part of the Roman Empire', in Garnsey, P., Hopkins, K., and Whittaker, C. R., eds., *Trade in the Ancient Economy*, 131–44 and 203–7. London

PUGLIESE CARRATELLI, G. (1948) '*Tabulae Herculanenses* 2', *PP* 3: 165–84

(1953) '*Tabulae Herculanenses* 3', *PP* 8: 455–63

PURPURA, G. (1984) 'Tabulae pompeianae 13 e 34: due documenti relativi al prestito marittimo', *Atti del XVII° Congresso Internazionale di Papirologia (Napoli, 1983)*, vol. 3, 1245–66. Naples

(1987) 'Ricerche in tema di prestito marittimo', *Annali del Seminario Giuridico dell'Università di Palermo* 39: 187–337

RATHBONE, D. (1991) *Economic Rationalism and Rural Society in Third-century AD Egypt, The Heroninos Archive and the Appianus Estate*, Cambridge

RAUH, N. K. (1986a) *Senators and Business in the Roman Republic, 264–44 BC.* Chapel Hill

(1986b) 'Cicero's business friendships, economics and politics in the Late Roman Republic', *Aevum* 60: 3–30

(1989) 'Finances and estate sales in Republican Rome', *Aevum* 63: 45–76

RAWSON, B., ed. (1986) *The Family in Ancient Rome.* London and Sydney

(1991) *Marriage, Divorce and Children in Ancient Rome.* Oxford

RAWSON, B. AND WEAVER, P.R.C., eds. (1997) *The Roman Family in Italy. Status, Sentiment, Space.* Oxford

RICKMAN, G. (1980) 'The grain trade under the Roman Empire', in D'Arms and Kopff, eds., 261–75

RODEWALD, C. (1976) *Money in the Age of Tiberius.* Manchester

ROSTOVTZEFF, M. I. (1957) *The Social and Economic History of the Roman Empire,* 2 vols. (second edition, rev. P. M. Fraser; first edition 1926) Oxford

ROUGE, J. (1966) *Recherches sur l'organisation du commerce maritime en Méditerranée sous l'Empire romain.* Paris

(1980) 'Prêt et société maritime dans le monde romain', in D'Arms & Kopff, eds., 291–303

(1985) 'Droit romain et sources de richesse non foncières', in Leveau, ed., 161–75

SAFRAI, Z. (1994) *The Economy of Roman Palestine.* London and New York

STE. CROIX, G. E. M., DE (1956) 'Greek and Roman accounting', in Littleton, A. C., & Yamey, B. S., eds., *Studies in the History of Accounting.* 14–74. London

(1974) 'Ancient Greek and Roman maritime loans', in Edey, H., and Yamey, B. S., eds., *Debits, Credits, Finance and Profits, Essays in Honour of W. T. Baxter,* 41–59. London

SALLER, R. (1982) *Personal Patronage under the Early Empire.* Cambridge

SANTORO, R. (1985) 'Le due formule della Tabula Pompeiana 34', *Annali del Seminario Giuridico dell' Università di Palermo.* 38: 333–50

SARTRE, M. (1991), *L'Orient romain.* Paris

SBORDONE, F. (1971) 'Nuovo contributo alle tavolette cerate pompeiane', *RAAN* 46: 173–82

(1972) 'Operazione di mutuo nel 48 d. C.', *RAAN* 47: 307–10

(1976) 'Preambolo per l'edizione critica delle tavolette cerate di Pompei', *RAAN* 51: 145–68

(1977) 'Actio petitio persecutio in una tabella pompeiana inedita', *AAN* 88: 121–7

(1978) 'Frustula pompeiana', *RAAN* 53: 249–69

SBORDONE, F. AND GIORDANO, C. (1968) 'Dittico greco-latino dell'Agro Murecine', *RAAN* 43: 3–12

SCHNAPPER, B. (1957) *Les rentes au XVIe siècle, Histoire d'un instrument de crédit.* Paris

SEAGER, R. ed., (1969) *The Crisis of the Roman Republic.* Cambridge

SHACKLETON BAILEY, D. R. (1965–8) *Cicero's Letters to Atticus,* 4 vols. Cambridge

(1977) *Cicero's Letters ad Familiares,* 2 vols. Cambridge

SHATZMAN, I. (1975) *Senatorial Wealth and Roman Politics.* Brussels

SIDEBOTHAM, S. E. (1986) *Roman Economic Policy in the Erythra Thalassa, 30 BC–AD 217.* Leiden (Mnemosyne, Suppl. 91)

STANLEY, P. V. (1990) 'The purpose of loans in ancient Athens: a reexamination', *MBAH* 9. 2: 57–73

STORCHI MARINO, A. (1993) '*Quinqueviri mensarii*: censo e debiti nel IV secolo', *Athenaeum* 81: 213–50

TALAMANCA, M. (1954) 'Contributo allo studio delle vendite all'asta nel mondo antico', *MAL* ser. 8, 6: 35–251

TCHERNIA, A. (1986a) *Le Vin de l'Italie romaine*. Rome

(1986b), 'Rêves de richesse, emprunts et commerce maritime', in *L'Exploitation de la mer. La mer comme moyen d'échange et de communication*, VIèmes Rencontres Internationales d'Archéologie et d'Histoire, Antibes (October 1985), 123–30. Juan-les-Pins

(1995) 'Moussons et monnaies: les voies du commerce entre le monde gréco-romain et l'Inde', *Annales (Histoire, Sciences Sociales)* 50: 991–1009

THIELMANN, G. (1961) *Die romische Privatauktion*. Berlin

THILO, R.M. (1980) *Der Codex accepti et expensi im römischen Recht*. Göttingen

THOMAS, J.A.C. (1957) 'The auction sale in Roman law', *Juridical Review* new series 2: 42–66

THOMPSON, W.E. (1979) 'A view of Athenian banking', *MH* 36: 224–41

THOMSEN, R. (1978) 'From libral *aes grave* to uncial *aes* reduction, The literary tradition and the numismatic evidence', in *Les Dévaluations à Rome*, vol. I, 9–30. Rome

THORNTON, M. E. K. (1971) 'Nero's New Deal', *TAPhA* 102: 621–9

(1975) 'The Augustan tradition and Neronian economics', *Aufstieg und Niedergang der römischen Welt*, vol. 2.2, 149–75. Berlin and New York

TORELLI, MARINA R. (1982) 'La *de imperio Cn. Pompei*: une politica per l'economia dell'impero', *Athenaeum* 60: 3–49

VELISSAROPOULOS, J. (1980) *Les Nauclères grecs*. Geneva and Paris

VERBOVEN, K. (1993a) 'Le système financier à la fin de la République romaine', *AncSoc* 24: 69–98

(1993b) 'La *Sententia Servilii* et l'endettement des cités libres (60 av. J.-C.)', *Euphrosyne* 21: 285–300

(1994) 'The monetary enactments of M. Marius Gratidianus', in Deroux, C., ed., *Studies in Latin Literature and Roman History*, VII, 117–31. (Collection Latomus) Brussels

VERLEY, P. (1985) *La Révolution industrielle*. Paris

(1991) 'La Révolution industrielle anglaise: une révision', *Annales (ESC)* 46: 735–55

VERZAR, M. (1985) 'L'Ara di Lucius Munius a Rieti', *MEFRA* 97: 295–323

VEYNE, P. (1957–8) 'La table des *Ligures Baebiani* et l'institution alimentaire de Trajan', *MEFR* 69: 81–135; 70: 177–241

(1961) 'Vie de Trimalcion', *Annales (ESC)* 16: 213–47 (repr. in Veyne (1991))

(1976; second edition 1978; abridged English translation 1990) *Le pain et le cirque*. Paris

(1991) *La société romaine*. Paris

VILAR, P. (1974) *Or et monnaie dans l'Histoire*. Paris

VULIC, N. (1923) 'Dispensator', in *Dizionario Epigrafico E. De Ruggiero*, 2. 2: 1920–3

WALLACE-HADRILL, A., ed. (1989) *Patronage in Ancient Society*. London and New York

WILSON, A. J. N. (1966) *Emigration from Italy in the Republican Age of Rome.* Manchester

WOLF, J. G. (1979a) 'Aus dem neuen pompejanischen Urkundenfund: der Seefrachtvertrag des Menelaos', *Freiburger Universitätsblätter* 65: 23–36

(1979b) 'Aus dem neuen pompejanischen Urkundenfund: die Kondiktionen des C. Sulpicius Cinnamus', *SDHI* 45: 141–77

(1985) 'Aus dem neuen pompejanischen Urkundenfund: die Streitbeilegung zwischen L. Faenius Eumenes und C. Sulpicius Faustus', in *Mél. Cesare San Filippo*, vol. 6, 771–88. Milan

WOLF, J.G. AND CROOK, J. H. (1989) *Rechtsurkunden in Vulgärlatein aus den Jahren 37–39 n. Chr.* Heidelberg

WOOLF, G. (1990) 'Food, poverty and patronage: the significance of the epigraphy of the Roman alimentary schemes in early Imperial Italy', *PBSR* 58: 197–228

WRIGLEY, E. A. (1988) *Continuity, Chance and Change. The Character of the Industrial Revolution in England.* Cambridge

YAVETZ, Z. (1963) 'The failure of Catiline's conspiracy', *Historia* 12: 485–99

(1970) 'Fluctuations monétaires et condition de la plèbe à la fin de la République', in *Recherches sur les structures sociales dans l'Antiquité classique*, 134–57. Paris

ZEHNACKER, H. (1974) *Moneta, Recherches sur l'organisation et l'art des émissions monétaires de la République romaine (289–31 av. J.-C.)*, 2 vols., Rome

(1979) 'Pline l'Ancien et l'histoire de la monnaie romaine', *Ktèma* 4: 169–81

(1980) 'Unciarium fenus (Tacitus, *Annales*, 6, 16)', in *Mélanges de littérature et d'épigraphie latines, d'histoire ancienne et d'archéologie (= Mélanges P. Wuilleumier)*, 353–62. Paris

(1990) 'Rome: une société archaïque au contact de la monnaie (VIe-IVe siècles av. J.-C.)', *Crise et transformation des sociétés archaïques de l'Italie antique au Ve siècle av. J.-C.*, 307–26. Rome

Index